CW01193037

MGM British Studios
Hollywood in Hertfordshire

MGM
British Studios

Hollywood in Hertfordshire

PAUL WELSH MBE

Copyright © 2020 Paul Welsh

Published by Elstree Screen Heritage

The right of Paul Welsh to be identified as the author of this work has been asserted by him in accordance with sections 77 and 78 of the Copyright, Designs and Patents Act, 1988

All rights reserved. No part of this publication may be reprinted, reproduced or utilized in any form or by any electronic, mechanical or other means, now known or hereafter invented, including photocopying and recording, or in any information storage or retrieval system, without the prior permission in writing from the publishers.

British Library Cataloguing in Publication Data
A catalogue record for this book is available from the British Library

ISBN 978-1-913218-97-3

This book is sold subject to the condition that it shall not, by way of trade or otherwise, be lent, resold, hired out, or otherwise circulated without the publisher's prior consent in any form of binding or cover other than that in which it is published and without a similar condition, including this condition, being imposed on the subsequent purchaser.

Typeset in Garamond

Printed and bound in Great Britain by
Biddles Ltd, King's Lynn, Norfolk

Contents

Foreword … … … … … … … … … … . 1

The Death and Birth of A Studio … … … … . 5

The Early Years (the 1940s) … … … … … 11

Hollywood Comes To Hertfordshire .. … … 29

The International Years (the 1960s) … … … 85

The 1970s and Beyond … … … … … … ..145

Appendix A: The Studios, From Start To Finish (and Beyond)… … … … … … … . 161

   1: Aerial Views. … … … … … … … ..165

   2: Site Plans. … … … … … … … … ..169

   3: During The War.. … … … … … … 183

   4: After The War . … … … … … … ..201

   5: Inside MGM British … … … … … . 207

   6: Samples of Correspondence. … … … ..217

   7: 'Foremost In Europe' … … … … … . 227

   8: The Backlot . … … … … … … … ..247

Appendix A: The Studios, From Start To Finish (and Beyond) *continued*.

   9: The Clock Tower . … … … … … … ..251

   10: The Ivanhoe Castle … … … … … ..255

   11: Final Visits. … … … … … … … ..259

   12: Demolition … … … … … … … . 263

   13: The Backlot Fades Away … … … … ..265

   14: The Site Today… … … … … … ..271

Appendix B: Remembering MGM British Studios… … … … … … … … … … . .277

   1: Local Road Names .. … … … … … . 279

   2: The Film & TV Heritage Trail … … . 283

   3: The Studio Way Woodland Trail . … . 285

   4: The Elstree Project… … … … … … 289

Appendix C: Filmography .. … … … … … .303

Foreword

MGM British Studios was described to me by Oscar-winning Director of Photography Ossie Morris as 'the Rolls Royce of British film studios' and actress Sylvia Syms told me 'It was the closest in feeling to a Hollywood 'dream factory' in this country.'

I guess that should be no surprise as the facility was owned and run by Metro Goldwyn Mayer for 26 years and during that time produced classic movies. Its short life was curtailed by a decline in UK film production and the near collapse of its parent company in New York and Los Angeles.

I had the chance to visit the studio once when it was still in operation but my strongest memory is after the cameras had rolled for the last time. The property company who had bought it allowed me three days and a set of keys to tour the now deserted studio and that memory is still with me over 50 years later.

Over the decades I have met and sometimes interviewed many of the stars, character actors and studio employees who worked there, many of whom are sadly no longer with us. They shared their memories of this now almost forgotten 'dream factory'.

MGM British Studios joined the list of lost studios such as Denham, Welwyn, Walton, Bray, Danzigers, Merton Park, Gainsborough, Lime Grove, Teddington and Wembley, but none of these were in its league.

Thankfully such familiar names as Elstree, Ealing, Pinewood and Shepperton are still with us, and are now joined by the likes of the gigantic home of Harry Potter, Leavesden. However, that 'touch of Hollywood' and the era in which it operated make MGM a one-off and we will not see its like again.

This book is a tribute to MGM British Studios and to all those who worked there. In the following pages I have tried to identify each television and film production that used the facility. I believe this is the first time such information has been gathered together in this way.

It is lavishly illustrated with photographs that have rarely or in many cases never appeared in print. Most of them are from my own collection; others are credited.

There are certain productions that were shot at the studio such as Stanley Kubrick's **'2001: A Space Odyssey'** and **'The Prisoner'** TV series that have whole books devoted to them. These will be touched on only briefly due to lack of space and to avoid duplicating much more detailed information already available in other publications.

In recent times a Facebook page created by Mike Grant has been devoted to all those who enjoy remembering the MGM British Studios. You are welcome to join us to share memories, anecdotes and even join our occasional get-togethers to explore the old studio site and enjoy a drink! I have spelt the word Borehamwood as Boreham Wood as this was the spelling generally used in the town and by MGM in the 1940s, 1950s and even the 1960s.

The old industry publication Kine Weekly proved a very useful source of contemporary information and I have read literally hundreds of editions covering the period 1944 to 1973. Over the years I have read several hundred biographies, autobiographies and film reference books beginning with "Immortals Of The Silver Screen" by Ray Stuart (Spring Books 1967) given to me by my late Mother 50 years ago and no doubt I have absorbed knowledge from many of them.

Books that also provided useful information in recent times for this effort include "The British Film Catalogue 1895-1970" by Denis Gifford (1973 David & Charles), "Halliwell's Film,Video and DVD Guide 2006" by John Walker (Harper & Collins) and "British Sound Films - The Studio Years 1928-1959" by David Quinlan (B T Batsford 1984) plus of course various websites, including IMDb.

In order to provide a context in which readers can assess MGM British Studios in the light of the state of the UK film industry or of worldwide filmmaking, I have on occasion included industry information in separate marked sections.

To try to recall all of the people I have chatted to about MGM over the past five decades is quite a task. There have been so many and include the likes of Charlton Heston, David Niven, Sir John Mills, Richard Todd, Richard Briers, Sylvia Syms, Honor Blackman, Derren Nesbitt, Deborah Kerr, Barbara Shelley, George Sanders, Janet Leigh, Jack Lemmon, Gene Kelly, Liz Fraser, Harry Andrews, Sophia Loren, Robert Douglas, Simon Ward, Donald Sinden, Stewart Granger, Nicky Henson, Ian Carmichael, Francis Matthews, Reg Varney, Adam Faith, Jess Conrad, Cliff Richard, Ingrid Pitt, Barbara Windsor, Martin Stephens and Anna Neagle to name but a few.

Behind the scenes people range from Oscar-winning cameramen such as Freddie Young, Jack Cardiff and Freddie Francis to MGM publicists such as Julian Senior and Paul Mills. In recent years as Chairman of Elstree Screen Heritage and in conjunction with the University of Hertfordshire I have recorded on camera interviews with a number of MGM veterans such as Mick Brady, Kelvin Pike and Alf Newvell and the aim is to make them available to the public, students and researchers. This would not have been possible without the stalwart efforts of Howard Berry and Bob Redman.

I was very lucky to interview all of the top management of MGM British Studios and what was then EMI Elstree Studios, so for the first time this book can reveal the facts behind the closure of the studio. They included Bryan Forbes, Ian Scott, Sir John Read, Sir Bernard Delfont, Nat

Foreword

Cohen, Jack King and Basil Somner.

Others who worked as crew or behind the scenes at MGM I spoke to include Mickey Hickey, Fred Zinnemann, Larry Cleary, Elliott Scott, Geoff Glover, Roy Parkinson, Tommy Ibbetson, Frank Westmore, Michael Balcon, Edward Dryhurst, Tommy McComb, Roger Garrod, Andrew Mitchell, Mick Brady, John Aldred, David Bowen, Jeremy Summers, Dennis Fraser, Derek Wells and Gordon Thomson. Others are mentioned in the text.

I must not forget Dame Agatha Christie who kindly wrote to me, or that famous lawyer Oscar Beauselinck who treated me to lunch at the Strand Hotel and told me the true story about the years he worked for MGM and in particular the cancellation of 'Man's Fate' and the closure of the studio. Then there was the kind help from Nick Soskin and David Carter, the archivist of Prudential who filled in vital gaps about Amalgamated Studios.

This will be a journey back in time aimed at the casual reader and film buffs alike, laced with anecdotes, bits of gossip, facts and most of all with a desire to ensure that although MGM British Studios is gone, it is not forgotten.

It is a matter of regret to me that I have yet to find a comprehensive list of films that made use of the post production facilities at the studios. Some of these were films not made at the Studio. I have also been unable to locate a list of adverts shot at the Studio, although I suspect they were few.

In the perfect world MGM would still hold a comprehensive archive of production records, call sheets and internal memos for all the films made at MGM British Studios. Alas such a holy grail simply does not exist for several reasons. First, the majority of the films were made by outside companies hiring space and would have taken such material with them at the end of production. Secondly the MGM of today bears no resemblance to the company when it owned the Boreham Wood studios. Lastly, I am aware much documentation went to landfill sites in Los Angeles when the Culver City studio was being cleaned out in the early 1970s and much material was destroyed at Boreham Wood at the time of closure.

I do know a number of production files were moved to Elstree Studios in 1970. However, in 1989 I was asked to sort them and arrange for MGM to collect the boxes as the building in which they were stored for 19 years was due for demolition. I did what I was asked to do but I later heard that MGM had dumped the material to save storage costs in London! I have recently been told they have been saved. Today they would have ended up for safekeeping in my garage. Putting together the information in this book has been a detective story but I hope a successful one, or at least a worthwhile attempt.

The book is published as a fundraiser for Elstree and Borehamwood Museum and Elstree Screen Heritage, a volunteer group dedicated to preserving the memories of all the studios that were or are based in Elstree and Borehamwood. Elstree Screen Heritage is a small band of brothers comprising of Bob, Ben, Brian and Maryse but supported at our events by a loyal group of helpers. Thank you also to Howard Berry of the University of Hertfordshire.

This is not the definitive work on this subject, as I discover new facts every year. If while reading this you feel you could add to our knowledge or have any material, please contact me. I also bow to the knowledge of 'The Prisoner' TV series experts, such as Rick Davy and David Lally, as well as the great work done by Kieran McAleer on exploring the backlot then and now for their walkabouts.

I want to acknowledge with gratitude that Hertsmere Borough Council has officially recognised this book as a worthy local element in the 'Hertfordshire Year of Culture 2020' programme, and that it has contributed funding towards our printing costs.

Finally I must give special thanks to Bob Redman who chased me to finish this book and has helped me get it published. Thanks are also extended to Anthony McKay, Mike Grant and Guy Nolan for their help.

Whether you are a fan of **'Where Eagles Dare'** or **'Fire Maidens From Outer Space'**, **'UFO'** or **'The Prisoner'**, I hope you will enjoy the following pages, so please join me in a look back at the wonderful MGM British Studios, when Hollywood came to Hertfordshire.

The Death and Birth of a Studio

Before the demolition crews arrived in 1973, for three years MGM British Studios stood empty. As a young fan of film, I approached the new owners and asked for permission to visit the studio complex. I was granted access for three days.

It was a marvellous but disturbing experience. When I arrived at the gatehouse on Elstree Way in Boreham Wood, I met a security man and his vicious dog, the only other living beings on the site. He opened the gate and let me loose.

I walked up onto the backlot and there before me were the sets built for **'Man's Fate'** and all the street sets, slowly decaying.

On its side lay a rusting cable car from **'Where Eagles Dare'**, and beyond that several staircases that led to…. nowhere. Plaster and wood-framed gravestones from **'One More Time'** lay scattered with other props. Discarded. I still remember how silent the backlot was, and how enormous it felt.

I walked past the cutting rooms that still contained reels of 35 mm film and editing machines. Workshops seemed as if the plasterers and carpenters had just gone off for the weekend, with half empty cups of tea and newspapers on the benches, along with the moulds for **'2001 – A Space Odyssey'** and other productions.

I ventured into the cavernous sound stages, now devoid of life, almost sensing the ghosts of Tracy, Gable and so many other stars who had walked on those well-worn wooden floors.

Then it was up into the dressing rooms which awaited forlornly the return of Liz Taylor and Richard Burton, and then on into the makeup department. Scattered on the floor were 10 x 8 photos of Grace Kelly, Robert Taylor, Victor Mature and Ava Gardner. And in the corner I discovered a chain mail glove, left over from **'Ivanhoe'**.

I walked along a corridor of offices and for some reason noticed a half-open door; it lead to a storeroom full of studio records and I spent hours reading through internal memos, contracts and documents. These private papers should all have been destroyed for privacy reasons. How bitterly I regret not being able to salvage them.

Another room held a set of scripts from

every film made at the Studio. Had home video cameras and digital cameras been available then, I could have made a thorough record of what I saw.

One of the greatest film studios of the 20th century was desolate and in ruins. But how had it come to this?

To answer that question, we need to start at the beginning, returning to the 1930s. When plans were made to build Amalgamated Studios by the Soskin family in the mid 1930s the area selected was vastly different from what I saw in 1970 and what you see today.

Until the arrival of the railway and the construction of the Elstree and Boreham Wood station in 1868, the area was very rural. Elstree village, up on the hill, was on the ancient Watling Street dating back to the Romans and was a well-known watering hole for coaches on the way from London to St Albans and beyond.

Boreham Wood was little more than a farming hamlet clustered around Theobald Street and the population just a few hundred. The railway brought life and expansion of business but slowly at first. Later it was nicknamed 'the bed pan' line, recognising it travelled between Bedford and St. Pancras in London.

The first film studio to take advantage of the cheap land, good locations, smog-free atmosphere and easy links to the capital was called Neptune and opened in 1914. Nobody could have foreseen it would lead to Boreham Wood becoming known as 'Britain's Hollywood'.

In the 1920s three more studios were to open; the Gate Studios located next to the station, British & Dominions where Charles Laughton was to star in his Oscar-winning title role of **'The Private Life Of Henry VIII'** and the massive British International Pictures where Alfred Hitchcock was to direct the first British talkie **'Blackmail'**. Only the latter survives today, as the world famous Elstree Studios, home to such diverse blockbusters as **'Star Wars'** and **'The King's Speech'**.

One more studio was to join the ranks in the 1950s and that was the 'infamous' Danziger Brothers 'New Elstree Studios' which was short-lived but ironically the only one actually sited in Elstree.

It has often been a source of annoyance to some local residents and purists that the Neptune Studio, now considerably enlarged into the BBC Elstree Centre, and Elstree Studios bear those names although they are obviously located in the middle of Boreham Wood.

Incidentally, I spell Boreham Wood as two words as that was the way it was commonly spelt when I was growing up in the 1950s and the way it was known when MGM arrived. Today it is generally spelt as one word. However, as often incorrectly thought, Elstree Studios did not take that name due to some snobbery value as Elstree was often considered 'stockbroker belt' and Boreham Wood 'working class'.

The reality was that when that studio opened in the 1920s Elstree was the name of the Parish, the railway station and a better known landmark than the farming hamlet of Boreham Wood. The film credits of movies made at the MGM British Studios chose to say 'Made at MGM Studios, Boreham Wood, Herts'.

Prior to the building of Amalgamated Studios

(later to become MGM), Boreham Wood was basically open fields, and the area around it remained so until an extensive building programme which between 1945 and 1956 alone saw the construction of many factories, roads and nearly 5,000 homes.

Paul Soskin was born in Kertch, Russia in 1905 and after arriving in this country soon became involved in the film industry, including a spell as an art Director at the British & Dominions Studio. Sadly, when Paul died in London in 1975 he left little behind in terms of records but we can piece together the rough details of how Amalgamated Studios came into being.

Paul had seen the breakthrough that the 1933 film **'The Private Life Of Henry VIII'** starring Charles Laughton had made in America, and it had been made at the British & Dominion Imperial Studio (B&D) in Boreham Wood. That studio was destroyed by fire in February 1936 and the owners chose to invest in the building of Pinewood rather than rebuild British & Dominion Imperial. Today the site is occupied by the Imperial Place office complex.

In October 1935 he persuaded his uncle Simon to join him in setting up the Niksos Trust with the sum of £2,000. Simon Soskin had made a fortune in China as a grain and general merchant and came to the UK in 1921. His nephew persuaded him to invest £350,000 in a proposed studio and its films, including £10,000 to buy the land. He was eventually declared bankrupt in 1939, claiming only £31 to his name.

The success of **'The Private Life Of Henry VIII'** started a boom in British film production and the Soskins took a gamble, forming Amalgamated Studios in November 1935 with capital of £50,000. They purchased farmland just down the road from Elstree Studios; this land faced onto the recently built Elstree Way which linked Boreham Wood to the A.1 trunk road from London. Appendix A-2 includes a map of the original site.

The only other building in sight was a luxury road house known as the Thatched Barn, which boasted a large outdoor swimming pool, restaurant, rooms to let and a bar. During the war it was the base for the manufacture of secret weapons and the training of agents due to go to occupied Europe.

Later, during the MGM years it was frequented by many stars and appeared in a number of films and television productions. Sadly, it was demolished in 1989 and replaced by a large modern hotel complex now owned by Holiday Inn.

The Soskins had ambitious plans for their new film factory, allocating a budget of £500,000 and employing consultant engineer Major C H Bell OBE who went to Hollywood to study studio layouts. The architects A. E. Stone & Partners were engaged and Sir Robert McAlpine & Sons appointed as the builders.

The Soskins made approaches to various film companies as possible tenants and announced they themselves would make four films a year, with a budget of £80,000 each. Originally they planned that the studio would have four self-contained blocks, but then announced it would have eight sound stages in six self-contained units, totalling 140,000 square feet plus eight acres of workshops and twenty acres of backlot. Appendix A-2 includes drawings showing the design of Amalgamated Studios. For photos of its construction see Appendix A-1

They met with Irving Thalberg and Louis B Mayer at Metro Goldwyn Mayer in Hollywood, who expressed an interest in renting two stages to produce four films entitled **'A Yank At Oxford'** (actually made at Denham), **'Silas Marner'**, **'The Wind and the Rain'** and **'Rage In Heaven'**.

In January 1937 the Soskins announced they were now going to make eight films, three of which would have a budget of £100,000 each and five with budgets of £50,000 each. These figures today may seem very low compared to television dramas costing one million pounds an hour, but even in the 1950s movies, albeit of the 'B' type, were being made for £20,000 each.

They expected the first film to be made would be for Columbia entitled **'Isn't Life Wonderful'** starring Ann Sothern (1909-2001). They were also planning two films starring Irene Dunne (1898-1990) one of which would be about Lily Langtry. Today Irene is a forgotten star but during her career she was nominated five times for an Oscar.

However, as 1937 progressed the cost of building and fitting-out escalated and it was rumoured the budget had ballooned to £650,000. In addition the British film production boom was beginning to stall. The writing was on the wall.

On 29th July 1937 the Soskins called in the receivers under powers contained in charges dated 10th December 1935 and 15th February 1937. It was the end of a dream for the Soskins. When the main creditor McAlpine foreclosed in January 1939 it found itself with an empty film studio on its hands.

Veteran film Producer and distributor John Maxwell had recently lost three sound stages in the fire at B&D and knew his own Elstree Studios (BIP) was already outdated, having been built before the advent of sound. He made an approach to buy the new studio and after negotiations eventually offered £220,000.

In the meantime J Arthur Rank, his rival, had been viewing the situation with alarm and with concern for his newly-built studios at Denham and Pinewood. Rank decided to make a move and employed 'the old boy' system by contacting Sir Malcolm McAlpine.

Exactly what transpired we can never know but Sir Malcolm accepted a lower bid from Rank of £182,500 with the purchase made via Emswood Properties Ltd, a holding company established for this purpose. Sir Malcolm wrote to Rank saying 'few things in life have caused me deeper thought than this deal with you,' stressing that his desire for their continued friendship was a key factor.

Rank had no intention of opening the studio for film production, and had even agreed a covenant that forbade such use for a period of 21 years! Instead he leased it to the Ministry of Works for 42 years at £7,730 per year for the first 21 years and £9,100 per year for the remainder. This apparently represented just over four per cent per year return on the capital investment, considered good at the time.

Although Prudential Assurance had burnt its

hands investing in the film world with Alexander Korda's London Films and the building of the 'white elephant' Denham Studios, it was always looking for new investments. Within two years Prudential had purchased the property from Rank.

By October 1940 the Government had moved 4,795 tons of paperwork from Whitehall to the vacant studio. This paperwork consisted of files from the Cabinet Office, Customs & Excise, Colonial Office, Home Office, Land Registry, Board of Trade and other departments but the majority was Ministry of Health records.

On 4th October the Ministry of Aircraft Production (MAP) wrote to Sir Horace Wilson, Secretary of the Treasury, urging that the studio space be allocated instead to aircraft production as part of the urgent effort to disperse such activity. 'You know only too well the importance of this work as bombs have already been within 50 feet of Handley Page at Cricklewood.'

An immediate decision was requested 'either to get rid of these records for good or dump them for the duration.' Of course, in October 1940 nobody knew the likely duration or indeed the outcome of World War Two. The Battle of Britain had been won by 22nd September but much more still lay ahead.

Within a week of the letter to the Treasury, an inventory had been completed. Several weeks later the Ministry of Works and Buildings reported that 20,000 sq. ft. had been cleared and handed over to Handley Page, with another 20,000 sq. ft. still being cleared.

What to do with all the files already stored in the Studio proved a major logistical problem.

One suggestion was to put most of the records on the backlot under tarpaulins; government departments were asked to dump as many records as possible. It was later reported that 46,000 police files removed from Ireland after the grant of Home Rule simply vanished. Eventually all of the records were removed, many of which were sent to Manchester.

By February 1941 77,000 sq. ft. had been given over to Handley Page and another 26,000 sq. ft. allocated to de Havilland. Striking an optimistic note, the MAP had agreed that Handley Page 'can have Building B for tea-making for their staff. We understand there was some trouble with the staff, which this arrangement might smooth.' Some things never change.

The Author found key documents describing this period in the life of the Studio during his research at the National Archive; readers will find examples in Appendix A-3: 'During The War'.

Aircraft company Handley Page Ltd quickly set about to use the 40 feet high hangar-like stages to manufacture parts of Halifax bombers.

Handley Page employee Peter Crawley recalled 'All the operations took place in the single large studio and upstairs there were some empty offices in one of which we set up our table tennis table. In one corner of the stage was the drawing office designing the patterns.

Adjacent were the pattern makers making the male and female patterns which were then used in the nearby casting shop to make sand moulds. The press tools were then cast in low melting point alloys and fettled to remove irregularities. In the off centre of the stage was the hydraulic press.'

A local resident and friend the late George Hawkins told me, "I moved to Boreham Wood in 1939 with the RNLI Depot and was enlisted into the local fire warden corps. I used to be positioned atop the studio clock tower which had a good view of the area, although we were not really a target for bombing raids. Only a handful of bombs were dropped on Boreham Wood throughout the war."

Fellow Handley Page employee Roy Renshaw remembered 'One morning we came in to find that the Germans had landed a bomb on the corner of a smaller shed but the soundproofed stage was OK' This bombing incident took place on 6th January 1941.

The White Paper on Defence published in February 1937 had taken steps to reduce the risk of air attacks delivering a knockout blow on sources of essential supplies by building new satellite plants ('dispersal units') The studio was designated as DU5 (dispersal unit 5), part of the London Aircraft Production Group, and the outer walls of the buildings were given a covering of camouflage paint.

Meanwhile, Prudential was planning ahead. In 1941 it applied for permission to build a fire station, in 1942 a compressor house and in 1943 a press shop.

The Early Years – The 1940s

In 1944 victory looked certain and MGM once again turned its eye to post-war film production in England. They had previously made movies at Denham but were looking for their own facility. At the time Sir Alexander Korda was working for them.

On 14th April 1944 Korda purchased Amalgamated Studios on behalf of MGM, who realised the facility would not be useable for some time. The purchase price from Prudential was reported as £225,000 although in June 1945 Korda persuaded MGM to pay a further £75,000 for 'immediate possession'.

In February 1945 Korda announced in Kinematograph Weekly that "We have acquired new studios at Elstree, the most modern in the United Kingdom, and intend equipping them so that they will be the most up-to-date in the world.'

Several months later in June Korda had a long private meeting with MGM's 'enforcer' General Manager Eddie Mannix and in October went to Hollywood to meet Louis B Mayer before resigning.

It cannot be overestimated how important the UK cinema income was to Hollywood companies. If for instance you look at two MGM films produced in the UK before the war, **'Goodbye Mr. Chips'** cost $1,051,000 to produce and made $1,717,000 in America and $1,535,000 in foreign earnings. **'The Citadel'** cost $1,012,000 to make, with American earnings of $987,000 and $1,611,000 in foreign earnings.

Studio records later revealed the true cost of acquiring the premises. MGM decided the original 30 acre site was not large enough and purchased 85 acres of surrounding farmland. The adjoining Thrift Farm (which was situated directly behind where the Toby Carvery and Premier Inn stand today) cost £16,161. Land at the rear of the site cost £35,766 and a corner site cost £10,248. Appendix A-2 includes site plans showing Thrift Farm and the rest of the site.

The purchase of Thrift Farm had greatly increased the studio backlot. In 1949 MGM introduced sheep and cattle to replace the original arable crop and I certainly remember sheep grazing right to the frontage on Elstree Way in the 1960s. There was great amusement at the local job centre when a redundant MGM employee went to sign on in 1970; when asked his occupation, he genuinely replied "I was the MGM shepherd."

The original studio land was valued at £18,000 and the studio buildings, including the cancellation of the lease charges, amounted to £386,052. The eventual reconstruction costs totaled £983,227 bringing the cost to a total of £1,387,279. The reconstruction costs were amended in 1949 to take into account professional fees and other outgoings and the figure was put at £1,021,745 which included a war damage reimbursement of £39,976.

In December 1944 MGM announced an impressive programme of production for their new facility once it was fully operational. They would make 12 to 16 pictures a year with a budget of £4 million, drawing on their roster of stars. They could, after all, boast 'more stars than in the heavens'.

The titles announced were quite impressive. **'Velvet Cloak'** would tell the life story of Robert Louis Stevenson, **'Return Of The Warrior'** would be based on an R.C Sheriff screenplay and **'Bricks Upon The Dust'** would tell the story of liberated Europe.

'Habitation Enforced', based on a Kipling short story, would tell the story of a Yank who becomes a ghost, **'Pastoral'** would use Neville Shute's novel about a bomber pilot's romance and Dicken's **'Pickwick Papers'** was soon added to the list. **'Lettie Dundass'** was to star Vivien Leigh and **'War And Peace'** would be directed by Orson Welles. **'Old Wives Tale'** would be based on a Arnold Bennett novel and **'Heart Of Gold'** would be MGM's first British musical, starring Pat Kirkwood.

'In The Queen's Service' would hark back to the days of Elizabeth 1 and **'Target Island'** would relate the true story of Malta's suffering in World War II. **'The Wrecker'** would be based in the Pacific Ocean, at least story-wise, with a screenplay by H E Bates. **'Four Roads To Paradise'** was an Eastern fantasy and **'Friday's Child'**, a Regency comedy.

The Andy Hardy series starring Mickey Rooney was a favourite of Louis B Mayer's so naturally **'Andy Hardy In London'** was an obvious choice, and because MGM could not resist milking success a sequel to 'Goodbye Mr. Chips' was proposed entitled **'Mr. Chip's Boys'**. They also hoped to start a training programme for young actors and Directors.

However, these films were in the future and in most cases, would not happen at all. In the meantime MGM needed to concentrate its efforts to convert what had become a temporary aircraft factory into a working film studio.

By late 1945 three quarters of the facility had been handed over, but it was decided that the

---

In the league of most appearances at MGM, Anthony Newley came second behind the great character actor Victor Maddern who turned up in 11 productions. Victor continued acting until his death from a brain tumour in 1993.

In third place came Margaret Rutherford (1892-1972) with 8 appearances and in fourth place the debonair Dennis Price (1915-1973). In joint fifth place came character actors Percy Herbert (1920-1992) and Herbert Lom (1917-2012) but eagle eyed viewers may find others to beat this list.

sound stages would need to be heightened by 18 feet and then reinforced for the extra lighting required for colour films. Work commenced on blocks A, B and C as soon as labour and steel could be obtained, as both were in short supply. In 1946 it was decided that block D would not have its roof raised but half of it kept for the production of black and white films and the other half converted into a music recording stage. Appendix A-4 includes photos taken during the redevelopment of the site in 1946. Appendix A-5 contains photos of the various departments created and the people who worked in them.

Although Handley Page had left by 14th February 1947 it took until June 1948 to complete redevelopment, including the repair of bomb damage. Other work on the block required replacing a concrete floor with a wooden one, filling in large press pits and demolishing the bases of furnaces, all at a cost of £71,000. The builders finished on 24th November 1948.

During the same time period, MGM applied to the local council for planning permission to lay out a car park, build a timekeeper's office, erect a workmen's canteen and erect eight Romney Huts as workshops. In 1947 they built an electricity sub-station, and that is the only studio building that remains on site today. The same year they submitted plans for a fire station building.

In 1947 MGM announced they were to produce a Technicolor version of **'Pickwick Papers'**, **'Secret Garden'** starring Margaret O'Brien and **'Young Bess'** on which pre-production began but the film was moved to Hollywood.

In November 1947 the former King of Romania was shown around the complex whilst in England attending the Royal Wedding of Princess Elizabeth. The studio phone number was then Elstree 2000.

At last the Studio was ready to house its first MGM production in 1948, some 12 years after the original studio had been built. However, the record books do not record that in fact four feature films and part of another British classic had already occupied the sound stages before that day arrived.

Two years earlier the Boulting Brothers had hired one of the big stages for 10 days and built one set for the classic crime thriller **'Brighton Rock'** starring a young Richard Attenborough. The picture was mainly shot on location and at the Welwyn Studios.

The first film to be shot entirely at MGM was to be known by two titles. Roy Parkinson recalled, "I came out of the army and 6 months later joined MGM on 31st December 1946 on the very good salary of £11- 4 shillings a week. I was assigned as first assistant Director on **'While I Live'** which was filmed from 5th May 1947 to 19th July 1947. I eventually worked on 21 films at the studio and was there until the end. The facilities were very good, especially Tommy Howard's special effects department. My first job at the studio was to go with a props man to stage 7 where there was a lot of stage furniture and allocate the desks to various offices around the studio."

The film told the story of a young girl composer who apparently falls to her death over a cliff but turns up again 25 years later. The main star was Clifford Evans who enjoyed a successful career up until his death in 1985.

The Producer was Edward Dryhurst who remembered, "I began my career as a youngster at the old Neptune Studios in Boreham Wood in 1920 and supplemented my income by playing the piano accompanying silent films at the little local cinema next to the railway station for £1 a week.

An American, Ben Goetz (1891-1979) was appointed by MGM as the Studio Head and when he heard I was setting up **'While I Live'** he offered me a special deal to use the studio in order to test out the staff and facilities. We shot it in 6 weeks and the sound track included the musical number 'The Dream Of Olwen' which was recorded at Watford Town Hall by the London Philharmonic Orchestra conducted by Sir Thomas Beecham with the piano played by Lady Beecham. The music proved so popular we later released the film again but this time called **'The Dream Of Olwen'** and it made a nice profit on a budget of £100,000. It was given a cinema release but sold directly to television in America"

The second film to go before the camera was entitled **'Idol Of Paris'** which was a costume drama set in the 19th century and had the flavour of a Gainsborough movie that had proved enormously popular in the war years. That was no surprise as the Director Leslie Arliss had been responsible for **'The Man In Grey'** and **'The Wicked Lady'**. Leslie was related to the actor George Arliss, the first Englishman to win a best actor Oscar for **'Disraeli'** in 1929. George was credited by Bette Davis for having given her a first chance in movies.

'Idol Of Paris' came in two weeks under its 14 week schedule and had been assigned a budget of £18,000 a week. It starred Michael Rennie who was soon snapped up by Hollywood and went on to star in the iconic science fiction thriller **'The Day The Earth Stood Still'** in 1951. He cemented his fame with the TV series **'The Third Man'** but in the latter part of the 1960s his career petered out with such films as **'Dracula vs Frankenstein'**. Always a heavy smoker, Michael suffered from emphysema and in 1971 died while visiting his mother in Yorkshire.

The supporting cast included Andrew Cruickshank who became a TV star in the 1960s series **'Dr. Finlay's Casebook'** and Donald Gray who enjoyed 1950s TV fame as Mark Saber, the one-armed detective.

The studio was now fully staffed. One of the earliest employees was carpenter Jim Hedges who later recalled, "The first set we built was for **'Brighton Rock'** but before that we had to make our own work benches. We had a pool of carpenters and the Producer would ask for a team of say 8 or 9 to work on that particular film. They used to have a rota so everyone had a fair chance."

The third film before MGM itself was ready to go into production was **'Spring In Park Lane'** which was one of a series of highly successful pictures with a London title that Herbert Wilcox Produced and Directed in the immediate post war years. They starred his wife Anna Neagle and both are remembered by street names on the former studio site. The budget was £230,000.

These were 'frothy' musical comedies which seem dated today but caught the public taste of that era. It has been said that **'Spring In Park**

The Early Years – The 1940s

> For British films this era proved a challenge to make a profit which naturally hurt production levels. An example was given in 1948 by the owners of the nearby Elstree Studios who made **'My Brother Jonathan'** that went on to achieve the second highest takings on the ABC cinema circuit in the UK that year.
>
> The film cost £198,000 to make and took £1,041,000 which on paper seems to be a very handsome profit. However, £416,000 went to the Government in the way of entertainments tax. The exhibitor took £375,000 and then the distributor their share resulting in the return to the Producer of the film only £6,000. In this particular case all the companies were owned by ABPC but the point was made.
>
> In 1947 the top ten money-making British stars at the UK cinemas were James Mason, Anna Neagle, Margaret Lockwood, John Mills, Stewart Granger, Patricia Roc, Michael Wilding, Deborah Kerr, Robert Newton and Trevor Howard.

Lane' holds the record for the greatest number of cinema seats sold in the UK. This was the time of 4,500 cinemas in Britain, when audiences would go once or twice a week. There are probably less than half that number of screens today. Anna commented "The film took £1,600,000 which was a great deal in the 1940s and I went on to become the number one British female star for six years in a row, which was very flattering."

Anna would return to Boreham Wood for the last time in 1984 to be a special guest at an Elstree Studios event which I organised to celebrate 70 years of film production in the town. She recalled fond memories of living with Herbert at the top of Deacons Hill Road in Elstree and at the top of Cowley Hill in the 1930s. "We named the house in Elstree 'Hartfield' after the title character's house name in 'Emma' by Jane Austen which I played on stage".

Herbert had been one of those responsible for building Elstree Studios in the 1920s and for launching Anna's screen career. He later criticised the high level of entertainments tax levied on film box office income, indicating that it could amount to more than three times the cost of making the film, which deterred people from investing in motion pictures.

Anna's on-screen partner was the debonair Michael Wilding who was destined to meet a young Elizabeth Taylor at MGM and to marry her. He later commented, "I dreaded the dance sequence in that film but it became my signature screen moment. I eventually had to retire due to increasing problems with epilepsy. I don't think I ever really enjoyed acting and preferred painting." Sadly Michael died following a fall in 1979. For her performance Anna Neagle was awarded the Picturegoer Magazine's Best Actress award; Wilding was runner-up for the Best Actor award to Laurence Olivier for his role in **'Hamlet'**

The final picture to take to the floor in 1948 was **'The Guinea Pig'**, directed by Roy Boulting, and told the story of a working class kid who goes to a public school and suffers from bullying. It was a big success but its star Richard Attenborough later recalled, "The crew made fun of me playing a schoolboy when I was actually 25 and I had to wear a school cap at all times to avoid them filming my bald patch!"

The shooting started on 29th January 1948 and went on for 16 weeks. Stage B was used to create the sets for Waterloo Station and the school hall. Roy Parkinson was First Assistant Director and told me "Dicky Attenborough asked me to place a bet for him on the Grand National as the horse was the same first name as his wife. He bet £5 and won over £200. When the horse ran again he drove his car onto the sound stage so we could listen to the result on his radio between takes. Roy Boulting happened to walk on the stage and he tore strips off both of us."

Amongst the supporting cast of children was 17 year old Anthony Newley who went on to appear in another 8 films made at the studio. He returned to Borehamwood for the final time in 1998 to appear in **'EastEnders'** at the BBC Elstree Centre and died the following year from cancer.

■ ■ ■ ■

The studio was now fully staffed and had been thoroughly tested, so MGM launched its own post-war production programme, bringing over from Hollywood an 'A list' Director and a top class cast.

The chief shop steward was Harry Downing who told me "I started at MGM in November 1946 and Ben Goetz made me full time chief shop steward in May 1948. I remember I set up a hardship fund for my members, and Anna Neagle and Michael Wilding each gave £25 and Herbert Wilcox gave £50 to start it off. That was a lot of money in those days when some people were paid only £5 or £10 a week.

I went to Spencer Tracy who had just arrived and he said put me down for £50. I later had to return the cheque as he had charged it to expenses on the film and the management would not accept it! I remember once Spence did not report back after lunch for filming and I was sent to find him. I eventually located him in the boiler room chatting away to the stokers about their wartime experiences in the merchant navy."

'Edward My Son' was chosen to launch MGM's production programme at their own studio in England. It was filmed from 9th June to 6th August 1948 and helmed by one of Hollywood's top Directors, George Cukor. The cast was drawn from tinsel town royalty in the form of Spencer Tracy and Deborah Kerr and ably supported by British character actors including Melvyn Johns who was engaged for £1,350, Finlay Currie at £100 a day and Ian Hunter who was guaranteed £5,000 for 17 days filming.

Future well-known character actor Laurence Naismith was hired as a double for Tracy in long shots. He was to be paid £50 to include time spent studying Tracy's walk and movements at the studio.

George Cukor arrived at the beginning of June and wrote home with his first impressions. "The trip on the plane was dreamy, quiet, uneventful and very pleasant. I immediately plunged ahead into preparation. You know the pressure is because Tracy wants to spend as little time as possible here and tends to get restless. I have been busy interviewing actors looking at sets, etc. After a really too short a period we go, ready or not, on Wednesday 9th.

I have found nothing but co-operation and pleasantness at the studio. I am very comfortably settled in a charming but slightly old fashioned suite at the Savoy. The food is not all it should be but the service and views very good. Metro have provided me with a very grand car and chauffeur so I am living in the lap of luxury."

So with the Director settled, Spencer Tracy was ready to go. He was accompanied to London by Katie Hepburn but as their long time affair was not public knowledge, discretion was the order of the day. When I was given a guided tour of the MGM Studio in Culver City by an old veteran in the 1980s he showed me some steps leading from the restaurant. He recalled "This is where Spence met Katie for the first time. The chap with Katie did the introductions and she said to Spence 'I hope I am not too tall for you.' and he replied jokingly 'Don't worry, I will soon cut you down to size.' They were to remain inseparable until his death although he remained married to his wife.

Freddie Young, the Director of Photography, who went on to win three Oscars told me, "I was told by MGM that Spence was a sick man and had recently suffered a heart attack. He had to be given two hour lunch breaks and finish promptly at 4pm which he did, regardless of whether we had finished a scene. We were doing long takes of up to ten minutes and sometimes he would forget his lines but could improvise rather than ruin the shot. The camera held 1,000 feet and we would use 960 feet in one take. Spence was a wonderful man."

The film was based on a successful stage play written by and starring Robert Morley who remembered "Herbert Wilcox offered me £20,000 and a share of the profits for a film version to star his wife Anna Neagle and Michael Wilding. It was a great deal of money but I felt they were wrong for the part. MGM offered me twice that sum and held the release until after the Broadway run."

Morley later commented that he thought the film version was terrible and Tracy's performance a mess, and a number of critics agreed. Deborah Kerr was generally praised for her performance.

Deborah Kerr told me "It was of course a great experience working with the unique Spencer Tracy and the talented George Cukor. My performance was undoubtedly aided by the old age make up which took hours to put on and even more painful hours to take off each day. The MGM make up department was excellent. The Studio itself was rather barn-like and large but was run very well and the dressing rooms very comfortable. It was never as cosy as say Pinewood or Shepperton and somehow did not have the same personality of the latter two."

A visitor to the set of **'Edward My Son'** recalled, "There was a relaxed atmosphere on set with Tracy engaging in banter with Cukor and the crew. It was fascinating to see that the studio roads had traffic lights that were linked to the sound stages and went to red when shooting was underway. All the publicity and production photographs were compressed into a two day session rather than spread through the filming at the request of Tracy. The shots were taken in the photography department; where necessary, small parts of scenery were reconstructed."

At the end of picture party, the studio management gave Spencer Tracy a cricket bat and the crew gave him a cricket cap and badge from their social club. Spence had been amused during filming with the interest the British had in such a game.

By this time the staffing levels at the studio were 376 technicians, 96 construction workers and 230 clerical staff.

In 1954 MGM announced they were going to make a comedy starring Spencer Tracy on location in Scotland, with the interiors shot at the studio. Tracy came to London for talks but the project was cancelled as part of cutbacks being undertaken and **'Edward My Son'** remained his only film made in England.

No sooner had that film wrapped than Hitchcock moved in with **'Under Capricorn'** starting on 9th August and lasting 10 weeks. It was not to be one of Hitch's best films and even one of its stars Joseph Cotten renamed it 'under corny crap'. Michael Wilding recalled "Ingrid Bergman started off with an odd Irish accent but gave it up half way into the film. Hitch had his foot run over by a camera and broke his toe."

The film was a drama set in 1830s Australia but filmed in 1940s Boreham Wood. One memorable thing did happen. BBC television, then in its infancy, visited the set for a television programme and this was apparently the first time ever for such a visit.

The filming moved at a pace as Hitchcock had decided to try 10 minute takes which resulted in 50 minutes of screen time in the can after just 29 days. The longest take was actually 9 minutes with walls that electronically slid out of the way and with props men removing furniture in split seconds as the camera crew moved along. Hitch would rehearse on one stage and then the technicians rehearsed before a final joint rehearsal. On one stage was a 100 feet composite set of an Australian homestead lit by 200 lamps.

At the time Ingrid Bergman said "Hitch is making the biggest change since the close up and the new technique is exciting." Joseph Cotten was reported as saying "It's a tiger shoot but I like it." and Michael Wilding remarked "The speed of this makes ordinary film tame." Hitch himself was quoted as saying "As far as I am concerned the whole picture was over four months before filming when I had finished working it all out on paper."

Years later he revealed "The film lost a lot of money and the bank that financed it reclaimed the picture. Bergman and myself took large salaries which seemed wrong on my part but I could not see why I should do it for nothing and she be paid a great deal. There were not enough humans in the film and Cotten was miscast whereas someone like Burt Lancaster would have been better."

Hitchcock had bought the rights for a token $1 and assigned a budget of $2.5 million but disliked costume dramas and made the film to please Ingrid Bergman. The film was scheduled to take 55 days and he later admitted the long takes drove everyone mad. He also felt the Boreham Wood crew had not forgiven him for being in Hollywood during the war and gave him a cold reception.

Ingrid Bergman later said in the 1970s "I got an Oscar for doing **'Murder On The Orient**

Express' at Elstree and everyone made a great fuss as I had done such a 'great' job doing a long speech. In fact I had done such long takes on **'Under Capricorn'** all those years earlier but because that flopped, everyone ignored that."

Michael Wilding remembered "All sound was dubbed after as Hitch would shout directions to the camera while shooting the long takes and the crew had to shift stuff to make way. I met Margaret Leighton on the film and thought she was a bit stuck up. We met again 14 years later in New York and married the following year."

Hitchcock's first assistant was Cecil Foster Kemp who later recalled "Hitch did not like extras walking about aimlessly in a scene such as the Governor's ball sequence. I hired bit part players and gave each of them a pamphlet saying how guests would have behaved in that era and also gave them imaginary roles so they would appear animated and move about properly."

Sound recordist Peter Handford remembered "I went to work for MGM but it was not a happy experience. Firstly they wanted only the head of sound at Culver City, Douglas Shearer credited on every film but the unions here resisted that and won the day. I found they were either hiring me out and making a profit on me or I was sitting around the studio for 9 hours a day with nothing to do as there was little happening so I left."

MGM sound man John Aldred told me in 1987 "I was engaged by Douglas Shearer and was one of the first employees to work for A W Watkins at MGM Boreham Wood. We spent a long time installing all the latest Westrix sound equipment shipped from the USA in strong wood cases which we all took home to use as work benches. We recorded the music for **'Under Capricorn'** at the newly opened ABPC Elstree Studios in their music stage but had to bring our own equipment as it was empty. I remember MGM also had to lay a new floor on their stage for the filming to allow for smooth tracking."

John also recalled some of the other early work he did at the studio. "We recorded the music for **'Spring In Park Lane'** on the MGM music stage and the jazz score for **'The Miniver Story'** with Ted Heath and his orchestra.

Miklos Rosza recorded all the music for **'Quo Vadis'** at the studio although that was shot abroad. One veteran recalled, "He recorded part of the score outside stage 7 at night with a band of woodwind, brass and percussion. He also recorded early Christian hymns outdoors to get night acoustics and all at night to avoid cars and aircraft. He used the Royal Philharmonic and BBC chorus with 100 singers but later complained his music on the film was drowned out by effects and dialogue."

In November 1948 two films went onto the floor at the studio and they were to result in a true life romance. **'Conspirator'** was the first adult role for MGM child star Elizabeth Taylor and she was cast opposite long time MGM heartthrob Robert Taylor who was flown over from Hollywood.

In the supporting cast was future star Honor Blackman, and 48 years later I invited her to unveil a plaque honouring Elizabeth Taylor's career. At the time Honor commented, "Whatever we think of Miss Taylor's films we have certainly been entertained for decades by her private life."

'Conspirator' was directed by Victor Saville, returning to England for the first time in nearly 10 years. Saville was not popular with some of the crew who felt he skipped off to the comfort of Los Angeles as soon as war seemed likely. This was confirmed by Honor who recalled a heavy lamp fell 'by accident' from the lighting gantry and landed very close to him.

Saville recalled that the Borehamwood facility was "A first class studio running in top gear" and was pleased to see production manager Dora Wright to whom he had given her first job in the industry back in 1933. He felt that MGM did not appreciate they had a star on their hands with Elizabeth although he admitted not being happy with this particular film.

The story revolved a Guards officer played by Robert Taylor and his young wife played by Elizabeth but for a change Robert turns out to be a traitor. Saville recalled MGM hired a detachment of real life Guards and built part of the barracks square on a sound stage. "The problem was that in any marching sequence, when as Director I shouted stop they would not do so until the Sergeant Major called out halt."

> At this time a survey was undertaken to identify the cost of film production. It identified that support features were being made for between £8,500 to £78,000. Main features were being produced at the nearby National Studios for £65,000 to £95,000 whereas at the other end of the scale **'Hamlet'** cost £550,000 and **'Bonnie Prince Charlie'** £600,000.

Freddie Young, the legendary cameraman, told me "Robert was the most handsome man I can remember on screen and was a nice fellow albeit quiet and not a tremendous personality. He aged badly and rapidly but in a way was relieved as he hated being 'the pretty boy' image. He was very loyal to MGM and stayed under contract longer than nearly all of them.

He told me once his agent told him to go see Louis B Mayer and ask for a pay rise. He entered his huge office with a long walk to his desk which was raised on a dais. Robert asked for the rise but Mayer burst into tears exclaiming he considered him to be like a son and to be patient and be happy that he was at the best studio. The agent asked what happened and Robert told him 'I never got any more money but I think I got another father.' which I thought was typical of Mayer and the studio system."

Robert later admitted he would get quite sexually aroused when playing scenes with Elizabeth and was therefore grateful for close ups when possible. He apparently liked to socialise with Ronald Reagan who was shooting **'The Hasty Heart'** just down the road at ABPC Elstree. Filming went on for 13 weeks but Elizabeth had eyes for another star who was working on another film at MGM.

The industry magazine Kine Weekly was less than impressed with the film and commented "Elizabeth Taylor is slightly more mature in figure than in mind. Robert Taylor plays the role of the fellow who wears scarlet, has a black heart and is politically red and can be excused if he occasionally gets his colours mixed up. It's vague, lopsided hokum.'

The Early Years – The 1940s

> The studio itself was now well established, and the industry publication Kine Weekly provided details of the facilities. It revealed that the workforce in 1947 had been 702, rising to 784 in 1948 and declining to 545 in 1949.
>
> A block consisted of two sound stages, one 11,520 square feet and one 7,100 square feet. B block consisted of one stage 18,820 square feet. C block housed two stages the same size as A block and D Block had two stages one of which was 11,500 square feet and one 6,000 square feet.

The national press tore the film to shreds with comments like "It's all rather embarrassing for everyone" (Daily Mirror) and "reaches the standard, almost, of a 'quota quickie' script, its flabby dialogue largely inept, acting not much better and the Director's grip on his material about as firm as though handling a wet cake of soap" (The Observer).

On 29th November **'Maytime In Mayfair'** commenced filming under the directorship of Herbert Wilcox who was still cashing in on the screen chemistry of his wife Anna Neagle and leading man Michael Wilding. It was a frothy bit of nonsense revolving around the fashion industry. Time was running out on these type of British films, although the fashion for 'kitchen sink dramas' was still a decade away.

Michael took note of Elizabeth but felt she was too young for any serious feelings. They met again when she returned to England a couple of years later to film **'Ivanhoe'** and the romance began in earnest. On 27th February 1952 they married with a great deal of fanfare and Michael went to Hollywood. It brought to an end his successful on screen partnership with Anna Neagle and in retrospect was not a good career move as in Tinseltown he was a small fish in a big pond. Subsequently he and Elizabeth divorced but remained friends. Ten years later Liz would be back at MGM with a new partner in mind, but more of that later.

Future film and television Director Jeremy Summers told me, "I started my career on this film as a teenager and things were much more formal in those days. You addressed Herbert Wilcox as Mr. Wilcox on the set for example. He tended to like keeping the same crew so I went on to work on **'Odette'** at the nearby Gate Studios. I think Wilcox moved his films from being made at MGM as he found them rather expensive."

In April 1949 John Huston arrived to supervise tests of supporting cast members for **'Quo Vadis'**, which was to star Gregory Peck and Elizabeth Taylor. However, in June it was announced that the projected had been postponed to the following year to due to the illness of Peck.

That same year Ruby Burke joined the studio as a canteen trolley service lady. This involved taking refreshments to the sound stages. Ruby recalled : "It was a great atmosphere and the stars lined up with the crew for refreshments. I remember Stewart Granger used to like bread and dripping, and would bet with me to see whether or not he would pay. Even when he lost he never paid!"

The final film to go into production in the 1940s was a sequel to the hugely successful **'Mrs Miniver'** which was made in Hollywood during the war and considered to have been a big propaganda success for the British war effort. The usual rule of thumb is that sequels never live up to the original and **'The Miniver Story'** was no exception.

A good supporting cast was assembled including John Hodiak, Reginald Owen, Peter Finch and Leo Genn. Greer Garson and Walter Pidgeon were reunited as Mr. and Mrs. Miniver but this time Mrs. Miniver was trying to save her daughter from a romance with an older man and dies at the end of the film.

Behind the scenes it was not a happy production. Director Hank Potter was replaced by Victor Saville and that did not please Miss Garson who also endured ill health with a serious case of influenza.

A young Richard Burton was tested for the role of Tom Foley but lost out to a now long forgotten actor named Richard Gale. One wonders what would have happened if Richard and Liz had met at this point in their lives. Robert Beatty also tested for the role won by Leo Genn. A young Peter Finch was cast when spotted on the London stage by Producer Sidney Franklin. Finch had come over from Australia the previous year having been seen by Laurence Olivier.

James Fox also turned up playing a child in the film. He remembers "My Father was working for a powerful film agency and took myself and my brother Edward to meet the Director. The part was offered to Edward who was not interested, so I made my screen debut and thoroughly enjoyed it. It was like working in Hollywood but actually in Boreham Wood as it was a very impressive studio."

Greer Garson told me decades later her two fondest memories of the filming was working again with Walter Pidgeon and making visits to Ayot St Lawrence to meet with George Bernard Shaw.

The film cost $3,660,000 to make but the critics disliked it and the public were lukewarm, resulting in a loss of $2,311,000. The author of the original story also successfully sued MGM for killing off Mrs. Miniver.

Walter Pidgeon stayed with MGM until 1956 becoming one of their longest serving contract stars and continued acting into the 1970s. At the end of his life he became a recluse due to balance problems and the effects of several strokes before dying in 1984.

Greer Garson had first made her name in the British MGM production of **'Goodbye Mr. Chips'** shot at Denham and enjoyed a decade of stardom in Hollywood. She later married a multimillionaire and retired from acting. She spent her final years a semi recluse due to heart problems and lost all her memorabilia in a fire, including her Oscar, although that was later replaced by the Academy.

MGM announced in 1954 she would be returning to Boreham Wood to make a film entitled **'Case Of The Journeying Boy'** but it never happened. Greer died in 1996 and her obituaries widely referred to her signature role of Mrs. Miniver.

The Early Years – The 1940s

KINEMATOGRAPH WEEKLY February 22, 1945

Metro-Goldwyn-Mayer
LONDON FILMS Ltd

WE have announced our plans for a long-term production programme of important British films. The first of these pictures to be released is "Perfect Strangers", starring Robert Donat with Deborah Kerr. Since the announcement was made our producers and writers have prepared and completed screenplays which are now ready for production. We have also acquired new studios at Elstree, the most modern in the United Kingdom, and intend equipping them so that they will be the most up-to-date in the world. Immediately these studios are released from their wartime occupation and as soon as the equipment is available, we will embark on our production programme at an annual expenditure of several millions of pounds, giving employment to thousands. As these pictures are assured of world-wide distribution they will make a great contribution to the essential post-war export trade of Great Britain.

ALEXANDER KORDA

Studio Head Ben Goetz looking positively benign
(Photo courtesy of Guy Nolan)

Cast and crew of 'While I Live'

Filming cliff-top scenes for 'While I Live' with Clifford Evans and Carol Raye

Michael Rennie as Herz in 'Idol In Paris'

The Early Years – The 1940s

King Michael of Romania visited on 27th November following the wedding of Princess Elizabeth.

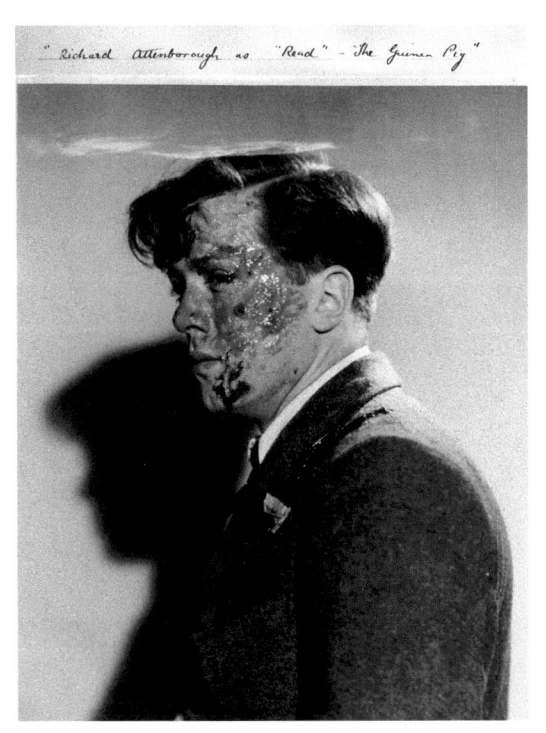

Richard Attenborough as "Read" in 'The Guinea Pig'

Spencer Tracy and Deborah Kerr in 'Edward My Son'

Spencer Tracy travelling on the 'Queen Mary' on his way to film 'Edward My Son'

Bernard Lee tested as "Soames" but not cast in 'Edward My Son'

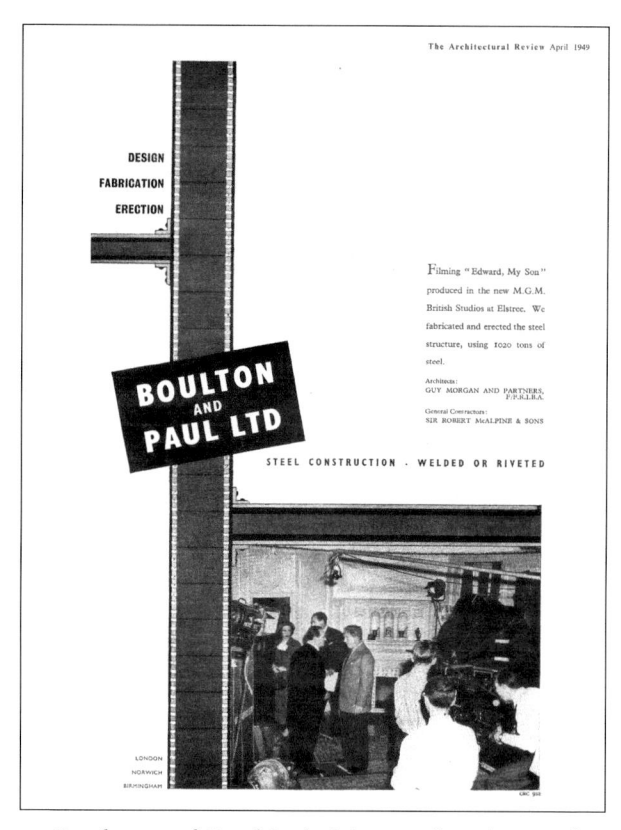

Boulton and Paul Ltd. fabricated and erected the steel structure of MGM

Michael Wilding discusses his role in 'Under Capricorn' with co-star Ingrid Bergman

Joseph Cotten as "Flusky" in 'Under Capricorn'

The Early Years – The 1940s

Elizabeth Taylor as "Melinda Chapin" in 'Conspirator'

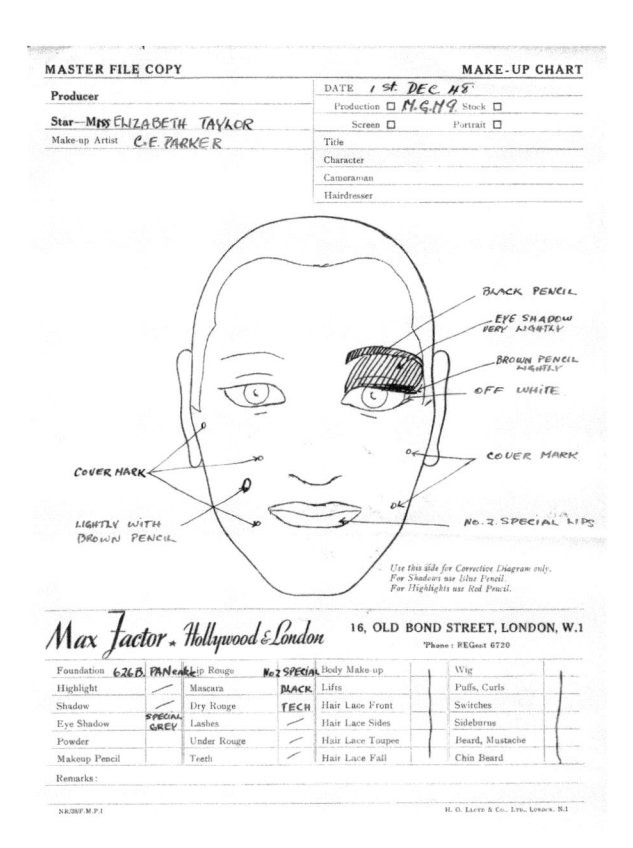

Makeup instructions for Elizabeth Taylor

Michael Wilding again, this time with Anna Neagle, wife of Director Herbert Wilcox

Cast and crew of 'The Miniver Story'

Mrs. Miniver (a.k.a. Greer Garson) cuts her birthday cake.
(Photo courtesy of Guy Nolan)

Robert Beatty tested for 'The Miniver Story'
but not cast

Richard Burton tested for 'The Miniver Story'
but not cast

Hollywood Comes To Hertfordshire – The 1950s

The 1950s began with a slow start, partly because the studio was gearing up for a major production. Only one film went before the cameras and that was another Victor Saville production entitled **'Calling Bulldog Drummond'** *which was little more than a glorified 'B movie' although it cost £506,883.*

WALTER PIDGEON was retained to play the 'boy's own' adventure hero Bulldog Drummond who is called in by Scotland Yard to help deal with a gang of thieves. He was supported by a cast that included Margaret Leighton and a young David Tomlinson. Saville later commented that he thought Pidgeon was miscast and regretted it was his swansong for MGM as a Producer and Director.

Roy Parkinson recalls working on actor tests for the epic **'Quo Vadis'** in February 1950 but remembered only a young Audrey Hepburn coming to the studio and failing to get the role. The film with a $7 million dollar budget was filmed abroad although stage 7 was used to record the music score.

Deborah Kerr starred in **'Quo Vadis'** when it was filmed in Italy and told me, "It was a great pleasure to star with Robert Taylor who was a dear man. He was incredibly shy and his incredible good looks were more of a burden than an asset to him. He was a private person, most unassuming, always correct and very professional."

1951 started with the production of **'The Hour Of Thirteen'** which at a cost of £287,882 was virtually a 'B movie' by MGM standards. The Director Harold French was paid £8,708 and London born contract star Peter Lawford (1923-

> The studio's social activities were becoming established with the first social evening staged at the Crown pub in Shenley Road. In March 1950 the MGM darts team beat the Pathe Labs team and progressed to the finals of the Boreham Wood Business House Cup tournament. The football team had their own pitch on the backlot.

> There is no doubt that for much of its life, the MGM British Studio was under-used. For instance, look at the film production in the nearby ABPC Elstree during the period 1949, its first fully operational year after being rebuilt and 1951. In that first year the studio produced six films including **'Stage Fright'** directed by Hitchcock. In 1950 it also produced six films including **'Captain Horatio Hornblower'** with Gregory Peck. In 1951 that increased to seven films and all that was on four stages totaling 60,000 square feet.
>
> The General Manager Vaughn Dean at Elstree commented that the Industry should aim for a minimum of 10 set ups a day and 2.5 minutes of screen time each day. He suggested that Assistant Directors should be encouraged into competing with each other and estimated that the average black and white film would involve 10% of the total production hours being overtime that had to be negotiated with the three unions – ACTT, ETU and NATKE. Post production should be completed within 10 weeks.

1984) was imported to play a jewel thief wrongly suspected of being a serial killer murdering policemen. It was actually quite a decent film and used locations in Hammersmith and Chiswick goods yard over an eight week period.

Lawford was one of those stars who had everything and lost it all. He had a contract with Hollywood's biggest studio, married into the Kennedy family and so had the ear of the President and was a member of the Rat Pack with Tinseltown royalty Frank Sinatra, Dean Martin and Sammy Davis Jr. However, he ended up broke and died from a mixture of drink and drug abuse.

Even in death he was not allowed to rest in peace. Lawford's ashes were interred in the same cemetery as the remains of Marilyn Monroe. In itself that was ironic as he is believed to have been the last person to have spoken to her and some conspiracy theorists believe he was involved in her 'murder'. However, they were not companions in death for many years as it was alleged his funeral expenses had not been paid and his ashes were disinterred and scattered elsewhere.

At the completion of the film, MGM announced after close consultation with New York and Culver City that the British studio was now ready for big scale, top bracket production.

For many years MGM had been toying with the idea of making a film version of **'Ivanhoe'** and now they had their own British studio with a large backlot and within easy reach of locations, so the go ahead was given. This was to become the most famous film to come out of the studio in the 1950s and no expense was to be spared.

MGM put their plans into action in 1949 and started planning the construction of a large exterior castle set on the backlot. Appendix A-10 shows key stages in the construction of the castle, from the architect's models to the completed castle.

MGM decided the reliable Director Richard

Thorpe (1896-1991) who had spent most of his career with the company would be put in charge. He would make five films at Boreham Wood but may be best remembered today for helming **'Jailhouse Rock'** in Hollywood starring Elvis Presley.

In 1949 MGM were trying without success to entice Laurence Olivier and then Errol Flynn to take on the title role. Stewart Granger thought the role was his and even in January 1951 they were talking about costume fittings. In March 1950 they announced filming had been postponed for 12 months; sets built and props gathered would be put into storage while casting difficulties were overcome.

Finally MGM decided to bolster the sagging career of their loyal contract star Robert Taylor who was cast despite his reservations about appearing in costume dramas. He eventually warmed to the film, describing it as a medieval western. Taylor stayed at the Dorchester Hotel in London during filming.

Elizabeth Taylor was less keen, and during filming was described as looking thin, ill and disinterested and reportedly mumbled so many lines that she later had to loop the whole dialogue when back in Los Angeles. While working on the film Liz was said to have visited the house in which she had been born and found it to be now a children's day nursery. Jack Hawkins tested unsuccessfully for the part played by George Sanders, having also lost a part in **'Quo Vadis'** to Ralph Truman.

Thorpe did a good deal of research and at one point found a 1913 version filmed at Chapstow Castle by Herbert Brenon for £3,500. In comparison, the cost of the 1951 version was put as £1,201,072 with £14,000 paid to the Director, the story costing £55,000 and set construction amounting to £60,000. In 1976 Variety trade magazine said the film grossed $6,258,000.

The castle set dominated the backlot for several years and some visitors to the town thought it was real. It was used again for **'Knights Of The Round Table'** and was rented out to Elstree Studios for the production of **'The Dark Avenger'** starring Errol Flynn.

Eventually the castle was demolished in March 1958 to make way for a giant Chinese village being created for **'The Inn Of The Sixth Happiness'**. Chief Shop Steward Harry Downing recalled, "On Ivanhoe the crew wanted the extra payment called 'height money' for working on the castle. I had to measure it to prove it was over the required 40 feet high."

Work started on building the castle in 1950 as they wanted it standing for a few months to help it 'age'. 25,000 metal tubular fittings were required and a significant wood framework. Trucks carrying timber, cement and stones to the backlot site travelled on temporary roads made from 2,000 railway ties. A moat was constructed around the front of the castle last, due to bad weather. Bulldozers carved out an area 10 feet deep over several days and filled it with 170,000 gallons of water.

The bottom was tarpaulin-covered and a rubber fabric mattress was anchored to the bottom to protect stuntmen. At first it was filled with chlorine water but 2 weeks later it was drained and filled with a milder antiseptic. Electrical cables had to be buried underground and the work was difficult due to a hard winter.

In total 50 sets were built at the studio, including a castle dungeon which required 2 five hundred gallon tanks containing crude oil and petrol. This was constructed in a temporary stage built on the backlot erected on scaffolding to allow piping for gas jets. Other fire scenes were shot indoors.

For one scene a stuntman wore an asbestos suit covered by a costume soaked in petrol. In his pocket was a battery connected to a strip of gun cotton and as the lamp hit him, he pressed a button and literally set himself alight. At the end of the scene he jumped into a bath of cold water. The potential for accidents was great and even Robert Taylor had his eyebrows singed.

More serious was an injury to one of his co-stars actor Robert Douglas who recalled, "They had machines that could fire 60 arrows at a time when the castle was being stormed. I was standing on the ramparts for a scene when one hit me under my eye and knocked me down bleeding. Being short I was wearing four inch heels which was lucky as otherwise it would have hit me in the eye and possibly killed me. Production was stopped, I was taken to hospital and was off for two weeks. The surgery meant I lost two film roles when I returned to Hollywood so I sued MGM. The trouble was you can't fight big studios so I only got a small amount and never worked for MGM again."

The film's female star Joan Fontaine had less fond memories of the film, remarking that it took 5 months to shoot and the Director was more interested in the performance of the horses than the actors. It took three months to train the horses and riders to act dressed as knights, not to mention having to manufacture 14,000 arrows, chain mail costumes and other props. Hatfield Woods doubled as Sherwood Forest; Richard Thorpe, Freddie Young, Robert Taylor and 9 MGM crew left on 22nd September for a few days to shoot scenes in the vicinity of Vipiteno and Bolzano in Northern Italy.

Johnny Goodman was the Third Assistant Director and told me "We had the best stunt Director, an American called Yakima Canutt. We had a big problem with the jousting scenes to get the men knocked off horses safely. We tried plastic corrugated lances, etc but people got injured but Yakima came up with a great idea. He erected a pylon at the end of the jousting field, employed jumping jockeys who were used to falling from horses and put a hook under their armour attached to a wire with the other end attached to the pylon. It was precisely measured that the wire was fully extended at the exact point where to the two jousting horsemen met and would pull off one rider in perfect timing.

They also used a little Irishman named Paddy Ryan to do the falls from the castle. He would have an arrow strapped to him which would spring out on cue and he would fall some distance into the moat. I asked him what it felt like before he jumped and he said 'I don't see the moat. I just imagine the cashier and I jump straight for him!' We did have some trouble with arrows sticking into the castle walls which were of course pretending to be stone."

Veteran actor Frank Williams, best remembered as the Vicar in **'Dad's Army'**, sums up very well the life of an extra on this film in his autobiography ('Vicar to Dad's Army' by Frank Williams with Chris Gidney, Canterbury Press 2002). "We were called to the studios at seven in the morning to get into costume and to go to make up. With two or three hundred people to deal with it was a time consuming process. When we were ready we were directed to the lot, an enormous open air space at the back of the studios.

We were filming a sequence in which this vast army of extras were attacking the castle. This required shooting arrows at it and we were arranged in ranks with the stuntmen who were skilled in the art of archery nearest the camera. Those of us who were less skilled or as in my case totally unskilled, were placed as far away from the camera as possible. This was just as well as when we were commanded to fire our arrows, I found that mine rarely travelled farther than the rank immediately in front of me. Midmorning we had a break. Tea or coffee and sandwiches were set out on long trestle tables and were very welcome after our exertions. Then we were back on the attack again.

At the lunch break, we were provided with packed lunches. In the afternoon we returned to the attack once more. About halfway through there was the statutory tea break, cakes and biscuits this time. At the end of the day having washed off our makeup and changed into our ordinary clothes, we queued to be 'signed off'. Then we joined another queue, presented the paper that the assistant had just signed and received our day's pay in cash."

Frank went on say "After about a week the extras changed position and now were the defenders on the castle ramparts. They soon figured that if they played dead when the first arrows arrived it meant they could spend the day laying down but the problem was that too many 'died' too quickly. That resulted in the Assistant Director having to assign which extras would die and when."

Overall the efforts were worth it as the film proved to be a big success when premiered at the Empire cinema, Leicester Square in June 1952 in the presence of the Duke of Edinburgh.

■ ■ ■

1952 saw the studio play host to three productions, one of which starred a legendary Hollywood song and dance man. However, it was 'the King of Hollywood' who arrived in the summer to make his first film away from his kingdom, partly driven by tax advantages.

Clark Gable had been with MGM from the 1930s, had already won an Oscar and was of course known the world over as Rhett Butler in **'Gone With The Wind'**, probably the most famous film ever made in Tinseltown. Those successes were over a decade behind him and after a break for war service Gable's career had not really taken off to the same level. He left America on 6th May but first travelled to Paris for a holiday.

Filming on **'Never Let Me Go'** was scheduled for June to September with interiors at MGM and locations in Cornwall at Newquay, Mevagissey, Mullion Cove and Kynanee Cove. Gable ordered a custom-made Jaguar sports car and elected to stay at the Dorchester Hotel in London. On one occasion he was approached in the lobby by a young man for an autograph and afterwards was told it was King Hussain of Jordan.

Roy Parkinson was employed on the production crew and recalled, "I remember having a drink at the Headlands Hotel at Newquay one evening with Clark. He had been golfing that day and said it had been tiring as quite a few spectators followed him around. I asked him if that worried him but he said he would have been more worried if nobody had shown an interest."

One young member of the cast was Kenneth More who went on to become a big star for the Rank Organisation a few years later. He later remembered "The casting Director warned me that Gable was sensitive about younger actors on screen with him and suggested the night before the screen test I go out and get drunk so my eyes would be puffy and I would look a bit haggard. It worked and I got the part but sadly a lot of my role including a big scene with Gene Tierney was edited out so I guess he saw the rushes."

The film's Director Delmer Daves was approved by Gable and he later commented "Clark was insecure, very polite but almost shy. He was inflexible as an actor but of course had a great personality. On location at Mullion Cove he was given a cottage to stay in but after one night complained it was too quiet and it scared him to death so we swopped and he took my room at the local inn. He loved his new Jaguar and took Gene Tierney for a pub lunch in Cornwall but she said after he really only wanted to talk about his late wife Carol Lombard, who had been killed in a plane crash during the war."

Years later the unit publicist assigned to the film Paul Mills told me, "I had to drive from Cornwall and back to pick up two pairs of shoes Gable had ordered from Paris and to tell the Dorchester he wanted a bigger suite when he returned from location. When Gable was driven down to Cornwall at the start of filming the car broke down with a petrol pump fault and they did not arrive until 1.30am but he took it in his stride and seemed very happy during the shoot."

The same cannot be said for his leading lady Gene Tierney who was borrowed from 20th Century Fox at her salary of $100,000 for 14 weeks plus $500 a week expenses. Gene had shot to fame in the classic movie **'Laura'** but sadly

---

In 1952 the Boreham Wood studio admin and overhead costs totaled £371,634. Of this amount £6,176 was allocated to **'Ivanhoe'**, £103,708 to **'The Hour of 13'** with the balance divided between the three 1952 productions. The salary of £55,846 for MGM's top man in England Ben Goetz was not included.

Veteran sound man Mickey Hickey told me, "In those days MGM encouraged us to buy our own equipment and rent it to the studio so it could be directly costed to each film. If MGM bought it, the capital cost would fall against the studio overheads." Mickey also remarked "Clark Gable was the fastest actor I ever worked with on post synching and a real gentleman."

Hollywood Comes To Hertfordshire – The 1950s

> Cinema-going in the UK had hit a peak in 1946 and the situation was still healthy in 1952 with 4,570 cinemas (that is individual buildings as opposed to the number of screens quoted today in the multiplex era) attracting an average weekly attendance of nearly 26 million at an average ticket price of two shillings (10p). However, within a year a dramatic decline began.

suffered mental health issues. They worsened when she contracted German measles during pregnancy and her baby was born handicapped. She was further devastated when she later met a fan who said she recalled meeting the actress at the Hollywood Canteen when she was pregnant but the fan had been ill with German measles. Thus Gene blamed her fame for her child's disability.

The makeup artist Frank Westmore was not very sympathetic and commented "I came over from Hollywood to work on what I thought was a horrible film. Miss Tierney was so fond of her bed we came to a unique arrangement to get her to the set on time in Boreham Wood. I would go to her hotel where breakfast for two was organised. I then did her makeup without causing the darling the traumatic experience of putting feet to floor as I would do her entire make up while she stayed in bed."

Gene Tierney herself recalled that she spent 2 hours a day for six weeks mastering enough basic steps to get away with playing a ballerina in this 1950s Cold War love story. In the film most of her dancing scenes were doubled by Natalie Leslie.

Gable left on 20th September having spent a total of 97 days in England and 11 days on weekend breaks to France. The film was not considered a success.

'**Time Bomb**' was little more than a B movie with imported Hollywood star Glenn Ford (1916-2006) tackling a bomb placed on a train containing naval mines on the way to Portsmouth. The action takes place at night in a railway siding and manages to convey a tense atmosphere although you know in films from this period the star is unlikely to be killed or fail his mission.

A good supporting cast was brought together including Maurice Denham, Bill Fraser, Harry Locke, Sam Kydd, Victor Maddern and Campbell Singer who between them turned up in most British films of the 1950s. For America it was entitled '**Terror On A Train**' and was allocated 37 days to shoot. That broke down to 24 days on location and 13 days of interiors at the studio spread between 24 March to 16th May. Locations included Willesden Junction, Elstree and Gunnersbury stations and the Chiswick and Hammersmith goods yard.

Ford was apparently paid $125,000. He enjoyed a successful film career although in private life he was a heavy drinker and sadly his last years were blighted by poor physical and mental health. The Director Ted Tetzlatt (1903-1995) had started off as a Director of Photography in the 1930s and graduated to directing, albeit his were usually unmemorable movies.

The next Hollywood star to arrive was Gene Kelly who at one point during his stay rented the London home of actor Robert Donat for 11 weeks at a cost of £371.

In the 1980s I spoke to Gene who recalled working at the Boreham Wood facility. "The studio staff were great and I enjoyed going to the local pub and having a drink with the boys. The equipment was not at the same level as in Culver City but we coped. The landscaped studio looked more like a country club and the restaurant food was excellent. Naturally it was a bit of a jolt to come from sunny California living a cosseted life to England that was still recovering from a terrible war but I enjoyed making both films there although neither proved a success."

I could not resist asking him about that dance sequence in 'Singing In The Rain' to which he responded "Everybody asks me that more than any other work I have ever done. To be honest, it was not a great memory as I was ill with a fever while shooting it and because water does not show up on film they added a sort of diluted milk mixture. I guess they should have retitled it 'singing in the diluted milk'."

Gene was here to make **'Invitation To The Dance'** and principal photography began on 19 August. This was his pet project and at the time he was not happy with the studio which he felt seem stretched to handle two pictures at a time, as the Gable film over ran. By Culver City standards he felt the crew worked slowly, the costume department was poor and the camera crew totally unfamiliar with moving a boom into certain marks at definite speeds to musical counts. Of course it could be argued he was unfairly comparing MGM British to the Hollywood facility where they had established departments that had been producing films for nearly 30 years.

The result was that after 3 weeks, only 11 minutes and 20 seconds of useable film had been achieved. At one point the union banned any weekend work, Kelly fell ill and a nasty accident was barely avoided when the anchors broke out of the concrete floor causing a tightrope walker to crash to the ground.

It was not an inexpensive film and was comprised of several sequences. The circus segment lasting 31 minutes cost $180,264, the 'Ring Around The Roses' sequence $158,370 for 34 minutes and the 'Dance Me A Song' section $137,812 for 28 minutes. They took 27 days of rehearsals and 56 days shooting although Kelly sustained a skiing injury during a break in Klosters.

The cartoon sequence was shot in Hollywood and cost $947,659 shot in 10 days with the animation bill amounting to $323,025. That part took 250,000 individual drawings and over 18 months to complete.

Kelly admitted MGM had no idea what to do with the finished product and it was tampered with over the next few years eventually being released in 1957. It grossed only $615,000 of which $415,000 was overseas box office.

A piece of studio trivia is that in June 1952 the studio wrote to Kelly to inform him that he would be issued with a ration book. It was pointed out that this was not essential while staying in the hotel except that without the personal points coupons, he could not buy sweets. The good news was that he was entitled to one and three quarter pounds of sweets each month plus a bonus of two pounds as an overseas visitor whether he stayed a week or a year!

Perhaps the last words should be from Gene who told me, "We shot four episodes but the studio cut one. MGM did not understand how to market the film which was experimental and not designed to be a major commercial film as with some of my other screen musicals.

The studio was still badly equipped after the war and fairly primitive in terms of equipment. I had to rehearse the crew on how to handle the camera crane as they had not seen it before and had to get used to a 5 day rather than 6 day working week but the crew were highly co-operative."

■ ■ ■

1953 brought five productions into the studio with mixed box office results but top stars of their day.

'Seagulls Over Sorrento' starred Gene Kelly and was directed by John and Roy Boulting. For the American release it was retitled 'Crest Of The Wave'. It was a modest story involving British and American scientists trying to sort out a problem with a new torpedo on a remote military outpost, blending laughs with drama.

Kelly was ably supported by two stalwart character actors in the shape of the future 'Carry On' star Sid James and the future 'M' in the James Bond movies Bernard Lee. Both could be guaranteed to enliven any film and no doubt enjoyed the location shooting in the Channel Islands.

The big film on the slate was 'Mogambo' which was a remake of a 1930s hit 'Red Dust' with Clark Gable reprising his role but with Jean Harlow and Mary Astor replaced by Ava Gardner and newcomer Grace Kelly.

On a practical note Gable moved from the Dorchester Hotel to the Connaught Hotel in London. He complained about the cold weather and found London boring so began to drink more. Lana Turner declined the role played by Ava Gardner as she did not want to go on

---

Meanwhile the old pre-war home of MGM British films which was Denham Studios had reached the end of its short life. Opened in 1936 at a cost of £1 million it was supposed to be the final word in dream factories and was huge. However, it was not well-designed and was expensive to run. After Richard Todd's film version of Robin Hood it finally closed its doors and during February and March the contents, totaling 4,000 lots, were sold off by auction.

A survey of 10,000 cinemagoers was undertaken by a trade magazine to gauge their reading habits. Only 5.8% read the film fan magazine Picturegoer compared with 50.3% reading the Radio Times and 49.9% reading the News Of The World.

location to Africa and Gene Tierney turned down the role played by Grace Kelly for the same reason.

It was an expensive movie to make with known costs at the time totaling £1,046,321 and a top Director was engaged by the name of John Ford, today best remembered for his western movies with John Wayne.

Ava Gardner wrote later "**Mogambo** was one of my more serious films and allowed me to get more involved in the part than usual. It was probably the pinnacle of my career. However, it was not a happy time as I decided to have an abortion and MGM arranged it for me in London. John Ford tried to talk me out of it but it was the wrong time for me to have a child personally and career wise. I did not tell Sinatra."

Filming started on 17th November 1952 and went through until March 1953. Gable had turned down 'Quo Vadis' as he disliked appearing in costume films. He disliked Ford as a person but got on well with the cast. Donald Sinden was cast as the young man in the story and he told me "Clark was a splendidly professional actor. I got cast when the Producer of **'The Cruel Sea'** made a show reel from the film for me before it was released. When I appeared in my first scene my skin had to be whitened as I had gained too much of a tan already and I was supposed to be just arriving in Africa. I did not find Ford an easy person and I became his whipping boy. I also remember that my chest hair had to be shaved to match Gable."

Cameraman Freddie Young told me, "With filming Gable you had to be careful as he had developed a slight shaking of the head. We would shoot the scene again without comment and it was usually okay. Two thirds of the film was shot at Boreham Wood with back projection. Ford could be quite hard on the actors except Gable. I remember once the Producer Sam Zimbalist turned up on set and Ford ordered filming to stop. When Sam got the message he complained to Ford the film was behind schedule who in front of the crew ripped out 6 pages of the script and said 'Now we are up to date!' In fact Ford had already decided he was going to scrap those scenes anyway."

Freddie remained with MGM until 1959. "I left as they asked me to take a pay cut despite the fact they had made a lot of money loaning me out to other companies for which I got no extra pay." Freddie went on to win three Oscars, although he never attended any of the award ceremonies and in 1996 I invited him and two time Oscar winner Freddie Francis to revisit Boreham Wood to unveil a commemorative plaque honouring the MGM British Studios.

When the unit went off to shoot in Africa, Roy Parkinson recalled, "I met Clark at Nairobi Airport and he seemed very pleased to see me, a friendly face in a foreign land. That evening we consumed quite a few drinks together before going into dinner at the New Stanley Hotel and had to concentrate on steering a straight line to the dining table!

There has been much talk about him and Grace Kelly but from my point of view as Production Manager, what goes on between artistes is nothing to do with me unless it interferes with production. All I can say about Clark was that he was no trouble, always most friendly and co-operative in every way. Ford never saw the rushes as he felt he knew what had been shot and filmed in such a way that it would be very difficult for anyone to edit the picture in any other way than he wanted it.

I remember one scene where Gable was supposed to be whipped by a native as a test of strength but he was not keen on it. Instead they decided he would stand against a board and the natives would throw spears close to his body. The prop boys had to stay up all night creating hollow spears which were attached to the board by a wire so when thrown they travelled down the wires and stuck into the board around Gable."

Elliott Scott was on the location and reported back to the studio "Ford does not decide until the night before what he is going to shoot. He does not abide by the script and thinks out new scenes daily. He shoots in small snatches so that it cannot be edited in any other way than he intended. There is a complete 2nd unit here which is an exact replica of the main unit with doubles, make up, wardrobe, 3 Assistant Directors, etc and in 9 weeks in Kenya have only shot 2 plates as Ford won't give away information or ideas on his wishes.

We flew out of Heathrow to Nairobi via Frankfurt then stopped for 90 minute lunch break. Then to Rome for a 90 minute tea break then to Khartoum for another 90 minute stop. We spent 2 days in Nairobi then flew 700 miles to the camp site which had its own one mile long airstrip."

While at the MGM Studios Clark endeared himself to the staff and one lady cleaner recalled years later "I was cleaning his dressing room and he walked in. I said "Oh Mr. Gable. I have loved all your pictures and I love your beautiful smile. To send himself up he took out his false teeth and said 'It's only Hollywood make-believe."

Ava Gardner was obviously preoccupied with the abortion and a stormy relationship with Frank Sinatra who visited the location and on occasions sang around the camp fire. Gable is supposed to have enjoyed an affair with Grace Kelly who was no puritan when it came to her leading men. Back in London they both stayed at The Savoy and on 15th April he drove her to Heathrow Airport for what was described as a tearful farewell on her part. Kelly had been paid a reported $850 a week on the film and of course went on to become Princess Grace of Monaco before her tragic death in a car crash.

'Knights Of The Round Table' brought medieval England back to Boreham Wood and put Robert Taylor back into chain mail. He disliked costume roles but was a loyal star to MGM eventually clocking up 24 years under contract. He was also comforted by a $6,000 a week paycheck.

This time he remembered about the food shortages in London and had some steaks flown in and gave them to the hotel chef with special cooking instructions. They came back overcooked to the dinner party and the usually placid Taylor was so livid, he stormed out.

Ava Gardner joined him as the leading lady but thought little of the film, calling it 'a bit of historical foolishness.' She was still suffering in her personal life with terrible rows with Sinatra and another abortion. On 9 July she sent a memo to the studio manager complaining about the non-arrival of morning coffee and afternoon tea on set which had previously worked so well on **'Mogambo'**.

That superb screen villain George Sanders was cast but pleaded to be let out of his contract as was on the verge of a nervous breakdown following chaotic filming of a movie in Italy with Ingrid Bergman. Sanders broke down on the phone several times when talking to the Producer and it was finally decided he was too much of a risk. The casting department recommended a new British actor making his mark called Stanley Baker who was under contract to Korda. It was agreed he would be good and at £6,000 fee for the film was a cheap option.

Baker went on to enjoy a successful screen career during the 1950s and 60s culminating with the classic adventure story **'Zulu'**. However, although now a wealthy man, his career then went into decline. In 1976 he was diagnosed with terminal lung cancer and spent his final months in his villa in Spain as the disease spread through his body. His final triumph was the award of a knighthood in his dying days.

One person not sorry to see Sanders go was make-up artist Frank Westmore who recalled "I hated George Sanders. It took over a week to get to the point of exchanging even a good morning and when introduced he would spare only two fingers of his right hand to shake mine. He was having a nervous breakdown and luckily was replaced."

Robert Taylor seemed to enjoy his time on the film commenting "It has been my good fortune to make several movies in England and there is nothing so beautiful as an English summer. The countryside is so green and everyone so friendly."

Roy Parkinson recalled "Taylor was such a professional, always on set on time, word perfect and tended to stay around in case he was needed. He was a continuity girl's dream as he always ensured he was dressed exactly as needed to match up with anything previously shot."

The production was hit by bad weather and by a couple of strikes. Firstly 200 extras turned up at the studio and started changing for a crowd scene. They had been engaged at 2 guineas a day but then demanded 3 guineas. The Studio refused so they walked and the dispute dragged on from 17th June to 20th July when MGM agreed to pay the extra money.

Then they had agreed to use real British soldiers with the War Office for a particular scene but the union objected so the Director decided to shoot one battle scene in Ireland. He then hit a problem when the extras in Northern Ireland objected to the heavy armour and then the Motion Picture Producers Association objected to the move. In the end the Eire Government allowed shooting there and provided 300 soldiers as extras.

The salaries for the stars were recorded as $111,666 for Robert Taylor, $130,000 for Ava Gardner as her box office appeal was on the increase and Mel Ferrer got $54,166. It was said the film itself cost £1,500,000 to make and shot for 14 weeks from April to August. I have been told that two complete films were actually made, one using an anamorphic lens and the other a wide angle lens both shooting simultaneously. They opted for Eastmancolor rather than Technicolor. It was the first British feature shot in

Cinemascope.

The castle set on the MGM backlot had once again proved very useful and was occasionally used by outside productions. Actor Harry Andrews (1911-1989) told me "We shot some scenes for a movie called **'The Black Prince'** there in about 1954. The star was Alan Ladd who was easy and charming but had a great complex about his height or lack of it. As I am over six feet tall I had to be certain not to stand too close to him in scenes or arrange to be sitting. Sometimes if we were walking together they would shoot from the waist up so he could walk along a raised platform."

'Saadia' was a romantic story of a French doctor in the Sahara not only having to deal with his love life but with a witch doctor, and it did little to impress the cinema-going public. Directed by Albert Lewin they imported Mel Ferrer, Rita Gam and Cornel Wilde to bolster its chances but to little avail. The studio had originally been thinking of James Stewart and Victor Mature but obviously lowered their sights.

The Casting Director at the MGM British Studios was Irene Howard (1903-1981), the sister of that great romantic lead of the 1930s Leslie Howard. For this film she reported in a memo "I could obtain a young actor named Richard Johnson for the part of one of the lieutenants at £65 a week for the 8 weeks and have obtained his release from several BBC commitments."

The final film of 1953 was also not a blockbuster but had a great cast with Clark Gable, Lana Turner and Victor Mature. **'Betrayed'** was a wartime story set in Holland, with Victor Mature as a traitor uncovered by Clark Gable in the resistance movement.

It was the end of the road for Gable and his long run as a contract star for MGM. Negotiations over a new contract had been underway since **'Mogambo'** and this film was a one-off extension. MGM were in the process of shedding their roster of actors under contract and were moving away from the boast of 'more stars than in the heavens' . The discussions had not gone well and Gable is reported to have told his agent to "take them as high as they will go and then tell them to stuff it" or words to that effect.

He remained angry with the management over the fact they never gave him a slice of the huge profits from **'Gone With The Wind'**. After completing **'Betrayed'** the onetime 'King of Hollywood' flew back to Los Angeles. After 24 years under contract, his last day was a morning photo shoot at their Culver City studio. He then drove out without any official send off. Just a few years later while changing a tyre at home he suffered a heart attack. Taken to hospital he seemed to be on the road to recovery but a few days later while in bed reading a magazine his heart failed. Gable was buried next to his beloved Carol Lombard and his longed for son was born just a few months later.

In the supporting cast was a young Ian Carmichael who recalled the experience. "Gable was quiet and reserved but always on set by 8.30 am and ready to go. Victor Mature had the gift of memorising the whole script in advance but was unworried by any last minute changes. On paper I had a good role but if I was in a scene with one of the stars they tended to shoot me over the shoulder or in long shot.

> It is interesting to note that a study in 1953 attempted to identify the average cost of making a main feature British film. It decided that the average such film cost between £100,000 and £110,000.
>
> On average the hire of a studio would account for 20% of the budget and 15% would go on hiring the actors with another 15.6% spent on labour and sets. The cheapest components were insurance at 1.5% and the story including script at 3.4%.
>
> By comparison I recently saw a British film, basically a short students' film extended to feature length with no stars and shot on location. It cost £1 million.

When I went to the premiere at the Empire in Leicester Square I was stunned to see Louis Calhern appearing in the film although he had neither been on location nor at the studio. It turned out they shot all his scenes in Hollywood after we completed the picture. I was cast after a brief meeting at Claridges with the Producer and Director. It was good money compared with what I had been earning but I must admit to having been disappointed with the film."

David Bowen, who was a boom operator and later a sound mixer at MGM, told me, "I remember Gable as a nice chap and very professional when doing the post synch on the film. He was very relaxed and we shared an interest in sports cars to talk about. What we found amusing was that he was always 'bumming' cigarettes from us and never seemed to have his own."

■ ■ ■ ■

1954 saw a STEP UP in activity with seven films filmed or partly filmed at the studio as well as one television series.

'The Vise' was a low budget television series produced by the, shall we say, economically-minded Danziger Brothers. They soon decided it would be more economical to create their own studio and the following year they did just that. They converted and extended a World War II engine-testing facility near Elstree Village and cheekily called it 'The New Elstree Studios'. It lasted only a handful of years but produced a large amount of support features and televised series. However, that story is for another book.

'The Dark Avenger' used the castle set standing on the MGM backlot but was based at the nearby Elstree Studios. It was another swashbuckler starring Errol Flynn but by this stage of his life he had almost swashed his last buckle. He was using both drink and drugs to 'enjoy' life and along with his smoking they were taking their toll on his health.

During one sword fight sequence Flynn misjudged a movement and left actor Christopher Lee with a permanently scarred finger. The Producers of the film had insisted Flynn lose weight for the role but when he turned up it was obvious he had failed. Heavy drinking meant his best work was done in the mornings.

Olivia de Havilland, who co-starred in several classic movies with him in the 1930s told me "I moved to Paris but was invited back to Hollywood for some event in the late 1950s. I was at a reception when someone tapped me on the shoulder and said 'Hello sport'. I turned round and for a second did not recognise it was Errol as he had aged so much and his eyes seemed dead. It was a big shock as when we worked together he had been so full of life and I had a big crush on him."

During his stay Flynn visited nearby Hatfield House, where Queen Elizabeth 1 was residing when she learned of her ascent to the throne. Errol continued working and indeed gave some excellent screen performances, ironically as a drunk. He always said 'Enjoy your first 50 years as after that it is all an anti-climax.' True to his motto at that age in 1959 he was in Vancouver to sell his yacht and died of a heart attack while visiting friends.

Jeremy Summers worked on the film as an Assistant Director and told me "The Ivanhoe castle on the MGM backlot was quite a visible local landmark. We were able to adapt it for use on this picture. We also shot at Tring Park a battle between knights on horseback. I was asked to go up a hill and cue the knights when to ride down via a walkie talkie when the camera crew were ready.

The trouble was they could see me in the shot so they decided I should don some armour and get on a horse so I could charge down the hill with them! We always had an ambulance on standby and the stunt riders were paid £10 if they had to fall off their horses. Flynn told me off once when I called him to the set. He arrived, saw the scene to be shot and just walked off saying his double can do that, 'Don't ever call me unless it is a close up shot.'"

'Beau Brummell' was MGM's big film of the year and starred Stewart Granger, Robert Morley, Elizabeth Taylor and Peter Ustinov who later said it was a film he really enjoyed making.

Granger had a reputation as being difficult and he once told me, "I admit I was a bit of a sod as I had no respect for the studio system or for most of the films I appeared in." This was reflected in a memo sent from Culver City before filming even began. It read "Granger is being temperamental. He wants the costumes to be pure white while costume designer Walter Plunkett has made them in Technicolor one (off white). Can lighten to Technicolor half but you must see if the cameraman in the UK is okay with that or persuade Granger. He also wants the sets built to suit his favoured profile regarding

---

It was reported that year that 32% of all box office takings in the UK went to the Government in the dreaded entertainments tax. Admissions to cinemas were down from 1,635,000,000 in 1946 to 1,275,776,000 in 1954. About 190 cinemas had closed during those years as the steep decline began and total box office gross had reduced rom £118,300,000 in 1946 to £109,992,000.

his nose."

He was not popular with the crew so he decided to offer to pay for their tea trolley each day on set. Head Shop Steward Harry Downing remembered "The problem was the crew started ordering more and more – tea, coffee, cakes, sandwiches, rolls – and he got a bit alarmed but did not know how to get out of it. I agreed I would tell them to stop if he agreed to give them each a tip at the end of the film." Granger later remarked "English film crews resented stars and were always looking for trouble that eventually destroyed the industry."

Both Granger and Liz Taylor disliked the Director Curtis Bernhardt who they considered was a bit of a martinet. On occasions Liz would go up and yawn in his face so overall it was not a happy production.

Locations were filmed at the 15th century Ockwell Manor near Windsor Castle. Eleanor Powell had first been announced to play the role eventually allocated to Taylor.

For some reason the film was chosen for the Royal Film Performance of that year, which seemed odd considering the subject matter.

'Prize Of Gold' was a good little crime thriller based in post war Berlin and England when an American soldier (Richard Widmark) is persuaded to smuggle gold to England by Mai Zetterling and gets fellow soldier George Cole and criminals Donald Wolfit and Nigel Patrick to help.

The film was partly shot on location in Germany by Director Mark Robson and moves along at a cracking pace. Robson (1913-1978) started as a prop boy at 20th Century Fox in Hollywood in 1932 then became an editor before progressing to a Director. His other film credits included Humphrey Bogart's last film **'The Harder They Fall'** and the 1974 disaster movie, in more ways than one, **'Earthquake'**. Nigel Patrick and Richard Widmark never gave bad performances, Donald Wolfit could eat up the screen and it is good to see George Cole in an early non-comedy role.

'That Lady' brought together newcomer Paul Scofield with Olivia de Havilland and Gilbert Roland with support from Dennis Price and Christopher Lee. It was a tepid romantic costume drama with locations shot in Spain between May to July under the directorship of Terence Young. At least a young Lee got to play several minor roles before being engulfed in 'Hammer horrors' a couple of years later.

'Gentlemen Marry Brunettes' was produced to cash in on the success of **'Gentlemen Prefer Blondes'** which had paired Marilyn Monroe with Jane Russell but this

> The end of 1954 saw over 300 redundancies as no MGM film had been made at the studio for quite a few months.
>
> The staffing levels varied each year. 1948 had seen 784 employed while 1949 experienced a reduction to 545 and a further decrease to 416 in 1950.
>
> During the 1950s the numbers were 364 (1951), 487 (1952), 680 (1953), 344 (1954), 502 (1955), 671 (1956), 662 (1957), 547 (1958) and 592 in 1959.

time the latter was paired with Jeanne Crain who was reportedly dubbed for some reason in this light comedy musical. The film went on location to Paris and Monte Carlo and was due to complete at Shepperton Studios but lack of room required the move to MGM. The end of picture party took place at the adjoining Elstree Way Inn.

'Flame And The Flesh' brought together Lana Turner, Pier Angeli and Carlos Thompson but was mainly shot on location in Italy. This was Turner's first film outside of America as she previously turned down **'Mogambo'** which she later regretted. The film was produced by Joe Pasternak (1901-1991) best remembered today for his musical films starring Deanna Durbin, Esther Williams and Mario Lanza.

'Stranger From Venus' was a B Movie known as **'Immediate Decision'** in the USA starring Helmut Dantine and Patricia Neal. This science fiction thriller was presumably meant to cash in on the spate of similar movies following the success of **'The Day The Earth Stood Still'**. The interiors were shot at the studio but a number of exteriors were filmed at the nearby Edgwarebury Country Club that also featured in films such as **'School For Scoundrels'** starring Terry Thomas.

Dantine (1918-1982) had started in small roles in classic films such as **'Casablanca'** and **'Mrs. Miniver'** and would return to Boreham Wood in the 1960s for **'Operation Crossbow'**. Patricia Neal (1926-2011) enjoyed a successful film career, a noted romance with the married Gary Cooper in the 1950s and later a long marriage to author Roald Dahl.

The film was directed by Burt Balaban (1922-1965) whose father was once President of Paramount.

One project announced that never happened was a film entitled **'Digby'** which was to be a comedy starring Spencer Tracy on location in Scotland and with interiors at MGM.

■ ■ ■ ■

Only five productions went before the cameras in 1955 and they were certainly a mixed bag.

'Another Time, Another Place' was a love triangle story involving Lana Turner, Glynis Johns and a young Sean Connery years before his fame as James Bond.

In her private life Lana Turner was embroiled in a stormy relationship with a shady character named Johnny Stompanato. He followed her to Boreham Wood and began to create problems at the studio. First he insisted they be given a nicer apartment which raised the rent from £75 to £100 a week and they ran up bills exceeding the £150 weekly expenses allowed. He would sit on stage 3 looking menacing and concerned that Lana did not look twice at her handsome co-star.

Eventually MGM had endured enough and the studio publicist Paul Mills told me "They decided to approach the Government and managed to get him deported as an undesirable alien due to his criminal connections." The story had a sad ending when in Hollywood Lana's teenage daughter found her mother and Stompanato in a stormy row and it resulted him laying dead on the floor with a stab wound. The ensuing court case became one of the biggest celebrity scandals of the 1950s.

'The Gamma People' was a strange story of the doings of a sinister scientist in a small European state with locations in the Austrian Tyrol. The two stars were Paul Douglas and Leslie Phillips.

The Director John Gilling (1912-1984) later became associated with Hammer horror productions including **'Plague Of The Zombies'** and **'The Mummy's Shroud'**. The female lead was played by Eva Bartok who was one of those European actresses who sprang to stardom in the 1950s and 1960s and then vanished. Bartok was once married to actor Curt Jurgens and had a much-publicised affair with Frank Sinatra. Her career on screen finished in the 1970s and it was reported at the time of her death in 1998 that she had been living alone in a run-down hotel in Paddington, the glory days of stardom long forgotten.

'Safari' went even farther for its locations in Kenya, at Archers Post 200 miles from Nairobi. However, the location was not a happy experience for cast and crew. Female lead Janet Leigh fell ill. Character actor Roland Culver told me "We had been filming at the studio for a few weeks when on a day off I played tennis and tore my tendon. It would have cost the company a fortune to scrap the footage and recast me so I was strapped up and was accompanied by a nurse and masseur on location in Kenya. It was very painful and they had to use a double whenever my character was required to walk, so not a happy time."

There were threats from Mau Mau rebels, £500 was stolen from the Production Manager's tent and Director Terence Young was seriously ill with a temperature of 102 degrees but carried on. The heat meant they had to bury film stock underground to keep at an even temperature. Problems with strong sun casting shadows on actors' faces caused the need for matching shots to be done back at MGM.

> In her autobiography ('There Really Was A Hollywood' published by Doubleday 1984) Janet Leigh recalled MGM British, "The studio is a lovely ride from town nestled in a pictorial residential area. Filming is different, not in equipment so much or in achieving performance but more in attitude and custom. There is a matron for your dressing room. Tea is served religiously every day on set. There are very civilised working hours including a 5 day week which fortunately Hollywood adopted soon after.
>
> In spite of the formality, there is an easy feeling, relaxed and much is accomplished. It was a productive atmosphere. Strikes were common occurrences at the studio. The electricians walked off at one point because there was too much dust. Unlike the States, the administrators displayed extreme calm, almost resignation. Another time there was a general token strike by all of the guilds. These interludes were used to work on script changes and have visits.
>
> Gene Kelly dropped in, Paul Douglas, Compton Bennett. We watched Clifton Webb on the set of **'The Man Who Never Was'**."

The film's star Victor Mature seems to have sailed through but he was very reluctant to do anything that looked a bit risky. He later commented "I may look tough but at heart I am a coward. Cecil B DeMille once asked me to wrestle a lion in one of his films. I said no way but he said the Lion was quite safe as it was old and had no teeth. I replied 'I don't even want to be sucked to death!'"

Victor was always ready to send himself up and another of his favourite stories was when he applied to join a snobbish golf club in Los Angeles. "They said 'Sorry sir, we don't allow actors membership.' and I replied 'Me an actor? Have you ever seen any of my films?'"

Producer Cubby Broccoli recalled "Victor was a nice guy and good fun but by his own words a devout coward. He insisted on two white hunters guarding him the clock round while in Africa. He was scared to death when he had to rescue Janet Leigh from a river in case of crocodiles and in one scene picked her up but dumped her into the river when something brushed past his leg."

In September a big film booked in to shoot one scene. Director Michael Anderson had just finished making **'1984'** at Elstree Studios and Noel Coward recommended him to Producer Mike Todd to helm his giant production of **'Around The World In 80 Days'** They turned stage 3 into the Reform Club for the scene involving such British stalwarts as Trevor Howard, Robert Morley, Basil Sydney and Ronald Squires.

One extra recalled "I went into the canteen during shooting and saw Clifton Webb, Noel Coward, Peter Ustinov and John Gielgud and felt quite star struck as they were big names then.'

'The Adventures Of Quentin Durward' brought back Robert Taylor under the directorship of Richard Thorpe with support from Kay Kendall, Robert Morley and a young George Cole.

It was the first MGM production into the studio for almost a year but perhaps it was

---

Ealing Studios closed in 1955 and was sold to the BBC for £300,000. The Head of Ealing Sir Malcolm Balcon told me, "We decided to close our own studio due to the overheads and changing production needs so I hired space at the MGM Studio. We made 6 or 7 films there, and at the time it was the best of Europe. They were well laid out, well equipped and the staff very good indeed. The studio proved its capability for the production of films of the highest standards."

Actor Norman Bowler, who later enjoyed television success commented, "I came straight out of drama school and was put under contract by Ealing/MGM. The scheme ended when Ealing folded altogether, but for a time there were 12 of us under contract including Maggie Smith and Shirley Anne Field."

The Ealing agreement with MGM was that they would back 3 films a year allowing use of the studio, partly financing each film and agreeing to distribute in the USA.

one visit to the well too much with regard to 'knights of old' storylines as the film was reported to have cost $2,500,000 but lost about $1,200,000. Even today Producers and studios tend to milk a vein until it is dry and the 1950s were no exception.

Rigger Alf Newvell recalls "I was asked if I would like a job at the studio for 6 weeks and ended up staying 14 years and 10 months. That was my first film and there was a scene where Taylor has to fight the villain hanging from bell ropes. Another rigger and myself were fit enough and able to swing from one rope to another easily but they would not let us act as doubles as we were not in the right union. They kept testing people with no luck so in the end we had to rig up hidden wires and pulleys and Taylor sat on a bit of wire and a pole. It all had to be wrapped up so he would not hurt his bum and we would be swinging him about."

■ ■ ■

1956 was a bumper year for production with a total of 14 films partly or entirely made at the studio, which was good news in the face of falling cinema attendances worldwide and the growth of television as the main entertainment media.

'The Barretts Of Wimpole Street' was an old fashioned romantic drama directed by Sidney Franklin and starring Jennifer Jones, Bill Travers, Virginia McKenna and Leslie Phillips.

During filming Jennifer Jones dedicated a plaque at 50 Wimpole Street (the original Barrett residence no longer existed) and unveiled a figure of herself as the character at Madame Tussauds.

Franklin (1893-1972) had been in the film business since the First World War and alternated the role of Director with that of Producer on such classics as **'Mrs. Miniver'** and **'Random Harvest'.**

Veteran actress Jean Anderson remembered "It was not a happy film. Jennifer was more of a star than an actress and had to be told every move. I played her companion but between takes she never spoke to me." Virginia McKenna recalled "Miss Jones was always pleasant but slightly aloof and sat apart." and Bill Travers commented, "She refused to rehearse scenes which I found very difficult as my background was the theatre."

'Stars In Your Eyes' was a low budget effort about four music hall pals who put on a show in a derelict theatre and starred Bonar Colleano, Joan Sims and Dorothy Squires.

It was directed by veteran Maurice Elvey (1887-1967) who was living on the streets of London aged nine, found work in the theatre and then moved into film production where he directed scores of movies.

Bonar Colleano achieved some success in British films after the war, often playing Americans but tragically died at an early age in a car crash. He left his widow and young son in dire financial straits due to Inland Revenue bills and other debts, although friends such as Sid James staged fund-raising efforts.

'Port Afrique' actually started on location on 24 October 1955 and was a mystery story set in Morocco. It moved back to MGM on 18th November and continued in production until the new year. Certain scenes were shot at nearby Elstree Aerodrome. It starred Philip Carey, Pier Angeli, onetime girlfriend of James Dean, and reliables Dennis Price and Anthony Newley.

Pier Angeli remembered "The Director very kindly gave me a present of my screen wardrobe at the end of the film which was lovely as you don't usually get to keep clothes you wear in a film." Sadly, Angeli was to take her own life in September 1971 with a drug overdose.

Christopher Lee had a supporting role and shared a room with Anthony Newley on location. He remembered that there was a lot of trouble with Arab terrorists at the time so one day while Newley was taking a shower, he put on an Arab accent and burst into the bathroom as if he was about to murder him and gave Newley quite a scare.

'Little Hut' started production at Elstree Studios but ran into problems with the electricians and carpenters . The men were insisting they provide the crew going to Italy on location despite their own union saying it was not necessary, the studio saying they could not be spared and the Italians saying they would not allow it. The film eventually moved from MGM to Cinecitta in Rome with just 10 British crew as the compromise. The budget was £600,000.

The film paid nearby Arkley Golf Course the sum of 20 guineas to shoot two simple scenes involving Ava Gardner and David Niven. It was at this golf course that years later racing driver ace Graham Hill crashed in a light aircraft and was killed.

Ava Gardner later described the film as "A real fiasco which I hated" and the movie's third star Stewart Granger commented "I ended up playing a straight man to Niven's moustache which he kept playing with when I was saying my lines."

'Odongo' continued the trend for stories set in Africa and imported Hollywood B-listers Rhonda Fleming and Macdonald Carey and returned to the studio in December 1955 after four weeks in Kenya at an animal farm situated 140 miles from Nairobi, run by a well-known white hunter named Carr Hartley. Production was suspended at one point when Rhonda Fleming, the cameraman and several crew members were struck down by a flu bug.

Also returning from Africa was **'Beyond Mombassa'** after four weeks location shooting. It starred Cornel Wilde and Donna Reed with support from Leo Genn and Christopher Lee.

Lee recalled "My first big role and the film was great fun to make. However, I did injure myself on location and even caught malaria but the veteran Director George Marshall kept everyone laughing. I was also attacked by a mechanical crocodile in the tank at MGM but survived."

'Zarak' was a drama set on the North West Frontier and told the story of a bandit chief who saves the life of a British officer. It starred Victor Mature and Michael Wilding who were now fading box office stars, plus Anita Ekberg for sex appeal.

This was still an era of strict censorship in America and the censors were unsettled that the script indicated people living together outside of marriage, that there were two open-mouthed kissing scenes and too much violence. When the film was completed they insisted on several cuts of suggestive dances, trimmed whipping scenes and ordered the removal of the line 'closed up for the night'. They eventually released the film with a certificate even though they felt it contained grossly suggestive costumes and dancing. Those were the days and heaven knows what they would have said about **'Last Tango In Paris'** which was released less than 20 years later.

'Fire Down Below' featured an all star cast of Robert Mitchum, Rita Hayworth and Jack Lemmon, supported by Herbert Lom and Bernard Lee. The production spent eight weeks on location in Trinidad and the Director cut the film in London but when it was sent back to Hollywood the studio completely re-edited it.

In 1986 Jack Lemmon told me, "To the best of my recollection, Boreham Wood studio was quite similar to the small studios in Los Angeles and in fact reminded me of the Sam Goldwyn lot. Certainly it was more intimate and had more ambience than the larger studios in Hollywood such as MGM or Universal. My entire stay in London was wonderful not only because of the ambience but because the facilities were excellent.

I do remember the experience was very joyous because it was my first opportunity to visit England and because of delays in the picture, which secretly delighted me, much to the chagrin of Irving Allen and Cubby Broccoli, the Producers, I was prepared to stay in London for the rest of my life. London has remained my favourite city in the world as the people are warm and gracious."

Jack recalled on another occasion "Rita Hayworth was happy until she overheard one of the Producers query a delay while lighting a set for her and his remark 'Whatever you do, you can't make her look younger' which made her cry and she played up a bit thereafter."

'Anastasia' was another all-star production with Ingrid Bergman playing a claimant to the Russian throne with Yul Brynner and Helen Hayes. This was the comeback film for Bergman after several years spent in 'exile' making films in Europe after her love affair with Roberto Rossellini had caused a scandal in America. The film used locations in Paris and Copenhagen as well as closer to home at Knebworth House. Bergman very much wanted to do the film but struggled with the standard acting methods after the more improvised work in European films directed by Rossellini.

Her fellow star and veteran Oscar winner Helen Hayes later recalled, "She had trouble with the emotional scenes and in the end we had to loop the dialogue later. I had not really wanted to do the film as I had recently lost my husband and it killed off my interest in carrying on with my film career." Hayes did occasionally return to movies and in 1970 won another Oscar for her supporting role in **'Airport'** which was collected by Rosalind Russell on her behalf at the ceremony. Hayes died in 1993.

Bergman's co-star Yul Brynner is probably best remembered today for **'The Magnificent Seven'** but he had a string of film hits and enormous success on stage in **'The King And I'** which he continued performing until his death in 1985.

Bergman was paid $200,000 for **'Anastasia'**

and it not only relaunched her Hollywood career but won her an Oscar which was collected by Cary Grant as she was in Paris at the time of the ceremony.

Part of **'Sea Wife'** was shot at the studio starring rising star Joan Collins and Richard Burton. The latter was drinking heavily on location and one MGM crew member told me "He offered me a drink in the bar but I was on early call so I declined and he took offence and stubbed his lighted cigarette out on my hand. I complained to the union representative and the next day I was called into the production office and asked not to make a fuss."

'Man In The Sky' was an aircraft test flight drama starring the ever reliable Jack Hawkins and directed by Charles Crichton. It was retitled for the USA market as **'Decision Against Time'** and was good entertainment in its day.

Hawkins always gave a good performance, ranging from his appearances in blockbusters like **'Bridge On The River Kwai'** and **'Ben Hur'** to the British crime classic **'League Of Gentlemen'**. Sadly an operation for throat cancer caused him to lose his voice in the early 1960s but he carried on with guest parts with his lines dubbed by other actors. Tragically he died whilst undergoing treatment to implant an artificial voice box in 1973.

'Bhowani Junction' was MGM's next big film into the studio for interiors and with some scenes on the backlot. It starred Ava Gardner who described her co-star Stewart Granger as "Great fun and a nice guy". Ava recalled "The scene that stayed with me was shot at the studio and involved the character played by Lionel Jeffries raping me. I found filming the scene very traumatic so I insisted the Director call Lionel to my dressing room for a cuddle to help me forget it."

The Director was George Cukor who was gay and well-known for his pool parties for young men at his Hollywood home. Francis Matthews was cast in the film and told me "I think Cukor picked me as he thought we could have some fun together, but I was straight and much more interested in Ava. As a result he gave me a difficult time on the film. I was his whipping boy for six weeks and I thought he was a vicious old man. It was my first experience at MGM and I was very impressed when I saw the other names on my dressing room floor which included Kay Kendall, Robert Taylor, Ava Gardner, Bill Travers, George Cole and Stewart Granger"

Apparently Cukor was forced to change the end of the story as MGM did not want Ava's character marrying an Indian. The film started without a finished script and Cukor had wanted to cast Trevor Howard so was not happy with Granger. Many of the cast and crew fell ill on location which sometimes hampered the filming. Some felt MGM butchered the film to reduce running time.

'The Man Who Never Was' was based on the true Second World War story of when the British dumped a body dressed as a courier carrying important invasion plans off the coast of Spain, knowing they would be intercepted by German intelligence before being returned.

It was directed by Ronald Neame in a factual style and starred the gay Hollywood actor Clifton Webb in the leading role. The part was originally offered to Trevor Howard who told me, "I turned down the part and later I came up against the writer, who was also a magistrate, for a drink driving offence. He obviously had not forgiven me as he banned me from driving for years!" Webb turned up for filming sporting a moustache and was told to shave it off as Royal Navy officers were not allowed one in real life. He refused and the stand-off was broken when it was agreed that he could grow a beard as that would have been permitted by the Navy. They shot on location in Spain for 10 days but Webb refused to eat Spanish food so had food flown over from Fortnum and Mason's store in London. He still ended up with an upset stomach.

In one scene the camera pans across London and the crew were able to achieve the shot by climbing Big Ben which luckily had scaffolding erected for repairs. The film was reissued in 1960 with 20 minutes of cuts. Peter Sellers provided the voice for Winston Churchill in one scene. At the end of the film Noel Coward gave a lavish party at his London home; Ronald Neame remembered Coward and Webb dancing together and very well as Webb had been a West End and Broadway dancer.

Stephen Boyd was spotted in a play and the Producers were so certain that he would be great in the role, they paid off the actor already cast. Afterwards Boyd was signed up by Hollywood and today is best remembered for his role in **'Ben Hur'**. Sadly Stephen died at the age of 45 from a heart attack on a golf course in California.

'Fire Maidens From Outer Space' must rank as the worst film ever to be shot at the studio and as such is worth watching. It starred Hollywood actor Anthony Dexter who had played Valentino in a bio pic during the 1950s and British character actors Paul Carpenter, Sidney Tafler and Harry Fowler who played astronauts travelling to the 13th moon of Jupiter. Luckily for them it was inhabited by a race of young ladies who apparently were descendants of Atlantis. Now that may seem far-fetched but no more than their spaceship, which seemed to have no more than two controls. During the flight they were able to smoke and make tea. They also had an adding machine that seemed to work out directions.

For location spotters you will see Stirling Corner on the A1 and the observatory at Mill Hill in North London. You will also notice the MGM Studio clock tower and administration building exteriors doubling as the space agency control which seemed to be staffed by just a handful of people keeping in touch via a phone! Luckily it turned out that the moon of Jupiter looked the same as MGM's backlot.

The film's props man Tommy Ibbetson recalled "It was a real bargain basement movie. They even tried to use product placement as a source of budget revenue so if a character asked the time, the other person would reply 'By my Timex watch it is noon' or something similar. I told the Producer it was rubbish and was told off by the studio for expressing such an opinion."

The female lead was Susan Shaw, the widow of Bonar Colleano, who developed a drink problem and sadly died in poverty. The Rank Organisation, for whom she had started her film career, paid the funeral expenses. Antony Dexter faded into obscurity and Paul Carpenter, who starred in a number of British B movies, by the 1960s was reduced to bit parts, acting as a dance hall escort and died of a heart attack in a theatre dressing room. Sidney Tafler and Harry Fowler enjoyed successful careers as character actors.

1956 also saw MGM put Bill Travers under contract, possibly with the idea of casting him in **'Ben Hur'**.

■ ■ ■

1957 proved another busy years with 14 productions going before the camera including an early adventure into television.

'I Accuse' told the true story of the Dreyfus Affair in which an officer was wrongly imprisoned. It was directed by actor Jose Ferrer who also starred along with Donald Wolfit, Anton Walbrook and David Farrar. The film was shot between March to June at a cost of just under £200,000 which included a bit of location work in Belgium.

'Action Of The Tiger' was an adventure story about an American who helps people to be rescued from the communists and is based around Greece and Albania. It starred 1940s MGM 'bobby soxers' heartthrob Van Johnson, who enjoyed a long career but in his heyday had to keep the fact that he was bi-sexual secret as it would have destroyed his career. In has been rumoured in some Hollywood gossip books that MGM persuaded his good friend Keenan Wynn to divorce his wife so Van could marry her to protect his image. As all the parties concerned are now dead it is hard to verify but it is known MGM did a number of interesting things over the decades to protect their investment in their stars and to preserve their images in a more innocent age.

'The Safecracker' brought back to Boreham Wood an actor who had been discovered at Elstree Studios at the end of the 1920s. Ray Milland was now an Oscar winner and returned to star in and direct in this wartime story of a safecracker who is persuaded to crack a safe in occupied Belgium.

For the film Milland took part in commando training at Abingdon including an 80 feet training tower jump. Locations included

---

It is interesting to see what the pay was like in the mid 1950s in British films. The distinguished stage actor received £1,000 a week as did Anton Walbrook. The other star David Farrar was not so lucky with £777 a week.

The supporting cast varied from £400 per day for Herbert Lom, £25 a day for Charles Gray, £50 a day for Ronald Howard, son of Leslie to £160 a week for George Coulouris, £416 a week for Harry Andrews and £166 a week for Felix Alymer.

To put that money into perspective, Walbrook worked for 15 days, Williams for 10 days, Andrews for 6 weeks and Farrar for 9 weeks.

Hatfield House, Wilton Park and Wrest House, the former home of American ambassador Whitelaw Reid.

Milland enjoyed a long film and television career over several decades and in later life told me "I spent many years as what they call a leading man, but with time you have to transfer to character roles which are often more rewarding. Ironically that was triggered when I took off my toupee that I had worn since the late 1940s when I appeared in the hugely successful **'Love Story'** in the early 1970s.

I remember for this film I did that training jump and sprained my ankle. The last time I had worn a parachute was in Hollywood when I was making a film called **'I Wanted Wings'**. Between scenes I was offered a flight in one of the aircraft and during the flight we ran into a bit of trouble and I thought I might have to parachute out. Luckily we landed safely and I told the props man I nearly had to use his parachute I was wearing for real. He said 'I am glad you didn't as it is a dummy one!'" The publicity at the time reported that Milland loaned the green Jaguar car that Marilyn Monroe used while filming **'The Prince And The Showgirl'** at Pinewood Studios.

It is interesting to see how the shooting schedule for a film like this was tackled in the 1950s. The first day was camera tests on stage 1 and the studio lot. Days two, three and four were location shoots in nearby Shenley Road and in London in Bond Street and on the Thames Embankment. Day five saw a move to Wilton Park, the Army Education Centre near Beaconsfield where they also filmed on days six and seven.

Two days were then spent at the parachute training school at Abingdon before on day 10 they went to Wrest Park which doubled as the German headquarters they were to burgle. Day 11 was spent at Hatfield House to shoot at a farmhouse and on a country road.

From day 12 to day 28 they shot at the studio on stages 1, 2 and 3 recreating the interior of a barn, an army nissen hut, quartermasters store, prison, aircraft interiors, conference room and the interiors of the German headquarters.

Day 29 found them back at Hatfield House for a swamp and woods scene and on day 30 they moved just out of the studio into Clarendon Road in Boreham Wood for exterior shots of the street and the house in which Milland's character lived. The last 2 days were spent back at the studio for some insert shots, utilising the exterior of a studio building and the car park to match into some stock footage of a dog race track. All this lasted from late July to the start of September.

'Barnacle Bill' starred Alec Guinness as a seasick naval captain put in charge of a pier and gave him the opportunity to play several characters as he had so successfully done in **'Kind Hearts And Coronets'**.

Guinness enjoyed a great screen and stage career with his films being as diverse as **'The Ladykillers'** and **'Bridge On The River Kwai'**. In the 1970s he appeared in Elstree and made **'Star Wars'** which won him a new generation of fans and made him a fortune thanks to a percentage of the profits. Ironically he grew to hate 'the Star Wars circus and fame', fearing it would overshadow the rest of his work .

Alec Guinness later recalled that he had taken the film out of friendship for the Director but that was a mistake as it turned out just to be a comedy and could have been much more.

'Island In The Sun' was mainly set on a Caribbean island and boasted an all-star cast of James Mason, Harry Belafonte, Michael Rennie, Dorothy Dandridge, Stephen Boyd, Joan Fontaine and Joan Collins.

'The Shiralee' was a social drama set in Australia directed by Leslie Norman and starring Peter Finch.

Peter died of a heart attack in the 1970s while publicising his latest film **'Network'** and I recall visiting his grave in the Hollywood Forever cemetery in Los Angeles. I found him interred in a wall crypt opposite Rudolph Valentino. I had previously been told he was buried outdoors near Tyrone Power but the cemetery worker told me he had been dug up and moved as 'his family felt he would be happier indoors.'

During production **'How To Murder A Rich Uncle'** was known as **'Uncle George'** and was a comedy directed by actor Nigel Patrick and Max Varnel. It also starred Nigel who was one of my favourite 1950s stars and in a small supporting role was a young Michael Caine. He recalled "I got the role as it was a toss up between myself and Sean Connery. I got my full pay although my part was cut in the final print". Michael appears in about six scenes but utters only three words.

Years later Producer Cubby Broccoli remembered "Caine was chatting to me and asked if I remembered when two young actors stood in front of him for this bit part in **'How To Murder A Rich Uncle'** and if I recalled the other actor I rejected. I said no and he told me it was Sean Connery."

'Davy' gave comedian and singer Harry Secombe his stab at screen stardom under the direction of Michael Relph but his future lay on the small screen and radio. Relph (1915-2004) had started as an Art Director before graduating into producing and directing. His distinguished body of work included **'The Blue Lamp'** and **'League Of Gentlemen'**.

MGM arranged a special showing at what they described as one of the smallest and loneliest army camps in England at Long Marston near Stratford Upon Avon. To entertain the troops they brought along Secombe who had been performing in panto in Coventry and Ealing contract starlet Shirley Anne Field.

'High Flight' was filmed during the summer and revolved on an RAF cadet blaming the Commanding Officer, played by Ray Milland, for the death of his father. Milland was supported by Anthony Newley, Helen Cherry and Leslie Phillips.

The film was shot using television techniques and avoiding long takes. This enabled them to shoot 26 and 27 set ups on 2 days on location, which is fast. The locations included the army school in Buckinghamshire and the parachute training school in Berkshire. They also used RAF College at Cranwell although shooting was delayed by rain. Interiors were filmed on stage 4 at the studio. During filming the production used the working title of **'The Willie Gordon Story'**. The end of picture party was held at the Royal Air Force Club in Piccadilly. **'Gideon's Day'** was one of those popular 1950s dramas based around a Scotland Yard police officer played by Jack Hawkins. The choice of Director was unusual in that they picked John Ford who had a known dislike of the British establishment and was more at home with John Wayne westerns but he did a competent job. Ford cast actress Anna Lee in a role in order to try help her off the so-called communist blacklist that existed in Hollywood during the 1950s.

Ford's salary for the film was reported to be $150,000 plus 50% of the profits and the film came in at just under its budget at $543,600. The Producers Columbia Films treated the film's release in the USA badly, first by delaying it and then releasing it in black and white, cut by almost a third, as a support feature called **'Gideon Of The Yard'** .

'OSS' was mainly filmed at the National Studios in Boreham Wood and was a television series of 26 half hour episodes starring Ron Randall, based in World War Two and shot in black and white. Guest stars included Anton Diffring, Leslie Phillips and Christopher Lee.

Francis Matthews told me "I did the pilot for the series at MGM with the great Director Robert Siodmak who taught me more about the close up and other techniques than anyone. When the series started I was in India on **'Nine Hours To Rama'** so was replaced by Leslie Phillips."

'Lucky Jim' was a comedy set in a university and starred Ian Carmichael, Terry Thomas and Hugh Griffith, directed by John Boulting.

Ian recalled "We shot on the largest stage at MGM for a couple of weeks on a vast set representing the quadrangle of the university. The Art Director Elliott Scott made it three-sided utilising as much stock property as possible. At 200 feet by 100 feet it was the biggest set built at MGM to date. It was not a happy film at the beginning and the Director Charles Crichton was replaced two weeks into the ten week schedule by John Boulting, which some of the other actors felt was my fault. Boulting soon settled it down and in the end it turned out to be a good and funny film."

'No Time To Die' was a story of prisoners of war escaping from a desert prisoner of war camp and in the USA was released as **'Tank Force'**. It brought back Victor Mature, ably supported by a British cast of Anthony Newley, Leo Genn, Alfred Burke, Kenneth Cope and Bonar Colleano. The film had an 11 week schedule with Director Terence Young, averaging four minutes screen time a day which regained 10 of the 15 days they fell behind on the desert location due to bad weather. The Producer was looking to keep the budget under £220,000.

1957 also marked the last time that the Ivanhoe castle was used prior to its demolition. It was dressed as a Scottish for an episode in a long-running Hollywood television series called **'General Electric Theatre'** and hosted by Ronald Reagan. The episode was appropriately entitled **'Time To Go Now'** and starred Finlay Currie.

■ ■ ■ ■

1958 proved to be another bumper year of production including television series and undertaking screen tests for a major MGM film.

Hollywood Comes To Hertfordshire – The 1950s

The tests for **'Ben Hur'** to fill the supporting roles began in February and more were undertaken in June and July, with up to 18 a day. The first tests were directed by the very experienced Charles Frend and the comments on each of the actors prove interesting reading.

For the role of Balthasar he tested Bernard Miles ("very sound actor"), Finlay Currie ("you are familiar with his work, need I say more") and Noel Purcell ("had difficulty remembering his lines perhaps due to sleepless night as his plane had been grounded at Dublin airport the night before – a more emotional actor than Miles"). The role went to Currie.

Nora Swinburn tested for Miriam and was described as "efficient, sympathetic personality" but the part went to Martha Scott.

For the role of the Sheik they tested Ian Wallace ("fine warm personality, takes direction easily"), Donald Wolfit ("professional and efficient") and Paul Rogers ("face absolutely right, thoroughly polished stage performer larger-than-life approach which may not matter"). MGM cast the alcoholic 'over the top' but always enjoyable to watch Hugh Griffiths.

Guy Rolfe went for the role of Pilate ("most impressive, looks magnificent and good actor") but lost to Frank Thring. Derek Godfrey tested for Drusus ("looks magnificent in Roman costume") and acted as the stooge for some of the others in their tests but lost out to Terence Longdon.

Andre Morell got the role of Sextus, having come across as a "very efficient sound actor who gave a well thought-out performance." Laurence Payne got the role of Joseph despite having appeared "a little casual and could be better but perhaps that is his attitude to tests". He beat Michael Gough who was described as "extremely sensitive".

Others tested for roles were Nigel Green ("extremely satisfying actor"), Robert Shaw ("limited performer, fairly inflexible"), Patrick Holt ("fairly inflexible") Christopher Lee ("had very good possibilities"), Ernest Clarke ("inflexible under direction"), Diane Hart ("very difficult to direct, forgot her lines and has ideas about her best angle"), Michael Horden ("intelligent, easy to handle") and Lionel Jeffries ("1st class actor, plenty of humour, got out of sick bed to do test").

These were all familiar faces to cinema-going audiences of the 1950s and for some roles the Producers were spoilt for choice. For MGM they knew they could cast all the supporting roles with quality actors for low pay compared with Hollywood.

Anthony Quayle recalled 'I was offered the role of Messala which could not fail to be a success and no doubt would have launched me in Hollywood. I turned it down and it went to Stephen Boyd. On the other hand I had a great part at Elstree in **'Ice Cold In Alex'** and I was informed would lead to many offers but nothing happened, so you never know.'

'Doctors Dilemma' was a medical comedy starring Dirk Bogarde, Leslie Caron and Alistair Sim with Anthony Asquith directing. He was often called 'Puffin' and usually turned up for work in a boiler suit.

Leslie Caron recalled that she was offered the part despite being five months pregnant and warned them that they could only photograph her in full shot for a few weeks before the situation would be impossible to disguise. Leslie felt the warning fell on deaf ears as "The Producer was a grandfather and did not remember, while Asquith and Bogarde were both homosexual, but at least Cecil Beaton understood and designed my dresses accordingly."

She felt Asquith reminded her of 'an absent minded professor' and remarked that Bogarde was a fine subtle actor but prone to vanity, although they became good friends. Bogarde considered the film to be one of his favourites and loved working with Puffin, who would crouch under the camera while directing and always walk around with a banana in his pocket every day, saying it was for lunch but would never eat it.

'Inn Of The Sixth Happiness' was a big budget production and required the demolition of the Ivanhoe castle in March to make way for the Chinese village set on the backlot. The set eventually took up half a million square feet, making it the largest ever constructed in Europe up until that time.

The film starred Ingrid Bergman and featured Robert Donat. The Director Mark Robson recalled "Donat was so ill I shot the close ups early just in case he did not make it so we could use a double in long shots. In between takes he retired to his dressing room. Cary Grant visited the set; they were a similar age but the difference so upset Bergman that it reduced her to tears."

Cameramen Freddie Young told me "He walked like an old man and he could not remember his lines which greatly upset him. He had a brain hemorrhage during filming and on the last day of shooting he was so ill we had to use idiot boards for his lines. The crew gave him a loud round of applause when he finished his last scene."

Although he had always been plagued by asthma, Donat was actually suffering from a large brain tumour. When admitted to hospital after finishing his role, he worried if the crew had been given their presents from him. The only money he left was his fee for the film. Donat started on the picture in April and spent five weeks filming which included his 54th birthday. He died in June while the production was on location in Wales. Props man Tommy Ibbetson told me, "Bergman used to wheel him around in a wheelchair and was sometimes in tears."

Curt Jurgens was cast as Bergman's love interest but was miscast as an oriental. Freddie Young recalled "We had to use contact lens to disguise his blue eyes and he had a lot of trouble with them. He was basically cast as he was as tall as Bergman." The actor Sean Connery was tested for the part. It was reported that Jurgens had to pay $50,000 to get out of a contract with a French film company to take the role and would fly home to Europe each weekend.

With a $4 million dollar budget the Producer could afford to import mules from Ireland, use real Chinese costumes and antiques and employ the RAF to supply bombers marked up to appear to be Japanese aircraft.

Actor Burt Kwouk, later famous as Cato in **'The Pink Panther'**, told me "This was the film in which I got my first decent role and the first time I was called Mr. Kwouk at a studio." For filming they recruited Chinese waiters from London.

The original plan had been to shoot locations in Formosa but there were problems with their government. Ingrid Bergman later said that 10 years after filming she went to see the real life Gladys Aylward who she had portrayed but the lady had died a few days earlier.

Chief shop steward Harry Downing told me, "The studio management asked if I would agree to an outside company coming on site to bring material for the set. I said 'Yes, provided they used their own vehicles.' but then they started using MGM vehicles and we found out the company concerned was on a union blacklist. I told the studio manager they must leave but he just laughed so I gave him to 5pm. Nothing happened so I called a strike of all staff. While we picketing at the gates, the lads stopped a lady from crossing the line. I said let her through as she is the payroll clerk and if we stop her, we won't get our wages on time!"

The film was premiered in November 1958 at the Odeon, Leicester Square with the proceeds donated to RADA to create an acting scholarship in memory of Robert Donat.

'Corridors Of Blood' brought the legendary Boris Karloff to the studio and the film was the first X certificate to be filmed at the facility. It was a 4 week shoot under the working title of **'Doctor From The Seven Dials'** referring to a 19th century poverty-stricken area of London. Filming began on 12th May and Karloff was paid $37,500 with the actual filming costing £90,000. The budget was partly funded by MGM although they wanted to withdraw halfway through but eventually agreed to allow filming to be completed.

Although Karloff liked the film, MGM had less faith and delayed releasing it for a couple of years, eventually putting it out as part of a double bill after Christopher Lee, in the supporting cast, had become a star in Hammer Films.

During filming a running gag by Karloff was to offer to sweep the set each evening and at the end of picture party the crew presented him with a broom. Actress Helen Cherry told me "Boris used to visit our house which was about a mile from the studio. My husband Trevor Howard and he were great cricket fans."

Francis Matthews was in the supporting cast and shared his memories with me "It was a great pleasure to work with Boris and he was a lot of fun. He was always thoroughly prepared and was professional. Between takes we would listen to the cricket commentary on the radio. He was a lovely man and a true English gentleman."

'The Angry Hills' was directed by Robert Aldrich and starred Robert Mitchum in a World War Two story set in Greece. The Director had wanted Alan Ladd and felt Mitchum gave a bad performance, possibly because he spent too much time socialising off set. When on location the Greek and British crews did not get along and the Producers eventually cut the film by 30 minutes.

'Count Your Blessings' under the directorship of Jean Negulesco brought together 'professional Frenchman' Maurice Chevalier, Deborah Kerr and Rossano Brazzi. The film was mainly shot in Paris and Hollywood. Child actor Martin Stephens recalled buying Chevalier a tie for his 70th birthday.

'Dick And The Duchess' was a TV series of 26 episodes that had started shooting in 1957. The pilot had already been shown in the USA on CBS who had bought the series starring Pat O'Neal, Hazel Court and Richard Wattis.

Hazel Court recalled "The series was very important in my life and it was unusual being an American sitcom filmed in England. The Producer Nicole Milinaire went on to become the Duchess of Bedford. It was a success and another unusual thing about it was in bedroom scenes with my screen husband I was actually allowed to have both feet on the bed as the normal practice on film was you kept one foot on the ground or had separate beds!"

Milinaire stayed at the vicarage in Totteridge which was rented from the Vicar who had gone away for the summer. During production the unit publicist suggested it might be a good publicity gimmick to invite a real Duke to visit the set. Eventually the Duke of Bedford arrived and things obviously clicked as within a couple of years they had married and Milinaire thereafter concentrated on turning the family stately home Woburn Abbey into one of the prime tourist attractions in England. She died aged 92 in 2012.

'Dunkirk' was a worthy Ealing film telling the story of the famous wartime 'victory' of saving hundreds of thousands of Allied troops from the beaches of Dunkirk. It starred John Mills, Bernard Lee and Richard Attenborough, all of whom spent a lot of the 1950s in screen uniforms although the latter two played civilians in this film. 4,000 troops and hundreds of locals were used in the beach scenes shot at Camber near Rye. 30 small boats were assembled at the naval dockyard at Sheerness, some of which actually took part in the real life adventure.

John Mills recalled working for 19 weeks on the film. Principal photography lasted 13 weeks including 5 weeks at Camber Sands and 6 weeks on the 70 feet by 42 feet model tank at the studio. The biggest travelling matte ever attempted in the UK involved a backing of 70 feet wide and 40 feet high with foreground blue backing increasing the effective width to 200 feet, requiring the use of forty-five 150 amp lamps.

The mile long 'mole' at the beach head was recreated by a 100 feet version constructed on the big tank at MGM with a further piece built in perspective to increase the apparent length to more than 300 feet. The interior water tanks at MGM had three full size launches and sections of a paddle steamer and a destroyer for night shoots.

Rigger Alf Newvell recalled a tragic incident while filming on location. "We were near a sluice by the sea and a car parked by the edge. There was a man and a woman and when they went to drive off he must have selected a forward gear instead of reverse and the car went into the water. I dived in and was able to get the woman out, then went back for the man who had his foot trapped behind the pedal. I eventually got him out but heard that he died later that evening.

A couple of days later his sister turned up and kindly gave me a fiver for my efforts although I did not want paying. Then the unit publicist said a magazine wanted to do an article about it and they paid me £25 so all the money went towards a new pram for my family. MGM and Ealing

Hollywood Comes To Hertfordshire – The 1950s

> During the year a number of promising newcomers were put under contract by MGM including Paul Massie, Ann Fairbank, John Turner, Shirley Ann Field, John Lee, Maggie Smith, Millicent Martin and Richard Johnson.

both sent me letters of commendation."

Director Leslie Norman recalled "It was a difficult film to make as for instance I had only 3 days to film the scenes with the army as extras whatever the weather, but we brought it in under its budget of £400,000." The film was premiered in front of Her Majesty The Queen in March 1958 at the Empire Cinema, Leicester Square.

'First Man Into Space' was shot mainly in and around a mansion in nearby Hampstead Heath. The film was directed by Robert Day and starred Hollywood import Marshall Thompson. The voice of supporting actor Bill Edwards had to be entirely redubbed by Bonar Colleano who was killed in a car crash before the film was released.

Thompson went on to television success in the 1960s hit series **'Daktari'** and died in 1982. For this film Producer Richard Gordon recalled he paid him peanuts by today's standards. The film was premiered in Albuquerque, New Mexico since MGM publicity had wrongly assumed the film had been shot there, as that was where the story was set.

> In the 1958/9 British film and TV yearbook the studio boasted it was the first studio in Europe to make pictures in cinemascope, stereophonic sound, technirama and Todd-AO.

'Nowhere To Go' was a taut crime thriller directed by Seth Holt who a few years later was destined to be killed in a car crash. The film starred beefcake actor George Nader who had to keep his homosexuality and friendship with Rock Hudson under wraps due to the prevailing climate in that era. The film is interesting to view for a very early screen appearance by Maggie Smith. It also features Harry H Corbett, later to enjoy TV fame in **'Steptoe And Son'** and Bernard Lee, both playing against type as criminals.

Nader later commented "The supporting players are much better in England. Take Bernard Lee for instance. According to his calibre as an actor he ought to be called a star and the character actors in England give such thoroughly first-rate performances."

'Tom Thumb' was directed by George Pal and starred Russ Tamblyn, ably supported by Peter Sellers, Jessie Matthews, Bernard Miles and Terry Thomas, who suffered from bad back pain throughout filming and lived on painkillers. To make Tamblyn, at 5 feet 8 inches tall, look small, sets were built twelve times as large as normal with the drummer's hat 12 feet high and with a 40 feet circumference. A quilt used as a coat was 20 feet wide, 35 feet long and sewn with 2 inch stitches to increase the oversize effect.

■ ■ ■ ■

1959 started with the production of a neat little drama called **'Serious Charge'** *in which do-gooder vicar Anthony Quayle tries to help a juvenile delinquent Andrew Ray who rewards him by accusing the vicar of attempted male rape. Ray, the son of comedian Ted Ray, played the part well and Quayle was as reliable as ever.*

The gang of juveniles included Jess Conrad and a young singer named Cliff Richard playing the role of Curly. Cliff told me, "My hair was straight so you would have thought they could have just renamed the character but instead they insisted on curling it each day. However, in the film I am seen singing 'Livin Doll' which became a big hit and helped launch my pop career."

The exteriors were shot in Stevenage Old Town and the film was directed by Terence Young who was now a regular at the studio.

'Libel' also went into production in January at the studio and on location at Longleat House. Directed by Anthony Asquith, the film brought together Olivia de Havilland and Dirk Bogarde, the latter commenting later "It was a load of rubbish and we knew it was over the top so we hammed it up tremendously."

Under contract to the Rank Organisation, Bogarde became a big romantic star in the 1950s and he became known as 'the darling of the Odeons' often being mobbed or screamed at by young ladies. He grew to hate that form of stardom partly because he felt it denied him decent roles and partly no doubt he felt the image was fake as he was gay. Had such a fact become common knowledge it would have destroyed his career.

At another studio Bogarde starred in a film with the bi-sexual Michael Redgrave which was called **'The Sea Shall Not Have Them'**. An actor told me he was driving around Leicester Square with Noel Coward when they passed a cinema displaying Bogarde and Redgrave's names along with the film's title and Coward quipped "I don't know why. Everyone else has!"

Bogarde retreated to Europe in the 1960s and 70s and when I met him late in life, he came across as a slightly unhappy and embittered man. I invited him to an event at Elstree Studios but he replied that he was retired from the screen and had no desire to meet former colleagues or look back at the past.

In November 1959 **'Libel'** became the first MGM film to be premiered at the Empire, Leicester Square

'The Rough And The Smooth' brought together smooth Englishman Tony Britton and the Hollywood heavy William Bendix. Director Robert Siodmack (1900-1973) had scored a number of hits in Hollywood such as **'The Killers'** and **'The Spiral Staircase'**. The Daily Cinema industry magazine described it as "An outstanding British production, polished, literate, beautifully acted with immediate appeal for most audiences" Kine Weekly commented, "Highly polished and stoutly carpentered sex melodrama, a strong cast and intriguing story."

'A Touch Of Larceny' brought James Mason back to England. The Producers had originally wanted the more bankable David Niven as

Mason had slipped a bit since his heyday of the 1940s starring in Gainsborough melodramas. Some in the industry had not forgiven some derisory comments he made about British films when he left for Hollywood.

Mason recalled, "It was a happy film for me as it meant I could spend my 50th birthday back in England. I was saddened by my co-star George Sanders as he seemed to have so little interest in his career or the film. In fact he ripped out all the pages of the script on which he had no dialogue and had no interest in the plot. I came up with the title of the film which seemed a good choice."

The Producer Ivan Foxwell commented at the time "I hope the USA like it due to the increasing cost of production. For instance I made **'The Colditz Story'** for £136,000 and took £270,000 in the UK alone. Neither figure could be achieved today."

'House Of Seven Hawks' was the story of a search for Nazi loot and brought Robert Taylor back to the studio for the final time where he had first worked a decade earlier. He commented at the time "People in the States say the Brits are cold and unfriendly but that is nonsense. I took advantage of doing some travelling to such places as Clovelly in Devon and everyone was always welcoming."

Like many stars of the 1930s his big screen career was coming to an end and he was to turn more to television in the last few years of his life. Taylor had always been a 60 a day cigarette smoker and it was to cost him his life when he died of lung cancer in 1969. The crew noticed between takes he preferred his own company and would usually walk off to the side of the stage or to his dressing room alone.

Actress Linda Christian loved raw and green herrings and had a barrel flown in for the end-of-picture party but many of the crew preferred a pint and a pork pie.

The Director Richard Thorpe spent decades working for MGM on both sides of the Atlantic and was appreciated as a fast and reliable Director, although due to this some criticised his work as predictable.

'Gorgo' has become a bit of a cult monster film and was a big production, with 18 months preparation. Art designer Elliot Scott designed complete sets one-fifth and one-twenty-fifth normal size. One set of the Thames around Tower Bridge occupied half a sound stage. On stage 3 they used the whole tank for a scene of the monster attacking a destroyer which was a 15 feet model.

The film had a budget of $300,000 and it took 10 weeks to build the miniatures at a cost of $75,000. They also built a mechanical model 65 feet long of the monster Gorgo which was towed around London as a publicity stunt. It was reported that to make the noise of the monster they use 4 jet engines with the sound bounced through a wind tunnel. While the Producers were at the studio they announced they would be returning the following year with a 39 episode TV series called **'Sinbad The Sailor'** but it never happened. **'Jazz Boat'** was a B movie light hearted comedy musical starring Anthony Newley in which he gets involved with a criminal gang, co-starring James Booth, Lionel Jeffries and Joyce Blair.

'Beat Girl' started filming in August and attempted to capture the late 1950s coffee shops and beatnik era. Adam Faith starred and he told me, "Looking back we had some awful dialogue that has dated badly but it was correct for that period. I had started as a trainee in the editing departments of the Danziger and National Studios in Elstree and Boreham Wood, then I got a break into pop music. For some while I still held on to my union ticket in case the singing career fell apart but it never did and I also drifted into acting."

John Barry was involved in the music for the film and he subsequently enjoyed a memorable and distinguished career as a composer of film theme tunes.

Christopher Lee remembered "My role was a good one and different. However, it was all a bit hectic as I was literally running between that film and **'Too Hot To Handle'** set which was also shooting at MGM at the same time."

Watch out for a young Oliver Reed as one of the crowd of beatniks in an early screen appearance.

'Too Hot To Handle' starred the unforgettable Jayne Mansfield whose short film career certainly made an impact on the 1950s. Tragically she was to be killed in a car accident a few years later.

Barbara Windsor was in the supporting cast but does not have warm memories of Mansfield and told me "She would not even say good morning to us so I approached her to say we would like to be friendly but she just ignored me."

Mansfield at the height of her fame could earn $35,000 a week appearing in Las Vegas but her film career was on the slide and the production ran into financial problems when there was doubt they could pay the studio. The film had a budget of £250,000 but fell 10 days behind and shooting halted several times due to alleged 'bouncing cheques'. Director Terence Young was at the helm and it may have soured his relationship with the studio manager.

Veteran MGM props man Tommy Ibbetson told me "The word around the studio was that when Young was appointed Director of **'Dr. No'** the manager said 'No way is he working here again.' and so we lost the James Bond films to Pinewood." Young had been the Director who had helmed the most productions at the studio in the 1950s totaling seven but is now best remembered for the classic **'Dr. No'**, **'From Russia With Love'** and **'Thunderball'** which helped establish 007 as the huge franchise it has since become.

When **'Too Hot To Handle'** was released the critics described it as 'sordid and nasty'.

The studio looked to have a busy future and in September they announced future productions utilising the facility would include two feature films, one entitled **'In The Nick'** and another **'A Gift From The Boys'** starring Yul Brynner and directed by Stanley Donen. They also expected to play host to a 23 week production of an ATV series entitled **'Men In Danger'** with an option for a further 39 episodes and an MGM-produced TV series called **'Raffles'**.

'The Day They Robbed The Bank Of England' was much as the title suggested and starred newcomer Peter O'Toole who not long after was to shoot to worldwide fame as **'Lawrence Of Arabia'**. The Producer said he got the idea after reading a book about three Americans who robbed the bank at the turn of the century.

'In The Nick' was a low budget crime comedy set in an open prison bringing together Ian Hendry, Anthony Newley, James Booth and Bernie Winters under the directorship of Ken Hughes.

Hendry looked like he would develop into one of Britain's top cinema stars but alcoholism blighted his career.

Certain scenes were shot at the nearby Knebworth House, a stately home that continues to be used as a film and TV location and is famous for staging outdoor pop concerts.

'The Wreck Of The Mary Deare' was mainly shot in Hollywood but about 3 weeks were filmed at MGM.

It brought together ageing Hollywood superstar Gary Cooper, the then 'king of the epics' Charlton Heston and newcomer Richard Harris who had been put under contract to nearby Elstree Studios. He recalled, "I was loaned from Elstree where I was under contract at £30 a week. Cooper was unwell and Heston was a prick who thought himself a great actor. They basically ignored me as the newcomer."

Cooper was indeed unwell and the year after making his final film called **'The Naked Edge'** at Elstree he died from cancer.

Charlton Heston told me "I remember Coop and myself dined at a restaurant in London called 'The Guinea' which served the best steak in London. My scenes were filmed, I think, about June and I stayed at the Savoy. It was a great pleasure to work with Coop even though he was obviously unwell and I enjoyed the MGM Studio and so chose it for my production of **'Caesar'** a few years later just before it closed."

It is interesting to read the casting suggestions for the supporting roles. The part of Mr. Petrie went to Alexander Knox but they considered Donald Pleasance, Ernest Clark, Richard Wattis, Raymond Huntley, Lionel Jeffries and Alan Cuthbertson. The role of Higgins went to Harris but they thought of Peter O'Toole, Percy Herbert, Eddie Byrne, Duncan Lamont and Patrick Allen. Felix Aylmer, John Welsh, Ronald Adam and Clive Morton were under consideration for the Chairman but it went to Cecil Parker.

One location was Waterloo Station and featured Gary Cooper. The camera was hidden but they required several takes, as every time Cooper appeared he would be swamped by autograph hunters. While in the UK Cooper took the opportunity to visit his old school in Dunstable where his English parents had sent him from America as a child. Today there is a pub in the town named after him.

MGM's costume department were sent over Charlton Heston's details for wardrobe purposes listing his shoe size as 12c, his height 6 feet 2 inches and waist 34 inches. During production MGM sent Michael Redgrave a letter of congratulations on his award of a knighthood.

A small part of **'Solomon and Sheba'** was shot at MGM and all the dubbing was done there. The studio was also home to the television series **'Rendezvous'**. The 41 episodes, each 30 minutes long were hosted by Charles Drake. 28 were filmed at MGM and 13 in the USA.

The guest stars list included Peter O'Toole, Gladys Cooper, Barbara Shelley, Donald Pleasance, Paul Massie, Lionel Jeffries, Ian Bannen, Samantha Eggar and Fraser Hines (as a school bully). Even the future star of **'The Prisoner'** Patrick MacGoohan turned up and it is one of the series I would love to see.

Other television work included shooting some beer commercials and a 90 minute TV film produced by Nicole Milinaire entitled **'The Night Apart'**.

'The Scapegoat' was a production brought to the screen by Alec Guinness and Daphne du Maurier about a man who swops lives with a lookalike French nobleman and gets entangled in his family life. The studio wanted Cary Grant but in the end Guinness played the dual role and invited Robert Hamer to direct. Guinness felt an allegiance to his former **'Kind Hearts And Coronets'** Director but Hamer was now an alcoholic and filming proved difficult.

The legendary Bette Davis was signed to guest star for a reported fee of £200,000 and 10% of the gross. She later commented "Guinness had my part cut to shreds so my appearance in the final product made no sense at all. Alec is an actor who plays by himself for himself. At least in this film he plays a dual role so he could play by himself."

At the end of 1959 MGM appointed Lawrence Bachmann as liaison representative for European production. He recalled "My remit was to keep the studio busy during quiet periods with support films, or if you prefer, B movie production. Each would have a low budget but where possible one star would be cast to give it some potential in the USA.

The first film I got going was **'Village Of The Damned'** which had been kicking around at Culver City for a couple of years but they were concerned about the subject matter. We aimed for a 5 week shoot with interiors at MGM and exteriors at Letchmore Heath using two cameras, one starting at each end of the village and leap-frogging so nobody was waiting around for someone to finish."

'Village Of The Damned' started on 12 November at Letchmore Heath and told the eerie story of the ladies of the village becoming mysteriously impregnated by an alien race and all producing blond-haired children. It was based on the novel called 'The Midwich Cuckoos', the title of which did not grab the Producers idea of what would sell to teenagers going to the cinema.

The token star was George Sanders who told me, "I went onto that film about one week after finishing **'Bluebeard's Ten Honeymoons'** at the nearby Danzigers Studios and had not even read the script. My screen career almost started in Borehamwood back in 1936 when I was signed by British & Dominions but the studio burnt down and with it my contract so I went to America.

I have never thought much of any of my films but they have provided a nice lifestyle and much better than working. I seem to remember having to provide my own clothes for the film." Sanders eventually took his own life in a lonely Spanish hotel room in 1972 leaving a note declaring his desire to leave 'this sweet cesspool of life.'

In 2003 BBC Radio organised a reunion of the Director and the cast at Letchmore Heath and I spent the day with them recalling the making of the film which has become a classic. Director Wolf Rilla told me, "I had no hand in the casting as I was signed only 7 days before production began and so I also could not alter the script. Some scenes still work but others look dated and I cannot understand how it has developed a worldwide cult following.

The budget was £87,000 and Sanders got £20,000. He seemed detached, health conscious and afraid of growing old. He ripped all the pages out of the script on which he had no lines and never seemed to bother to learn his lines but memorised them after a couple of rehearsals. I remember young Martin playing chess with him on set and beating him, and Sanders demanded a piano on set so he could play to relax.

When we started the film it had no agreed ending. The idea of the wall sequence came to me while driving to MGM and seeing a wall demolished. To create the sequence when a car drives into a wall killing the driver, we simply filmed the car reversing and ran the film backwards. I was not very happy with the final film and MGM said 'What are we supposed to do with this rubbish?' I was against the glowing eyes that they added to the American release print.

They offered me the sequel but I declined as it was going over old territory. I did get invited to the set of the remake in 1995 with Christopher Reeve but there seemed to be an army of people employed. It cost a lot of money but ended up not very good." Wolf eventually left the business and died in 2005.

Producer Ronald Kinnoch remembered "The MGM casting Director Irene Howard and myself saw 178 children for the 12 children's parts which we reduced first to 36 and the final selection took six weeks. We were looking for children with a similar appearance. We used the Three Horseshoes pub in the village to feed and water the crew and cast and made a donation to the village hall fund as a 'thank you' for the locals' tolerance of us."

Aldenham House doubled as the manor house in which Sander's character lived and also acted as a 'green room' for the cast to relax between takes. During the War it had been taken over by the Government and converted by the BBC to become a monitoring station for all broadcasts in Occupied Europe including communication with resistance movements.

The children were paid £11 a week. Five were reunited in 2003 by now of course middle-aged. Peter Preidel was a caravan salesman, Carlo Cura a nightclub owner and Teri Scoble an actor. Martin Stephens, the lead child and so was paid

---

Excluding a couple of dips, the number of first feature films produced in the UK increased throughout the decade. The figures were 1950 (62), 1951 (53), 1952 (53), 1953 (61), 1954 (58), 1955 (46), 1956 (63), 1957 (77), 1958 (82) and 1959 (87).

more, had become a successful architect.

Martin told me "I made 10 films between the age of 7 to 10 and I was just over 10 when I made this. I was asked to read a part from the script and a week later offered the role. I remember Sanders was very professional but a depressive and hypochondriac. Barbara Shelley was lovely and Wolf Rilla a good Director, but I had little to do with the other kids as I was either filming a scene without them or doing my schooling.

I do remember the weather was awful both cold and wet. I thought the end sequence a bit simplistic and the sequel **'Children Of The Damned'** very poor and I gave up acting after **'The Witches'** in 1966. I feel very detached watching my younger self on screen."

Some of the other now grown up children recalled the smell of glue when they had their blond wigs attached. joking they were early glue sniffers and also having their heads clamped in place for close ups of their staring eyes.

Barbara Shelley told me "It was my favourite film and I remember supplying my own clothes. Martin was a very cool and excellent child actor. All the children were marvelous and George was easy to work with, although a bit distant. He could be very humorous and witty which I think frightened some people. I was shocked when he killed himself a few years later."

MGM sat on the film and gave it a half-hearted release, only to find they had a hit on their hands with the picture grossing a reported 10 times its budget on the initial release. Lawrence Bachmann recalled "MGM had wanted to shelve it but the boss Sol Seigel got behind it." The optical effects to give the children glowing eyes cost about £10 to create on an optical printer. As the alien children controlled humans by staring at them, the publicity department came up with the advert tag 'the eyes that paralyse'.

In 2013 another reunion was held at Letchmore Heath with a frailer but still lovely Barbara Shelley. The alien children were represented by Martin Stephens, Teri Scoble, Lesley Scoble and Peter Preidel. It felt odd to sit in the village hall next to Martin in almost the same position he had sat in 54 years earlier when they shot the inquest scene in the hall.

Peter told me "I was the youngest of the alien children aged six and it was my only film. I got the role because my family were friendly with actor George Baker and we heard they were looking for children who could stand still and stare, which not every six year old can do. When the film came out my father took me to our local cinema and the manager made a big thing of having one of the cast present but when it came time to show the film they would not let me in as it was an X certificate!"

In 2013 I also hosted a screening of the film to an audience at the University of Hertfordshire organised by Howard Berry and Bob Redman. There were a number of students present who thoroughly enjoyed the movie, but one or two said to me afterwards how shocked they were with living conditions in 1959 as shown in the film. The idea of no central heating, mobile phones or playstations and people washing up in the sink came as quite a culture shock.

So ended the 1950s at the MGM British Studios.

Hollywood Comes To Hertfordshire – The 1950s

Jack Hawkins tested as "Tigellinus" in 'Quo Vadis'. The role was given to Ralph Truman.

Walter Pidgeon and Margaret Leighton under the observant eye of Robert Beatty

"On the set of 'Hour of 13' Director Harold French discusses a point of procedure with the stars, Dawn Addams and Peter Lawford"

Peter Lawford as "Revel" in 'Hour of 13'

MGM British Studios

A scene from 'Ivanhoe' which was never screened. Can you spot why?

First night crowds in Leicester Square at the premiere of 'Ivanhoe'

Filming on location at Hatfield House

Cast and crew of 'Ivanhoe' on the set

– 70 –

Hollywood Comes To Hertfordshire – The 1950s

Finlay Currie as "Cedric" in 'Ivanhoe'

Jack Hawkins tested as "De Bois Guilbert" in 'Ivanhoe'

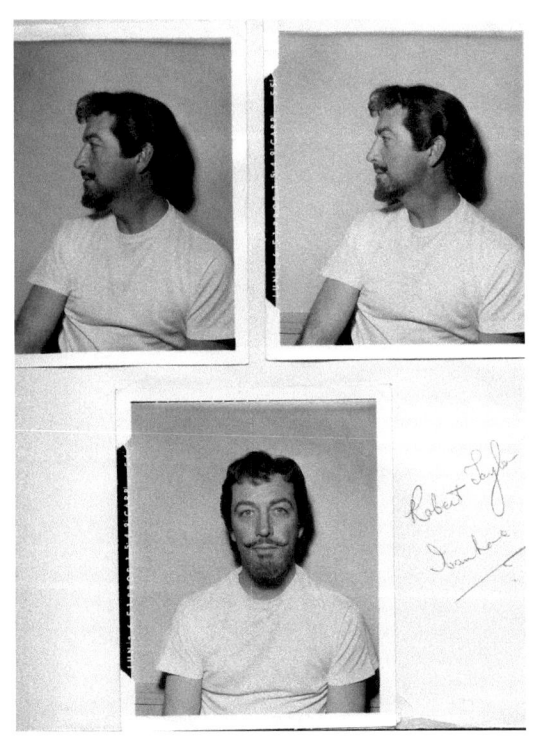

Robert Taylor in makeup tests for 'Ivanhoe'

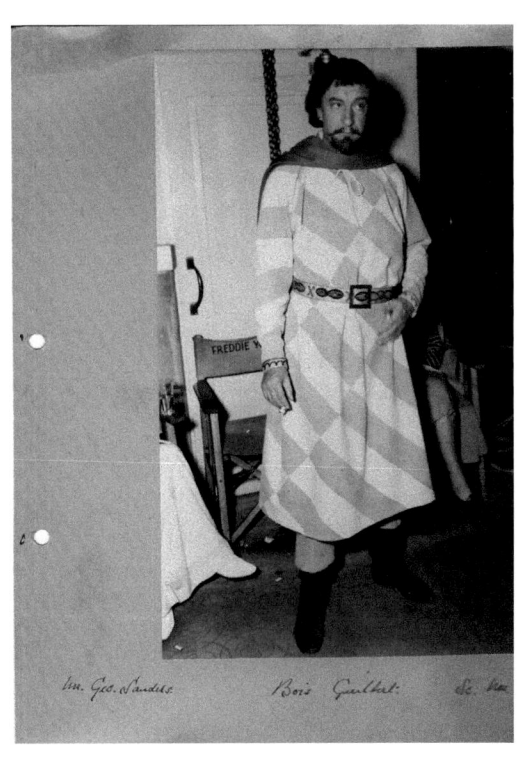

George Sanders as "De Bois Guilbert" in 'Ivanhoe'

Delmer Daves discusses 'Never Let Me Go' with Clark Gable at MGM

'The King' returns from a weekend in Paris

Clark Gable and Gene Tierney relax on the lawns outside MGM

Victor Maddern as "The Saboteur" in 'Time Bomb'

Hollywood Comes To Hertfordshire – The 1950s

Gene Kelly in full flight in 'Invitation to the Dance'

While relaxing during filming of 'Seagulls Over Sorrento', Gene Kelly shows off his previously unsuspected cricketing skills

Grace Kelly and Clark Gable relax between takes in 'Mogambo' while the 'continuity girl' studies the script

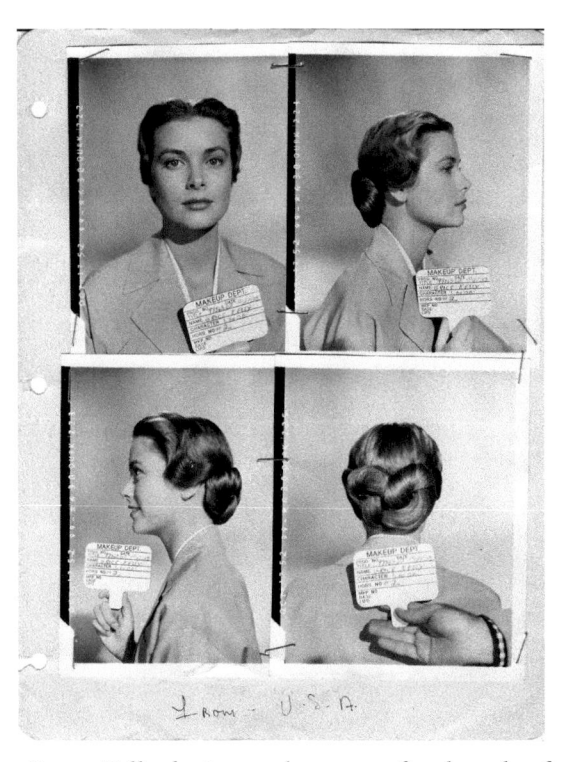

Grace Kelly during makeup tests for the role of "Linda Nordley" in Mogambo'

Cast and crew of 'Mogambo'

Ava Gardner and Robert Taylor take a coffee break while in costume for 'Knights of the Round Table'

Stanley Baxter as Mordred in 'Knights of the Round Table'

Poster for 'Betrayed'

Hollywood Comes To Hertfordshire – The 1950s

Victor Mature and Clark Gable in 'Betrayed'

Mr. and Mrs. Lex Barker (a.k.a. Lana Turner) try to decide how large a tip to leave in the MGM restaurant during her visit to film 'Betrayed'
(Photo courtesy of Guy Nolan)

An elegant Errol Flynn enjoys a day at the races away from filming 'The Dark Avenger'

Errol Flynn controls his steed, with the help of a friend, a cigarette and the mounting steps

While Lana Turner explains the plot of 'Another Time, Another Place', her companion Johnny Stompanato admires her daughter Cheryl Crane

Waiting for David Niven to complete his travels 'Around the World in 80 Days'

Poster for 'Safari'

David Niven, this time sharing the beach in 'The Little Hut' with Ava Gardner

Hollywood Comes To Hertfordshire – The 1950s

Yet another African classic, 'Odongo'

Off to Nairobi to film 'Beyond Mombassa': actors Cornel Wilde, Leo Genn and Donna Reed with blonde Jean Wallace, the wife of Cornel Wilde

What has caught the eye of the two ladies standing behind Ingrid Bergman on the set of 'Anastasia'?

Yul Brynner celebrates his birthday during a break in filming 'Anastasia'

Producer Sol Siegel and Director George Cukor arrive from New York on 8th July 1956 to start work on 'Bhowani Junction'

Stewart Granger and crew film on location in Pakistan for 'Bhowani Junction'
(Photo courtesy of Guy Nolan)

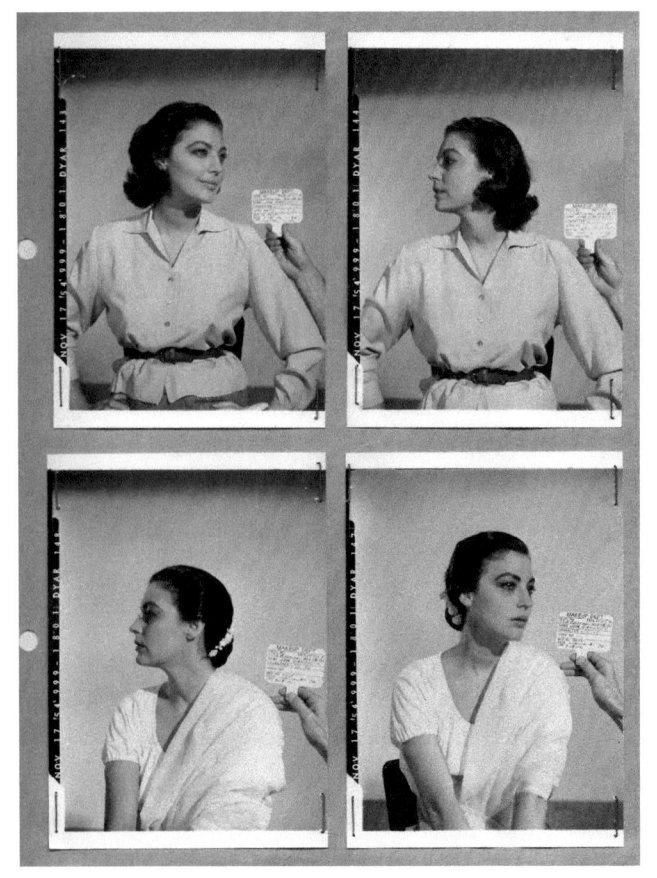

Ava Gardner prepares for 'Bhowani Junction'

Clifton Webb (centre) chats with Producer Ronald Neame and Lt. William Maybourn during filming of 'The Man Who Never Was'

Hollywood Comes To Hertfordshire – The 1950s

Commander Robert Fleming coaches 'Commander Ewen Montagu' (Clifton Webb)

Back from a week filming on location in Spain, complete with duty free

Perhaps not the finest moment of MGM British…

During filming of 'Space Maidens From Outer Space' a strange statue is discovered on the backlot

MGM British Studios

Getting to grips with the high-tech 'vehicle entry device' (a.k.a. a ladder)

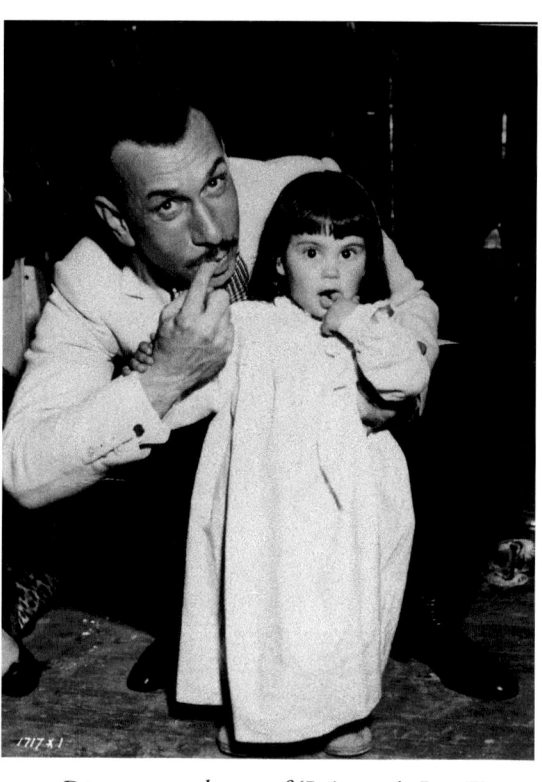

Director and star of 'I Accuse', Jose Ferrer with his young co-star Rachel Lemkov

André Morell tested as "Simonides" in 'Ben Hur' but not cast

"Sssshhh, can't you see I'm busy?" filming 'The Safecracker'

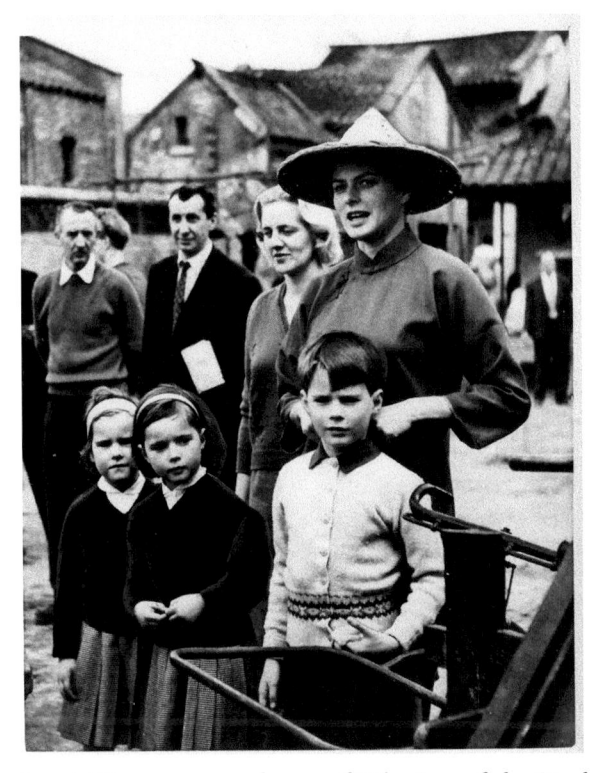

Hollywood Comes To Hertfordshire – The 1950s

Ingrid Bergman on the set of 'The Inn of the Sixth Happiness', with son Robertino and twin daughters Isabella and Isotta

Curt Jurgen, looking decidedly non-Oriental

Robert Donat makes his final film appearance

Russ Tamblyn, star of 'Tom Thumb' leaps ALMOST as high as the studio lights

MGM British Studios

Peter Sellers and Terry-Thomas play two villains

Star of 'The Rough and the Smooth' William Bendix flies back to the States with his 'super-portable radio'

Cliff Richard risks a serious injury while filming 'Serious Charge'

The stars of 'Captain Nemo and the Underwater City' are captivated by... a violin

— 82 —

Hollywood Comes To Hertfordshire – The 1950s

William Bendix impresses Tony Britton with his extraordinary fashion sense

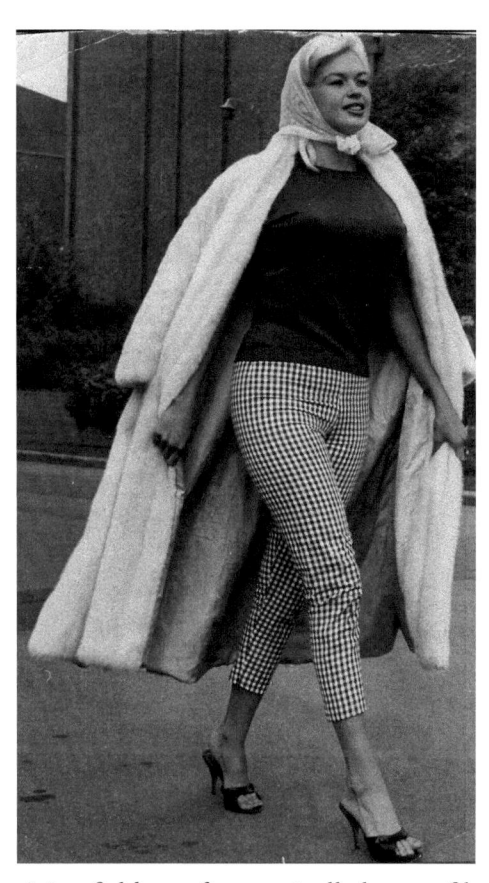

Jayne Mansfield goes for a typically low profile stroll around MGM while filming 'Too Hot To Handle'

Yes, it could be your daughter with Adam Faith in 'Beat Girl'

Gorgo steps out to start his reign of terror…

— 83 —

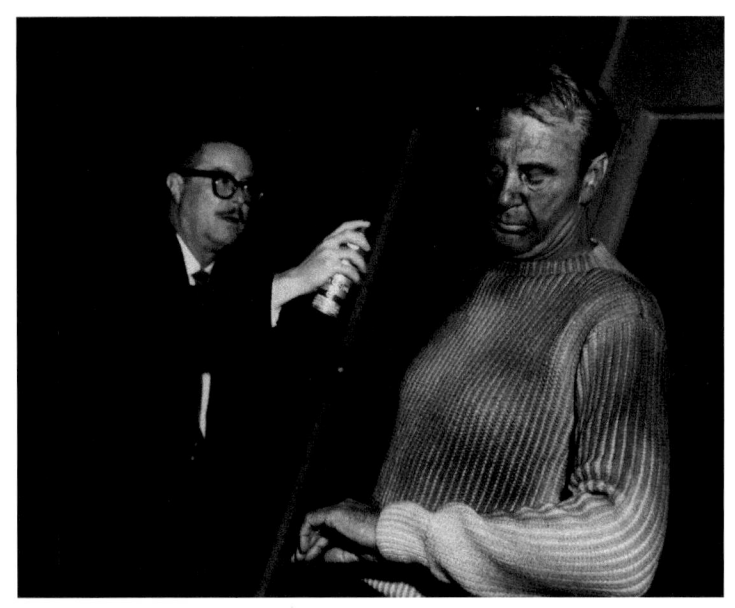

Realistic oil and dirt from a spray can for Gary Cooper before his next take on 'The Wreck of the Mary Deare'

George Sanders and Barbara Shelley under-react to their son's slightly strange appearance in 'Village of the Damned'

On the way to school, past the film crew at Letchmore Heath

Another strange-looking visitor to 'The Village of the Damned' (the Author in 2007)

Photo courtesy of Ken Morris

The International Years – The 1960s

The new decade of the 'swinging sixties' brought a mixture of productions to the studio.

THERE WERE PLANS for extensive use of the studio, along with Pinewood, for the massive production of **'Cleopatra'** and set building started on three stages. However, Elizabeth Taylor fell seriously ill, bad weather forced a change of plan and the film was shot in Italy.

The studio was also expecting to house another big production called **'The Four Horsemen of the Apocalypse'** but during location work in Paris, due to bad weather only 6 days out of 24 days saw any filming and the movie was relocated to Hollywood.

'The World Of Suzie Wong' utilised a big outdoor set at the studio plus real-life locations in Hong Kong. The original leading lady Frances Nuyen was reportedly sacked as she was pining for her boyfriend Marlon Brando, and then the Director Jean Negulesco was fired and replaced by Richard Quine, so it was not a great start for this romantic drama.

The final line up was William Holden, Nancy Kwan, Michael Wilding and Sylvia Syms. Kine Weekly described it as 'an infallible money spinner with a fascinating story'.

'Confessions' which was also called **'Let's Get Married'** brought together Anthony Newley, who was becoming a fixture in film made at MGM British Studios with James Booth, Lionel Jeffries and Bernie Winters in this musical comedy. Newley got to sing the song 'Let's Get Married' written by Lionel Bart. The Director Peter Graham Scott thought it was a poor script and that the film turned out badly.

'Macbeth' was a television production made in colour for Hallmark Hall of Fame; various running times from 90 minutes to two hours have been quoted. It starred Maurice Evans, Judith Anderson, Ian Bannen and future **'Sherlock Holmes'** Jeremy Brett.

'The Millionairess' was a comedy based around a wealthy woman falling in love with an Indian doctor. The cast included Peter 'goodness gracious me' Sellers, Sophia Loren, Dennis Price and Alistair Sim. Sellers was reportedly paid

£37,500 for his services.

During the filming Loren stayed at the Norwegian Barn, a house in nearby Barnet Lane. On 30th May her jewel collection worth £185,000 plus sentimental value was stolen. In 1992 the burglar Raymond 'the cat' Jones surrendered himself to the Boreham Wood police and confessed to the crime. He said he had posed as a chauffeur and drove into the grounds of the adjacent Edgwarebury Country Club with his partner. They burgled the Barn and later sold the jewelry for just £44,000. Two years later, his partner claimed that he committed the crime alone. The police decided to take no action.

The day after the robbery Loren reported to the set for filming although there was naturally a great deal of tension. Apparently this resulted in Sellers fainting and being taken off to hospital while they shot around him.

During filming Sellers fell in love with Loren and became obsessed with her, but it was unrequited love as she was already happily married.

In one scene Dennis Price was supposed to appear in a water scene with Loren but felt unwell. They asked his stand-in but he could not swim. In the end, to avoid delays Director Anthony Asquith did the swimming scene himself.

'Invasion Quartet' was a more modest comedy offering about a Home Guard officer and some army hospital patients spiking a gun on the French coast. Bill Travers was joined by funny men Spike Milligan and Eric Sykes. Kine Weekly commented "Scatty World War Two comedy or rather, a skit on **'Guns Of Navarone'**. Idea is bright, types effectively portrayed and staging good, but treatment is uneven and romantic interest negligible."

'The Green Helmet' was a drama about sports car racing with Bill Travers being the lead, supported by American import character actor Ed Begley and home-grown, or at least via South Africa, Sid James.

Locations included a visit to Portmeiron in Wales and closer to home a village garage near Letchmore Heath. During filming a £5,000 Jaguar sports car was accidentally wrecked.

'Secret Partner' was a modest crime drama starring Stewart Granger and Bernard Lee under the direction of Basil Dearden. Some critics described this effort as little more than a 'B movie' and a sure sign that Granger's stardom was on the decline. This is probably true but the plot is quite engaging, although Granger must have felt his star was slipping when compared with his earlier productions at the studio.

The studio itself makes a fleeting appearance when Bernard Lee, playing a police officer, arrives at an apartment block. The entrance he walks into was actually the entrance to the MGM front administration block, beneath the clock tower.

'Five Golden Hours' was a black comedy in the vein of **'Kind Hearts and Coronets'**. It was based in Italy and featured George Sanders, Ernie Kovacs, Cyd Charisse and Dennis Price. The film was shot during October and November with locations in the Italian Alps.

Kovacs had been a hit on American television and is credited with having introduced many television comedy techniques still used today. Sadly, a year later he was dead at the age of 42

The International Years – The 1960s

> 1961 saw 30 year MGM veteran Matthew Raymond removed as the studio's Managing Director 'by mutual agreement' and Maurice Foster made General Manager. Born in 1902 Raymond joined MGM in 1931 as a chartered accountant.
>
> One MGM manager suggested he fell victim to internal politics, while another veteran alleged Raymond was caught using studio labour and materials for private use at his home.
>
> According to Aida Young, he never recovered from the way he was treated by MGM, and died in 1967.

after crashing his car, apparently while attempting to light his cigar.

Mr Topaze was a comedy directed by Peter Sellers starring himself, Nadia Gray and Herbert Lom mainly set in France.

During 1960 the studio was used for a number of activities, including the shooting of a television pilot entitled **'Sirocco'** directed by Peter Graham Scott, tests and looping on **'The Fair Bride'** and shooting plates for **'Matilda Shouted Fire'**.

Albert Finney was also subjected to lengthy tests for the lead role in **'Lawrence of Arabia'**. At the time the possible cast was very different to the eventual one; Cary Grant was suggested as General Allenby, Kirk Douglas as the reporter and Horst Buchholz as the Sheik. Had David Lean gone with that cast, one wonders if it would a proved a better or worse film, or simply just different.

In his book 'Albert Finney In Character' (Robson Books 1992) the author Quentin Falk says that over £100,000 had been spent building interior and exterior sets at MGM for the test which consisted of five scenes shot over four days. They fully-costumed the actors and shot 1,400 feet of wide screen 35mm film. That expenditure seems amazing at a time when the studio was still churning out 90 minute, albeit 'B movies', for less than that sum.

Apparently Finney then rejected the film role and a long-term contract from Producer Sam Spiegel. Of course the role went to Peter O'Toole who gave an excellent performance but physically was a world apart from the real Lawrence. The Director David Lean later said they he had spotted O'Toole at a screening of the MGM Boreham Wood made film **'The Day They Robbed The Bank Of England'** and arranged a one day screen test at Elstree. Before it was over he had decided the actor was his man. Finney went on to a very successful career, including his film role as Poirot in **'Murder On The Orient Express'** made in the Elstree Studios 14 years later.

1960 also saw the production of a high quality adventure television series starring Patrick McGoohan entitled **'Danger Man'**. 39 episodes of the 30 minute variety were produced with an airing in the UK in 1960 and in the USA in 1961. In ratings terms it was not a runaway success in

America and it was several years before another series, this time one hour episodes, was made.

In some ways the character McGoohan played was a television version of James Bond. It has been said that the actor turned down that role and the part of Simon Templar in **'The Saint'** series due to a moral stance on the womanising nature of the characters.

The famed scriptwriter Brian Clemens told me "I script-edited and I wrote the first one, the pilot episode in fact. I nicked the idea for the plot from Hitchcock. Patrick was very professional but a very strange man though, a very strange man. I don't know whether he went off on benders but he would suddenly become very remote, but I couldn't fault him as a human being. He was very pleasant, enjoyed a joke and was always kind to me.

MGM studios were very superior. The backlot I thought was actually too neat whereas the backlot at ABPC Elstree was fascinating because it was more like a bomb site."

Actors who worked on the series often recall McGoohan as being very professional, someone who demanded high standards, very in control but a bit remote as a person. He insisted he was not involved in love scenes and preferred not to overdo violence or shooting.

Director Peter Graham Scott recalled, "I directed several episodes but one of the things

---

Film makers could not fail to be aware of the decline in cinema attendances since the 1950's. In 1957 and 1958 the figures fell by 17% each year. In 1959 that was worse, at 20%, and in 1960 and 1961 attendances still fell, by 14% each year.

By 1961 attendances had declined to 449,114,000 admissions, and that resulted in the closure of 323 cinemas in that year alone.

Not surprisingly, it was the biggest cinemas that were closing; in 1961, 120 cinemas in the 500 to 1,000 seater capacity closed, another 60 in the 1,001 to 1,500 category and 44 in the 1,501 to 2,000 capacity. The 'picture palace' cinema was fast becoming a dinosaur. In 1961 there were only 136 left with a capacity of 2,000 plus.

UK box office gross takings continued to decline. In 1950 the total was £105,200,000 and by 1958 that had declined to £83,400,000 Two years later it was down to £64,300,000

In 1950 there had been nearly 30 million attendances weekly, or about 1,500 million over the year. In 2012 the total attendance figure for the year was 172 million. Gross takings that year were £1,172,037,248

Both figures are impressive by comparison with the last two or three decades, but of course not so impressive when compared with those of 60 years ago and adjusted in real terms.

I did not like was that McGoohan's character always came out on top, so it was a bit one dimensional. If three men were lining up to fight him, he would always win and you always knew he was going to beat them."

Not everyone was a McGoohan fan amongst fellow actors. Character actor Peter Arne, who was gay, commented "He was homophobic and I would never work with him again."

■ ■ ■ ■

1961 saw the studio play host to the first in a series of very successful B movies based on an Agatha Christie created character. **'Murder She Said'** *brought to the screen the one-off Margaret Rutherford as Miss Marple in this adaptation of '4.50 From Paddington'.*

Rutherford was paid £16,000 a film and made the part her own, much to the dismay of the author who later wrote to me saying "Miss Rutherford was a splendid actress but totally miscast in the role and the films bore little resemblance to my books."

The film used Paddington station as a location and nearer home, Radnor Hall in Elstree as Ackenthorpe Hall. Radnor Hall was an empty building owned by the local council who rented it to MGM for £50 and demolished it the following year. The unit spent 6 days filming there which required repairing windows and hanging curtains for exterior shots, using the interior as temporary dressing rooms and a canteen.

Years later Agatha Christie commented, "I thought the film was poorly photographed, badly produced and lacked atmosphere. I hated Miss Marple replacing Poirot in the stories. MGM asked me if they could film **'Murder On The Orient Express'** but I refused as they no doubt would have replaced Poirot with Marple and had Rutherford driving the train!"

Muriel Pavlow told me "Margaret Rutherford was a delightful person and I thoroughly enjoyed the little bits we did together in the film."

In the supporting cast was a young Richard Briers who went on to become one of the country's favourite actors. Just four months before his death in 2013 I spoke to Richard on the phone, oddly enough while walking past the old MGM studio site, and he commented "It was a very impressive studio especially for a young actor. I think I worked on that film only for a few days at most and was paid the princely sum of £25 but that might have been a month's wage for the average working man in those days."

'She'll Have To Go' was a comedy about two brothers who plan to kill their young female cousin to prevent her inheriting the mansion in which they live. However, they both end up falling in love with her and end up killing each other. Alfred Marks and Bob Monkhouse play the brothers with additional comedy support from Hattie Jacques. Filming started on 17th April and shooting took place on stage 2 for four weeks which included a swimming pool set.

In **'Postman's Knock'** a village postman gets involved with a criminal gang posing as postmen, resulting in various comical twists and turns with the acting supplied by Spike Milligan, Barbara Shelley and Warren Mitchell.

'The Light In The Piazza' was a romantic drama set in Italy starring Olivia de Havilland,

George Hamilton, Rossano Brazzi and Yvette Mimeux with Guy Green directing.

Olivia told me "While filming and towards the end of the production, Rossano and I thought it would be entertaining to take George Hamilton and Yvette Mimieux out to dinner, duplicating in real life a romantic scene from the film. We went to a quite fashionable London restaurant hoping some of the spirit of the movie would develop at the table. It did not. George sulked and Yvette barely said a word. The experiment was a total and somewhat expensive disaster.

As to how the Boreham Wood plant compared to those in Hollywood in terms of efficiency, I thought the Boreham Wood studio a perfectly wonderful place in which to work. There was only one disadvantage, the long drive in the early morning from a London hotel and the long drive back at night. I have one other complaint. It often took twice the normal time to receive delivery from the laboratory of the rushes, which was sometimes a great handicap."

Rain during the location work in Italy in June meant some scenes had to be shot in Enfield, Middlesex. Associate Producer Aida Young told me "It was a marvelous experience making this film although Arthur Freed, as Producer, was more interested in touring Europe exploring his hobby of growing orchids. I got involved with what I will call 'sexual politics' on that film which opened my eyes but I prefer not to discuss. But overall it was a wonderful film to work on."

'Satan Never Sleeps', also known as **'The Devil Never Sleeps'** utilised the still-standing exterior Chinese village set from **'The Inn Of Sixth Happiness'** and was not a happy film. Both the star William Holden and the Director Leo McCarey were drinking heavily. Holden's co-star was the gay actor Clifton Webb who had shot to screen fame in **'Laura'** during the 1940s.

Webb had aged a great deal and was suffering a deep depression from the loss of his mother who had been his constant companion. His close friend Noel Coward had little sympathy, making the quip 'At 70 Clifton must be the oldest orphan in history.'

Holden seemed to spend his career feeling that acting was not a real job for a man although he enjoyed a number of successes. Alcoholism was his eventual downfall when he tripped on a bedroom carpet while alone in his penthouse a number of years later. Too drunk to summon help or to stem the bleeding from his head wound, he succumbed to his injury and was not found for several days.

During shooting the set was visited by the famous Hollywood gossip columnist Hedda Hopper. During her heyday in the 1940s and 1950s she could help make or break a career in Hollywood . Hopper was first promoted by MGM as a rival to the well-established Louella Parsons who had a virtual monopoly on Tinseltown gossip via syndicated newspaper columns, magazine articles and radio programmes.

Her power base was the William Randolph Hearst chain of newspapers. Some say Parsons got her job when aboard a yacht she witnessed Hearst shoot at Charlie Chaplin and kill instead a well-known Director of that era. The whole thing was allegedly hushed up and her reward for silence was a gossip column. By 1960 the power of both Hopper and Parsons was on the wane as the studio system collapsed and new stars simply ignored them.

'The Inspector' was a drama about smuggling in Europe, with a strong cast of Stephen Boyd, Dolores Hart, Donald Pleasance, Leo McKern and Harry Andrews.

The film was due to shoot in Tangier but the Moroccan government did not want the casbah to be portrayed yet again as a den of thieves, hence the move to MGM where sets were built on the backlot.

'Village of Daughters' was another low budget comedy churned out to keep the studio busy, featuring the ever-reliable Eric Sykes and John Le Mesurier.

'I Thank A Fool' paired Peter Finch and Susan Hayward in a crime melodrama. It was originally announced that Ingrid Bergman was to star.

During production the studio was affected by a 24 hour strike by 170 maintenance workers. Peter Finch recalled, "We filmed in the anal wastes of Ireland and back at MGM. Susan Hayward was always worrying that I kissed her on the correct side of her face in any love scenes."

'Nine Hours To Rama' was an historical drama set in India where they shot on location. In the supporting cast was Francis Matthews who recalled the star Horst Bucholz was 'behaving like a Nazi during the filming so it was not a good experience.'

The story was about the man who shot Mahatma Gandhi and the publicity tag was 'the murder that changed the lives of millions'.

Kine Weekly commented 'A film given the full cinemascope and deluxe colour treatment. Overall excellent and the pageantry and crowd scenes are excellent.'

'Zero One' was the next television series into the studio and starred Nigel Patrick in 39 episodes each of the 30 minute variety, with the storylines based around airport security. They started filming on the 6 November and each episode was given a 5 day schedule. Guest stars included Cecil Parker, Margaret Rutherford, Warren Mitchell and Kieron Moore. Director Peter Graham Scott remembers " **'Zero One'** was just **'Danger Man'** with a much funnier actor. Dear old Nigel Patrick could make anything amusing. He was a very clever character and a great light comedian. The scripts were rubbish but the Americans loved it."

'The Password Is Courage' was directed by Andrew Stone and starred Dirk Bogarde. It told the true story of a World War Two escape by Allied soldiers. For one scene they used nearby Radlett Station, draped it with Nazi flags and had extras dressed in 1940s clothes and as German soldiers. Oblivious to all this, one elderly resident walked into the station and demanded to buy a ticket to London.

The Producers bought a 1929 Derby made steam train (No 42325) engine and 40 redundant cattle wagons. The train was derailed for the film at the Scratchwood sidings just south of Elstree Tunnel at the western edge of what is now London Gateway services for the M1 motorway. After filming the spectacular crash scene the train was sold as scrap and cut up on site.

MGM unit publicist Julian Senior told me, "I started at the studio on that film and still remember going up to watch them shooting on the backlot. The catering wagon was there serving hot tea and rolls and the crew were having a break. I got my tea and roll and sat down on the chairs provided but noticed nobody else was seated. I was then tapped on the shoulder by the union representative who told me 'We don't sit because if we stand during our breaks, we get time and a half as too busy to breakfast but if we sit it's normal rate.' Nobody was actually working but such was the way unions worked in those days."

Julian Senior was one of over 65 film and TV veterans interviewed as part of The Elstree Project described in the section entitled 'Remembering MGM British'. I have included extracts from that interview.

The Director Andrew Stone insisted on realism with no model work, no back projection and no make up for the actors. He insisted on using 'raw' sound, not later looped, even though the sound recordist insisted he would not be held responsible. Cameraman Eric Cross said it was the hardest job he ever had.

For one sequence the film company hired three train coaches on the normal scheduled London to Exeter line for shooting interiors on the train, which required several stations seen passing through the window to be 'dressed' with German soldiers.

The film premiered at the London Coliseum on 10th October 1962.

A return to comedy came with the low budget **'Kill Or Cure'** which shot during May and included the use of the nearby Haberdashers School as a location. For an exterior scene the crew had to put up a fake tree which could be shaken to simulate wind and the leaves were provided by the studio estate department. The comedy revolved around a murder in a health farm and the laughs were provided by stalwarts Terry Thomas, Eric Sykes, Dennis Price and Lionel Jeffries.

'In The Cool Of The Day' was a love story set in Greece and starred Peter Finch, Jane Fonda, Angela Lansbury and Constance Cummings. Angela Lansbury later said she thought the film was so awful, she had erased it from her mind.

The Producer John Houseman commented "I produced it for two reasons, both bad and I prefer not to remember. The first reason was a holiday in Greece which was the main location shoot. The second was to keep my agents happy as I had a lucrative MGM contract. After the location we went back to the hostile atmosphere of the MGM studio in Boreham Wood. I felt utterly helpless and impotent as I watched the film drift towards its shameful close."

MGM hired a chauffeur for Peter Finch who was living nearby at Mill Hill and he reported often driving the star home in the small hours, stone drunk.

Next up was a comedy about air hostesses entitled **'Come Fly With Me'** with Dolores Hart, Karl Malden and Hugh O'Brien. Malden later commented "I did not do the film because of the fluffy story or the Director (Henry Levin) who anyway was lost with actors but for the chance to go to Europe for the first time. Dolores became a good friend to my family and she eventually left acting to become a nun."

During production the working title was **'Champagne Flight'** and **'The Friendliest Girls In The World'** was also considered.

As 20% of the action took place aboard an aircraft the studio built a duplicate interior of a

135 seater Boeing 707 which was 152 feet long. The fuselage was built in 10 feet lengths on 10 feet high wheeled units on stage 3. Immense cycloramas were erected around the stage walls with white painted floor which was blanketed with fibreglass clouds as necessary. The cockpit for the four weeks shoot was recreated to be 100% accurate but could be dismantled in sections to allow for camera angles.

Kine Weekly commented 'A thoroughly enjoyable deluxe trip in exciting company with first class photography, crisp dialogue and the music is catchy.'

■ ■ ■ ■

The frighteners were put on by the next production when Robert Wise directed **'The Haunting'** *which has become something of a classic. The budget was reported as $1,125,000 and filming in England was considered the best way to keep within that budget. Wise was not impressed with English crews, considering them clock watchers and was mystified by all the union rules.*

The film starred Richard Johnson, Russ Tamblyn, Julie Harris and Claire Bloom. Johnson was cast because he was already under contract to MGM British, as was Russ Tamblyn who was under contract in Hollywood. Tamblyn was not keen but was threatened with suspension.

Julie Harris recalled the old 'pea soupers' of the era; the fog was once so bad that it took three hours to travel the 12 miles from her London hotel to the studio.

Robert Wise remembered they chose Ettington Hall near Stratford Upon Avon because it could also be used as a hotel for the cast. He also recalled "We gave the job to a chap called 'Terry the Tinsmith' at the studio to create the spiral staircase but I had to climb it to prove to the cast it was safe. To get the effect of the breathing door, it was one side a laminated wood and on the other side a big 6 by 4 going across it and a big props man pushing it back and forth to create the effect."

One of the stunt people working on the film was Connie Hilton. "On that movie I plunged to my death down a flight of stairs and hanged myself. Around that time I also fell from London Bridge pretending to be Sophia Loren in **'The Millionairess'** and broke my ankle performing a falling down the stairs stunt for **'Gorgo'**."

Kine Weekly summed up the film with a review that said 'brilliantly spooky tale that is a masterly example of a proper chiller which should hold audiences spellbound.'

'Cairo' was a crime drama based in Egypt directed by Wolf Rilla and starring Richard Johnson and George Sanders.

The production of B movies continued with **'Dead Man's Evidence'**, a spy drama set in Ireland and starring Conrad Phillips, who had achieved television fame as William Tell.

A more gritty film was **'Saturday Night Out'** starring Bernard Lee which told of the adventures of a group of merchant seamen on shore leave in London. One scene interestingly shows the pop group The Searchers playing in a pub.

Plans were announced for MGM to film **'Robinson Crusoe'** with a budget of £246,864 excluding actors and Director's fee with 8 weeks at the studio and 7 weeks in the West Indies. The project seems to have been abandoned.

'The Dock Brief' was a legal comedy starring Peter Sellers and Richard Attenborough. Some felt the witty dialogue was a bit lost on most audiences, not helped by the low key performance given by Sellers.

'Private Potter' was a drama based around a soldier who sees a religious vision. It starred Tom Courtenay and was helmed by Finnish Director Casper Wrede (1929-1998) who spent most of his career on television productions.

The Evening Standard declared 'A triumph for Tom Courtenay' and The People newspaper said 'sincere and provocative so full marks'. The Kine Weekly were less impressed and described it as 'acceptable double bill material'.

'Live Now Pay Later' was a comedy about a salesman starring Ian Hendry, Liz Fraser and John Gregson. Interiors were shot on stage 2 and the household goods required for the film had to be insured for £30,000.

Hendry looked like he might become a major British star in the 1960s but his increasing alcoholism and troubled marriage to equally heavy drinking actress Janet Munro (**'Swiss Family Robinson'**, **'The Day The Earth Caught Fire'**) damaged his career. By 1980 he was bankrupt and appearing in an afternoon soap opera called **'For The Love Of Maddie'** at ATV in Borehamwood. He died four years later aged just 53 years old.

The studio's next production was another 'B movie' entitled **'The Marked One'** filmed in 3 weeks on stages 8 and 9 with locations including nearby Shenley Road at its junction with Drayton Road. This crime drama starred William Lucas and Zena Marshall.

'Maniac' was a Hammer Films production shot between May to July with location work in the Camargue region of Southern France. The crime drama starred Kerwin Matthews.

'Follow The Boys' was a comedy musical starring Connie Francis and Russ Tamblyn. Set in Europe, it was mainly shot on location in France and Italy.

A gripping little thriller about a kidnapped child was released as **'Tomorrow At Ten'** with the alternative title of **'Golliwog'**, a reference to the child's doll. It cast John Gregson as a police officer tracking down kidnapper Robert Shaw. Although made as a 'B movie' it stands up very well half a century later.

Gregson went on to television fame in **'Gideon's Way'** but sadly died prematurely from a heart attack while out walking on holiday in the 1970s. Shaw became a Bond villain in **'From Russia With Love'**, achieving success in Hollywood before his untimely death from a heart attack while out driving.

'Master Spy' was made under the working title of **'Checkmate'** and was a spy drama starring Stephen Murray, June Thorburn and Alan Wheatley, best remembered as the Sheriff of Nottingham in the successful **'Robin Hood'** TV series. Film buffs looking for use of the MGM facility will notice the studio gatehouse and the exterior of the post-production block appearing in certain scenes.

Some work was done on the all star **'List Of Adrian Messenger'** Directed by John Huston including a 12 day shoot of a fox hunt in

Ireland. It is an interesting murder mystery with an all-star cast but is flawed for several reasons. One is that George C Scott plays an Englishman who is investigating the crimes but his accent tends to drift across the Atlantic on occasions.

The gimmick is that several big name guest stars make cameo appearances but with their faces disguised. The trouble is that make up applied to their faces is so obvious the viewer becomes distracted from the story trying to guess who it is under the make up. At the end of the film each guest pulls off the make up and smiles at the camera and you find out it is Frank Sinatra, Robert Mitchum, Burt Lancaster and Tony Curtis.

The murderer is Kirk Douglas who also hides under various disguises during the story. The cast also included veterans Clive Brook, Herbert Marshall and Gladys Cooper. The female lead is played by Dana Wynter, who grew up in Boreham Wood in the 1930s and is best remembered today for her role in **'Invasion Of The Bodysnatchers'**.

'King Of The Seven Seas' or if you prefer, **'Seven Seas To Calais'**, was a costume drama starring Australians Rod Taylor and Keith Michell with a plot revolving around Sir Francis Drake searching for treasure. The model work for the Spanish Armada scenes were shot on the newly-built outdoor water tank. The Director Rudolph Mate (1898-1964) had been a noted Director of Photography before turning to directing in the late 1940s and his Hollywood successes included **'D.O.A'** (1950) and **'When Worlds Collide'** (1951).

'Four Hits And A Mister' was a short film lasting 14 minutes starring musician Acker Bilk and directed by Douglas Hickox.

'Murder At The Gallop' was shot under the working title of **'Funerals Are Fatal'** and brought Margaret Rutherford back to the studio as Miss Marple.

Unit publicist Julian Senior told me "Margaret invited me to her home in Gerrards Cross for tea and she spent a good deal of the time talking to a plush toy! She would say 'I am not a comedienne, I am an actress.' but I was bowled over by her because she was a great, amazing woman."

The Director, George Pollock (1907-1979), enjoyed a successful career in the 1940s as an Assistant Director on a number of films including **'Oliver Twist'** and **'Brief Encounter'** before directing B movies at MGM and ending his career directing episodes of the 'TV series **'Danger Man'** and **'Gideon's Way'**.

Television returned to the studio in the form of the series **'One Step Beyond'**. The first two series had been filmed in the USA but the third series included 13 episodes that were filmed at the studio between 28 November 1961 to 28 February 1962 and this was reported as the first time British television had linked up with a major American network.

The 13 episodes, each 30 minutes, shot at MGM were 'Eye Witness' with John Meillon and Anton Rodgers, 'Nightmare' with Peter Wyngarde, 'The Confession' with Donald Pleasance, 'Avenger' with Andre Morell, 'The Stranger', 'Signal Received' with Mark Eden, 'The Prisoner' with Anton Diffring, 'The Sorcerer' with Christopher Lee and Alfred Burke, 'The Room Upstairs', 'The Tiger', 'The Villa', 'The Face' and 'Justice' with Clifford Evans.

Throughout the 1940s, 50s and 60s the studio employed a number of familiar names within the Industry as permanent staff.

Dora Wright (1903-1988) was unusual in that she was a female production manager but she was highly regarded. Her career began in 1932 as a continuity girl and became the production manager for the Crown Film Unit during the war before joining MGM in 1946.

Freddie Young (1902-1998) was the studio's ace cameraman but he told me "I left MGM in 1959 when they asked me to take a pay cut despite the fact they had made a lot of money hiring me to outside productions". Freddie went on to win three Oscars.

German-born Alfred Junge (1886-1964) had entered the business in the 1920s and remained at MGM until **'Barretts Of Wimpole Street'** . He was responsible for creating the Ivanhoe castle which stood on the backlot for several years. Junge was born in Germany and worked in the film industry there from 1921 until joining Elstree Studios at the end of the decade. He then worked for Gaumont British and MGM at Denham before the war before being appointed production designer at MGM in 1947.

Elliot Scott (1915-1993) was an art and production designer who remained in the business until the late 1980s with his last credit being **'Indiana Jones And The Last Crusade'** at the nearby Elstree Studios for Steven Spielberg and George Lucas.

Tom Howard (1910-1985) was the MGM wizard of special effects and during his career earned two Oscars, for **'Blithe Spirit'** and **'Tom Thumb'**.

A W 'Watty' Watkins (1895-1970) headed the post production facilities at the studio. Watty started at the British & Dominions Studio in Boreham Wood in 1929 advising on the installation of sound equipment. In 1933 he became sound recording Director at Denham Studios and moved to the newly opened MGM British Studios in 1945 where he stayed until his retirement in July 1969, his last production being the **'Goodbye Mr. Chips'** remake. He was captain of the MGM cricket team and thankfully did not live to see the demise of his beloved studio. He died on a golf course in February 1970.

1962 saw a major investment by MGM in their 115 acre facility. The decision was made to construct two new sound stages each 3,750 sq ft (75 feet by 50 feet) towards the front of the facility. An additional large stage 100 feet by 120 feet was constructed to the rear of the main studio facilities plus an outdoor tank 100 feet by 150 feet with a sky-backing and wind and wave machines.

New office accommodation was erected along with extra cutting and dressing rooms. On the post-production side alterations were made to the recording theatre to enable dubbing in 2 theatres simultaneously, the building of a fifth viewing theatre and a new sound transfer suite.

A new accounting system was introduced along with the purchase of a fleet of cars. Car parks were extended and all roads resurfaced. The restaurant and canteen were redecorated, plus a bar was added.

New processing labs meant film from the set could be processed in 2 or 3 hours, allowing Directors to approve shots quickly if needing to strike sets or release artistes. The new lab could process 30 to 40 million feet a year of 16mm, 35mm, 65mm or 70mm film, becoming the only studio with such a facility.

The MGM British Studio could now boast 10 stages totalling 93,000 square feet. A stock of plants and trees were available with 5,000 square feet of greenhouse space and a vast stock of sets and props.

Stages 1 and 2 had sound-proof interconnecting sliding doors opening to 32 feet by 22 feet high. Stage 3 was 18,820 square feet with an interior tank 80 feet by 32 feet by 11 feet deep with armoured plated windows for cameras.

Stages 4, 5, 6 and 7 also had interconnecting doors and stage 6 had 2 tanks one 37 feet by 20 feet by 11 feet deep and the other 17 feet by 9 feet by 8 feet deep.

Stage 7 was also used as a music recording stage, and was equipped with a projector, footage indicator and echo/vocal chambers.

Stages 1,2,3,4 and 5 were 45 feet high to rails carrying lighting cradles with catwalks above with 15 feet height room. Stages 6 and 7 were 34 feet high. Compressed air, gas and water was available to all stages.

There were 12 executive suites and 7 suites for art Directors. Make up and hair dressing departments each had 7 private cubicles.

There were 22 cutting rooms, a library with 5,000 stock shots, 1,800 plates and 8,500 sound effects. In addition there were 30 artistes dressing rooms, some with bath or shower and large crowd dressing rooms.

For incoming productions, facilities and services were not charged except where required. Labour was not allocated to a production but taken from a pool of labour on a day-to-day basis.

The studio now boasted it was the first studio in Europe to produce films in Cinemascope, stereophonic sound, technirama , Todd-AO and Eastman colour.

MGM announced the forthcoming production programme would include films entitled **'Over The Rainbow'**, **'It Shouldn't Happen To A Dog'**, **'Lassie Come Home'**, **'Charlie Is My Darling'** and **'Hedda Gabler'**. There were also plans for a film called **'I'm In Charge'** with Bruce Forysth, Bernard Breslaw and Hylda Baker. Forsyth fell ill just before filming was scheduled to start2 and the production was cancelled.

One film not originally planned for MGM and based at Shepperton was **'The Day Of The Triffids'** which camera operator Geoff Glover told me "We did about 3 weeks work at MGM on that film as when they saw what had been shot, they felt the film was too dull. We shot the lighthouse scenes to be inserted and they were directed by Freddie Francis. On the stage they used a ground-hugging fog effect which for atmosphere had a green liquid added and the camera crew ended up with green-stained trouser legs."

■ ■ ■ ■

1963 saw another interesting selection of films go before the cameras with mixed success. In Los Angeles the managements of 20th Century Fox, MGM and Columbia discussed the idea of closing all their studios, selling the land and relocating to a 2,500 acre new studio to be built near Malibu. They would share such a facility but remain independent. The plan came to nothing.

'Impact' was a crime drama starring Mike Pratt who would find later TV fame in **'Randall And Hopkirk'** with Conrad Phillips. Bricket Wood rail station was used as one location which also features in the classic supernatural thriller **'Night Of The Demon'** made at Elstree Studios.

'The VIP's' was an all-star **'Grand Hotel'** style MGM glossy production partly made to cash in on the very public love affair between its stars Elizabeth Taylor and Richard Burton, which had recently started on **'Cleopatra'**.

Co-starring was Australian Rod Taylor who insisted on a dressing room on the same floor as his fellow stars but they took up so much

---

In 1962 Howard Thomas, Managing Director of ABC television explained the cost breakdown of making a TV series in the UK.

"A series of 26 episodes could cost say £295,950 to shoot and you might recover £3,000 an episode or £78,000 from a UK TV sale. You might gross £45,000 selling it to Canada, £20,000 from Australia, £13,000 from the Commonwealth and £20,000 from Europe. After deductions that would be about £75,000.

In other words, to make a profit you need to sell in America, generating a gross of something like £200,000 from a network sales and the odds on that are about 50 to 1."

space he was allotted what he called a 'broom cupboard'. In fact MGM had to rebuild and redecorate the dressing room allocated to Taylor. No doubt he was compensated by an alleged affair with a young Maggie Smith who was in the supporting cast.

Guest stars included Dennis Price, Richard Wattis, the legendary Orson Welles and Margaret Rutherford playing one of her dotty characters which gained her an Oscar, collected on her behalf by Peter Ustinov. Rutherford had at first declined the role, saying it amounted to little more than a couple of joke lines, but the part was built up to give her character more of a role.

The production began in January and rehearsals started on closed sets. A passenger lounge was built on a sound stage with the set measuring 185 feet by 85 feet on two levels and they put gauze on the windows to simulate fog. Altogether the studio built 28 sets, having taken hundreds of photos at London Airport.

During filming Burton suffered from a bad eye and Taylor experienced leg trouble, resulting in some scenes being shot with her sitting down.

The scriptwriter put a little in joke for the character played by Orson Welles who at one point exclaims 'My accountant is lost somewhere in the woods called Boreham. The telephones are out of order; how can phones be affected by fog?'

Taylor and Burton stayed at the Dorchester Hotel in London in adjoining suites. MGM took a gamble and did not insure Taylor for the film due to the high cost of premiums following her health impact on **'Cleopatra'**. Both stars behaved on set, partly due no doubt keen that the filming be completed on time as they were tax exiles and did not want to risk exceeding their allowed time in the UK. Burton did cause one problem when he got involved in a brawl at Paddington Station which apparently resulted in a back injury that remained for the rest of his life.

The two stars were well paid for their efforts with Burton getting $500,000 for 10 weeks plus $20,000 a week if any overrun plus 10% of the gross profits. Taylor got $750,000 for same period plus $50,000 a week for any overrun plus the same profits share. Despite Burton's run of bad films over the previous ten years, they were both very marketable due to the media frenzy surrounding their love affair.

Rigger Alf Newvell recalls that Liz Taylor could take a joke. "I had to hold her hand while she climbed some stairs on the set to see Burton and she had this big ring of diamonds flashing all over the place under the studio lights. I said 'A real one would not do that. You must have got it from Woolworths.' and she replied 'I bloody did not, get out of it you cheeky sod' and that's how she was like. One minute I would look at her and say 'What a lovely figure' and on another occasion think 'Who is that fat little woman?' She could put on weight while you looked at her."

Sound department veteran John Grover recalls working on **'The VIPs'**. "I had started at MGM at the end of the 1950s as a trainee or what was called a numbering boy. The pay was £6 a week from which I had to pay £5 for board and lodgings nearby. I often ate chips and gravy in the MGM canteen to make ends meet. Liz Taylor was due to shoot some scenes on a Friday but never turned up. We were all called back on the Saturday which was great as we were paid time and a half even though again she failed to appear. Eventually she turned up on the Sunday with a crate of champagne and after we all had a drink she completed her scenes perfectly."

Roy Parkinson remembered "We had Orson Welles on a four week contract and he was always short of money. Just before he left he asked for £100 in cash for the false nose he wore which he said had been made in Rome."

'Murder At The Gallop' based on 'After The Funeral' by Agatha Christie, saw Margaret Rutherford reprise her role as Miss Marple, supported by Robert Morley and Flora Robson.

Shooting started in January but was hampered by one of the worst winters of the century. Extra sets were built indoors. The stable set also converted into the old coaching inn to match up with the stables in Aldenham and the King's Arms Hotel at Amersham. The interior of Marple's house was built on stage 4 as were the interiors of the pub and sub post office. The old Enderby House was constructed on stage 5. Other locations shot in February included Church Farm, Aldenham, Hillfield Park, Aldenham, Elstree Police Station and Denham village.

An old-fashioned crime drama featuring Mickey Spillane called **'The Girl Hunters'** also starred Shirley Eaton and Hollywood veteran Lloyd Nolan. Spillane (1918-2006) apparently sold more than 225 million copies of his crime novels and this film was a very rare example of a novelist playing on screen his own character creation.

Kine Weekly commented 'This is a highly-coloured melodrama but it has sudden action and enough rough virility to attract Spillane fans and others. Mickey Spillane certainly looks the part, Shirley Eaton seems to wear little else but bikinis and Lloyd Nolan is almost monosyllabic.'

'Clash By Night' was a neat little drama about a group of prisoners who get free when the prison bus crashes and take refuge in a barn which later burns down. A reliable cast of Terence Longdon, Jennifer Jayne, Harry Fowler, Alan Wheatley and Peter Sallis, nowadays best remembered for **'Last Of The Summer Wine'**, were assembled and filming started on 11th March with 2 weeks on stage 7 and one week on location.

The next TV series into the studio was the ambitious and well-made **'Espionage'** series. This was an anthology series of 24 television plays each lasting an hour. Three episodes were even directed by the distinguished Michael Powell, one of which starred Stanley Baxter who told me "I did the episode at MGM with Roger Livesey. I remember he had a distinctive hoarse voice and he came up on the first day and apologised for his sore throat although he had sounded the same throughout his 30 year screen career!"

The Producer worried that Powell was taking too much time directing the episode. If he saw rehearsals going on too long he would walk up to Powell and say 'Don't you think we could summon up the nerve for a take?' which was not well received."

At the time it was reported that the series was aired in the very important American market up against **'The Beverly Hillbillies'** and **'Ben Casey'**, resulting in poor ratings and NBC dropping the option for further series. That wiped out the possibility of the Producers making any profit.

The series had been produced as a joint venture between NBC and ITC with a budget of £40,000 an episode with a schedule of 9 days filming each show. In Hollywood it was estimated that would have been reduced to 6 days as they worked 8am until 10pm with less restrictive practices.

The series was expensive compared with other one hour series such as **'The Human Jungle'** at £28,000 per episode and £23,500 for **'The Saint'** both made at the nearby Elstree Studios where **'Espionage'** was originally due to have been made. Lew Grade apparently bought into the series after seeing the pilot which was shot at a cost of £50,000 and without seeing further scripts.

The shows were sometimes a bit 'talky' by today's standards but had varied stories and good casts. An episode entitled 'To The Very End' featured a young James Fox and made good use of the nearby High Canons mansion, which featured often as a film and TV location and was for a while home to Tom Cruise when he was filming **'Eyes Wide Shut'** many years later.

Another strong episode was entitled 'The Weakling' which featured good performances from Patricia Neal, John Gregson and a young Dennis Hopper who can be seen being chased around the studio fields and Thrift Farm by German soldiers in this World War Two story.

Another television production was a half hour pilot for Screen Gems directed by Don Taylor. The tentative title was **'The Eve Arden Show'** but it was shown as **'He's All Yours'**. The plan was to make the series at MGM at a cost of £20,000 an episode starring Eve Arden as a manager of an American travel agency who is posted to London and comes into conflict with a fellow manager played by Jeremy Lloyd. It was cancelled after one series, which Arden blamed on poor scripts.

'Swinging UK' was a 28 minute short entitled **'Go Go Big Beat'** in the USA and featured pop groups of that era including Migil 5, The Searchers, The Merseybeats, The Tremeloes and The Four Pennies with disc jockey Alan Freeman as host.

'Echoes Of Diana' was another 'B movie' which got underway on 18th March with a three week shoot on stages 8 and 9, plus location work including the exterior of a house in nearby Theobald Street. The plot revolved around a reporter uncovering a spy ring and starred Vincent Ball.

Another all-star cast film to go into production was **'The Chalk Garden'** with John Mills, Deborah Kerr and Hayley Mills who played the part originally offered to Sandra Dee but she pulled out after becoming pregnant.

A supporting role was also planned for Gladys Cooper but it was reported Dame Edith Evans visited the Producer and Director and virtually intimidated them into casting herself. Out of respect for the veteran actress, Deborah Kerr deferred to her throughout filming. Director Ronald Neame felt the Producer Ross Hunter damaged the film by insisting on glossy sets and adding wall-to-wall music.

Kine Weekly described it as 'Extremely well-made and for the most part beautifully acted. This is a genuine thriller.' The film premiered in April 1964 at the Leicester Square Theatre.

If you have a hit film you can be sure a sequel will soon follow and thus it was when MGM put **'Children Of The Damned'** into production after the hit **'Village Of The Damned'**. The seven week schedule started on 13th May on location and on stages 4, 7 and 6; on the latter was constructed the interior of the church crypt. The film starred Ian Hendry and Alfred Burke, who did their best under the directorship of Anton Leader.

The location was St Dunstan's In The East Church in London where William Penn, founder of Pennsylvania, was baptised in 1644. Filming also took place in St Dunstan's Lane, Idol Lane and St Dunstan's Hill. A stagehand was required to dangle from the church tower to paint out the clock face to avoid reflection.

Back at the studio, four dressing rooms were converted into playrooms for the children and a large executive suite converted into a classroom. During filming they had two full-time teachers and three chaperones.

'It's All Over Town' was another low budget musical featuring The Bachelors, Dusty Springfield, Frankie Vaughan and The Hollies supported by comedy actors Lance Percival and Willie Rushton.

This kind of film was made to support the major feature in double bills at the cinema. Many such B movies were great entertainment.

However, one veteran Producer told me "You had to be careful not to make them too good as they then might be paired with a weak main feature which then did badly at the box office and you ended up with less money."

'Night Must Fall' was a crime drama remake starring Albert Finney, Susan Hampshire and Sheila Hancock. The film had previously been made by MGM in the 1930s but this time round proved a bit of a disaster. Finney later said "The film fell very heavily between two stools. We ruined the melodrama by trying to make it a psychological thriller and could not pull that off either."

The Director Karel Reisz later commented "The thing fell to pieces in our hands, just disintegrated. I knew it wasn't working after about three or four weeks but I could not put my finger on it and we just saw it through."

One of the most famous and catchy theme tunes to come out of MGM was attached to **'633 Squadron'**. It was the creation of the resident composer Ron Goodwin (1925-2003) responsible for scoring 19 films shot at the studio including the equally catchy theme tune for the Miss Marple movies and **'Where Eagles Dare'**.

The film was based around a World War Two Mosquito squadron starring Cliff Robertson, **'West Side Story'** star George Chakiris and Harry Andrews. Location work was undertaken at Bovingdon which had been an American air force base during the war. It is said Clark Gable, Jimmy Stewart and William Holden had spent time there while serving in the war. The pub scenes were shot at The Three Compasses in nearby Aldenham.

When Cliff Robertson arrived at the studio he said he was unhappy with the script he had originally approved and there were fears he would walk but he agreed to last minute rewrites. The film's reported budget was $1.3 million but it proved a big success, recouping that in the UK alone.

It was the first picture made at MGM by the Mirisch Company. Scottish lochs doubled for Norwegian fjords. The 2nd unit was directed by Roy Stephens advised by Captain John Crewdson's film aviation service. The main unit was directed by Walter Grauman with technical advice from Captain Hamish Mahaddie.

The two planned weeks at Bovingdon stretched to four due to the rain. The company purchased eight Mosquitoes, two Messerschmitts and a B 25 bomber, causing Walter Mirisch to enquire whether they had gone into the airline business. Had they held on to those aircraft, their value today would run into many millions of pounds.

Geoff Glover, the camera operator, told me, "They flew three Mosquitoes and we used the B25 bomber as the camera aircraft using two cameras. Once we were shooting scenes over Scotland, then the North Sea but lost our way and ended up over Norway. Then we ended up over the coast of England by Clacton and nearly headed for France, but luckily found our way back to Bovingdon airfield."

Kine Weekly summed the film up as 'The accent is on authentic combat thrills throughout the film and these will excite audiences.'

Two other productions were due to be shot at the studio in 1963. In May a 26 episode TV series called **'Harry's Girls'** was due to start but ran into problems with the actors union Equity. The other unions were angry with Equity as MGM were up against a deadline because the series had been pre sold to NBC. The result was that 20 technicians lost their jobs when MGM moved production to France.

The Director Stanley Cherry later recalled that proved a disaster as it was too noisy to film in the streets of Paris. They filmed mainly on sound stages but the crew were drinking all day, resulting in 20% of each days filming having to be reshot. In the end it was dropped by NBC after one season showing from September 1963 to January 1964.

'The Golden Head', a feature film, began shooting with Hayley Mills, Lionel Jeffries and a cameo by Otto Preminger, to be filmed in Cinerama. However, the studio were unhappy with Director James Hill so shooting was stopped. The film was later recast and filmed elsewhere.

■ ■ ■ ■

In 1964 another in the Agatha Christie murder mysteries entitled **'Murder Most Foul'** *went before the cameras with Margaret Rutherford as Miss Marple and a supporting cast including Ron Moody and Dennis Price. This was the screen version of Christie's 'Mrs McGinty's Dead'.*

Kine Weekly commented "Like all Christie's tales the plot is involved and full of false trails but this one lacks a little of the essential sustained pace although it's still good fun. Will make a useful double feature with **'Rhino'**.

Rigger Alf Newvell remembers "Margaret Rutherford called the crew together and handed out presents but only to the camera crew and we were a bit peeved. Ron Moody saw we were upset so he asked for all the other crew's names and half an hour later a secretary brought down an envelope for each of us containing £5 which was very handy in those days."

'The Americanisation of Emily' brought Julie Andrews to MGM as an established star. Back in 1947 she had attended the studio as a young girl for an unsuccessful screen test.

The World War Two romantic comedy co-starred James Garner and Melvyn Douglas but after a short while problems with the unions forced the production to move to Hollywood. Liz Fraser had a supporting role and told me "In those days the unions were all powerful but often made stupid demands. The Producers got fed up and simply moved the film to Los Angeles and I found myself in Hollywood."

James Garner later said it was his favourite film; Julie had been a joy to work with and gave an excellent performance. He also revealed the American Navy refused to cooperate due to the plot and the film flopped. Until 2005 it remained unavailable to be shown again due to legal disputes.

'A Shot In The Dark' brought Peter Sellers as the immortal Inspector Clouseau to the studio supported by Herbert Lom, George Sanders and Elke Sommer.

Crew members recall that Sanders started up a pool that every time Sellers caused the actors to break up in a particular scene, they would have to donate £5. They raised about £200 and Sanders suggested the money be donated to the nearby Home of Rest for Horses. Sophia Loren was originally offered the role played by Sommer but declined so the script was rewritten to put the main emphasis on the Seller's role.

During filming Sellers fell out with Director Blake Edwards and when he saw the finished film apparently hated it and offered to buy and destroy it. It was later reported that the film failed to make a profit due to cost overruns and delays due to Seller's behaviour on set.

On 12th March an empty sound stage was hired by Elstree Studios to shoot a scene starring Cliff Richard and the Shadows.

'Hysteria' was a Hammer film that started filming on 10th February and completed on 23rd March. The Director was veteran Freddie Francis who told me "It was a crime drama and starred an American actor called Robert Webber who I developed a strong dislike for, which is unusual for me. We had a newcomer in the female lead and he made her feel small which destroyed her confidence. He was not a nice chap and it was not a happy picture."

Sean Connery returned to the studio, along with Ian Bannen and Harry Andrews for an army detention camp thriller called **'The Hill'**. The film spent five weeks on location in sandy wastelands at Almeria in Spain where an area 500 yards by 200 yards was cleared. The hill was created by using 10,000 feet of tubular steel and 60 tons of timber and stone. The film returned to MGM for two weeks of interiors.

Boom operator and sound mixer David Bowen told me, "The Director insisted on thorough rehearsals for everything so he could then shoot the scenes quickly."

Television production returned with a second series of **'Danger Man'** but with each episode now one hour. Filming started 9th March and lasted until 9th April 1965. In total 26 episodes were made at MGM, with episodes 27 to 32 shot at Shepperton.

Sidney Cole, the Producer, commented "McGoohan was very professional, always listened to his Directors and helped fellow actors. It was very difficult for him as he is in every shot as the stories are seen through his eyes. That's not true for instance with **'Gideon's Way'** or **'The Saint'**. For a top rate Director we paid up to £1,000 an episode. Back in 1959 **'The Four Just Men'** cost us £12,000 an episode but by 1964 **'Danger Man'** was costing twice that amount. Luckily the series went down well overseas, especially in Canada."

MGM props man Mick Brady told me "It was a wonderful studio, great atmosphere, the best technology and wonderful amenities. McGoohan was a very nice man, he would join us in the Elstree Way pub for a couple of pints and a game of darts.

One thing I remember for one episode we were flying around all over the place on local locations. Luckily we had a catering wagon with us. There was one scene that required a phone box in somewhere like Ridge village and there was only one. As we approached we saw another film unit from Elstree Studios coming from the other direction intending to use the same box.

It was a bit of a stalemate until our location manager offered tea, coffee and sandwiches to the other crew while we filmed our shot. Normally we would have taken our own prop phone box but it all worked out."

Mick was still working at the studio in 1970 when it closed. "It was a big blow to most people as it seemed to come out of the blue. The next thing we knew was a couple of weeks later we were out of the gate and gone. You never wanted to take a day off as there was always something going on, something good, it was wonderful."

It is reported that when the decision was to made to transfer production to Shepperton it necessitated quite a rush to complete all the episodes in order to avoid the costs of transferring scenery to the other studio.

Producer Aida Young told me "I did about a dozen of the episodes but McGoohan was difficult in that he wanted you on call 24 hours a day. Understandable as it was his show, but I was recently married and it got to the point where my husband got fed-up so I left the series. MGM was a beautiful studio and everything so clean and well-maintained compared with other studios. In the end I don't think the management cared."

One interesting aspect of watching episodes of **'Danger Man'** is to spot studio buildings and local locations with for instance in 'A Room In The Basement' and 'Whatever Happened To George Foster' which between them feature the studio car park, the clock town and administration building and Shenley Road .

Two films got underway in May but with somewhat different budgets. **'Murder Ahoy'** was the last of the series of films starring Margaret Rutherford as Miss Marple. On 11th May Miss

Rutherford planted a tree in the flower bed in front of the front administration block to mark her 72nd birthday and was presented with a silver shovel to mark the occasion. Her co-stars, including Lionel Jeffries, attended the short ceremony and the tree remains today.

The front part of the training ship was an actual ship at Greenhithe but the aft was built in the studio, taking 30 men two weeks and was mounted on a six feet rostrum to allow characters to come up from below deck. A ship's mast was erected on the backlot for shots up the rigging and a model built on the tank to use against stock footage shot at St. Mawes in Cornwall.

'The Yellow Rolls Royce' was another star-studded production shot in England, Italy and Yugoslavia under the direction of Anthony Asquith wearing his trademark boiler suit. He was only just recovering from a car accident that had resulted in hospitalisation for 11 weeks and the need for a physio to visit the set several times a week to work on his damaged elbow and fingers. Rex Harrison commented "I had always wanted to work with 'Puffin' who is a great Director and to work with Miss Moreau who is a superb actress, and we worked perfectly together.'

A problem arose when Shirley Maclaine turned up with her own non-union hairdresser. Chief Steward Harry Downing told me "We could not permit that, but Shirley would not relent so her hairdresser did her hair in the Elstree Way Inn next to MGM and she was then driven into the studio."

This was an expensive film with the stars salaries reported as $560,000 for Shirley Maclaine, $275,000 for Ingrid Bergman, $240,000 for Rex Harrison going down to $99,000 for Alain Delon, $75,000 for Omar Sharif, $75,000 for George C Scott and $67,660 for Jeanne Moreau.

One veteran crew member recalled "We built a Spanish grotto on one stage. I remember Asquith wore a boiler suit and kept his script in a pocket on the side of a baby's rocking horse on wheels. He often sat on it when directing and seemed to live on bananas and complain. Studio security were reluctant to let him in on the first day when he arrived dressed that way'.

For the film the production office purchased a 1931 Rolls Royce but it was pale blue so they applied 24 coats of yellow paint. A standby Rolls was located and purchased in Cornwall for £250 although a larger sum was spent making it identical. During 18 weeks on location on the Continent both cars worked without problems. Dunlop had to cast 14 tyres from a defunct 1930 tyre mould. The cars were transported to Europe for filming on separate aircraft at a cost of £900 each per journey.

Props man Mick Brady remembered "Vincent Korda was the art designer. He would come on the set in the morning when we were doing it and had a shooting stick. He would sit on it all day issuing instructions."

Camera grip Dennis Fraser recalled on one occasion on location the car was being driven by a stunt woman and was loaded with extras; it went off the road down a hill but was saved by some trees. Dennis was travelling in front on the camera car and managed to get down and secure the car with ropes. On returning to the studio he was thanked on set in front of everyone by the Director for saving the 'star' of the film.

Actress Moira Lister appeared in scenes with Rex Harrison but it left her with unhappy memories. She later recalled "We were called in to rehearse and I realised the kind of man he was and I was very disillusioned. He gave my role no consideration at all. He just sat down and crossed out half a dozen of my lines without the graciousness of saying 'Terribly sorry but this scene is too long.' but just said 'We are doing this.' I think Rex felt he was the star and therefore everything should be done exactly as he wanted it."

Ingrid Bergman had considered turning down the role which she thought did not make sense but ended up enjoying the film and especially working with the Director. During filming a party was held on the Ascot sequence set for Margaret Rutherford, who was working on another film, in order to present her with the Oscar she had won for **'The VIPs'**.

'Young Cassidy' started under the directorship of veteran John Ford who was offered $50,000 plus 5% of the Producer's profits. Ford was drinking heavily and lasted only a couple of weeks before falling ill and being replaced by Jack Cardiff. It had been offered to Joseph Losey but he wanted to scrap all footage shot to date by Ford and MGM would not agree.

Sean Connery was first offered the starring role but had to withdraw as the scheduled clashed with the new James Bond movie. He was replaced by Rod Taylor after Richard Harris, Richard Burton and Peter O'Toole had all declined the part. Maggie Smith, Michael Redgrave and Julie Christie were supporting cast.

The shooting schedule allowed for seven weeks location work in Ireland and one week in the studio. Carpenter Jim Hedges recalled "On that film I was away in Ireland and had one day off in four months. I had planted my runner beans in my garden when I left and by the time I got back they had grown, flowered and come down again." Cardiff remembered that Redgrave was nervous about doing a long speech in an unbroken take but persuaded him to do it as a rehearsal which in fact he was filming and Redgrave was word-perfect. Julie Christie was taken ill with appendicitis during filming, which was completed on 24th September.

'The Alphabet Murders', known as **'The ABC Murders'** during production, filmed from 16th November through to 19th January 1965.

It starred Tony Randall as Agatha Christie's Poirot and Robert Morley as Hastings. Head of Production Lawrence Bachmann recalled "I had all the screen rights to the Agatha Christie material other than what had been previously filmed or stage plays. It amounted to about 400 short stories and 70 novels. I had originally planned a TV series and made **'Murder She Said'** more or less as a TV pilot but MGM wanted it released as a film. **'The Alphabet Murders'** had a budget three or four times greater. There were plans for another Miss Marple film called **'The Body In The Library'** but it never happened.' A rough cut was edited together in just two weeks by Director Frank Tashlin and Editor John Victor Smith.

MGM brought into the studio a star-studded World War Two adventure story with an all-star cast headed by George Peppard, probably remembered best today as the cigar-chewing leader of **'The A Team'** on television. Entitled **'Operation Crossbow'**, its supporting cast was indeed stellar and included Sophia Loren, Jeremy Kemp, Anthony Quayle, John Mills, Lilli Palmer, Paul Henreid, Patrick Wymark and Richard Todd.

Richard Todd later explained the challenge of being a guest star. "It was a few days work at the studio spread over three weeks although it was great to work again with my **'The Dam Busters'** colleagues Director Michael Anderson and Director of Photography Erwin Hillier. I appeared in a scene with Trevor Howard and John Mills. It can be difficult to come in on cue when it's a long scene but you only have a few words.'

Director Michael Anderson spent six months researching the story, including a visit to Germany and interviewing people who had been connected with the real life Nazi rocket programme. He told me in 2003 "I had worked at MGM before. It was an excellent studio and it was good to have my star of **'The Dam Busters'**, Richard Todd, in a cameo role. We made four films together and he inspired other actors and crew members by his steadfast and memorable performance in **'The Dam Busters'** and is one of our finest actors.

I was no stranger to Boreham Wood and the nearby Elstree Studios was my first love. I started there as a teenage actor in 1936 but when I discovered that acting was neither a lucrative nor a permanent profession, I used my contacts to convince someone to hire me as a runner and worked my way up. I used to cycle from St Johns Wood every day.

After the war I directed some small films that attracted some pleasant critical attention and did well enough at the box office. I was called into Elstree and told I was being given a massive assignment. It was **'The Dam Busters'** but I was cautioned that if at any time they didn't like what I was doing, I would be fired. I have never told anyone that before. That's when Richard Todd came into my life and I will be grateful to him forever as he was the star and had to approve me as a relatively unknown Director."

Props man Mick Brady recalled "We were on location just outside Cromer ; we did all the launchings on a big launch pad we made up there for the doodlebugs. We had this thing that was firing stuff out of it but it never actually took off."

Veteran rigger Alf Newvell told me "The only thing I remember about Sophia Loren is her nose. She is a beautiful woman but when she was laying down, all I could think about was her nose which looked so big, like the Blackwall Tunnel. She was so beautiful sitting up but seeing her laying down put me right off."

Cameraman Erwin Hillier recollected "Sophia Loren only worked for about ten days but was very professional, always on time and script perfect. Her husband Ponti only visited the set a few times. George Peppard was a tough cookie as he had a love-hate feeling towards MGM as he felt they were not paying him enough."

MGM had planned to film **'Journey's End'**, the classic war story but after some pre- production work, the project was cancelled.

The year ended with the filming of **'The Secret Of My Success'** from 5th October to 17th November including locations in Portugal. The film was a lame crime comedy starring Shirley Jones, Honor Blackman, James Booth and Lionel Jeffries playing several roles.

Shirley Jones is best known today as the stepmother of David Cassidy and for having starred with him in the 1970s TV series **'The Partridge Family'** rather than for her big screen career. Kine Weekly thought 'This ingenious story is told with even good humour and considerable invention. A clever British comedy.'

■ ■ ■ ■

1965 saw a slowing down in production.

'Lady L' was a big budget movie mainly shot on location starring Sophia Loren, David Niven, Paul Newman and Peter Ustinov. Filming started in Paris on 19th November 1964 and ended in the UK on 2nd April. **'Lady L'** had its world premiere in November 1965 at the Empire, Leicester Square.

Another all location movie was **'The Comedians'** with Elizabeth Taylor and Richard Burton. **'Dr Zhivago'** was other such MGM production. These films represented the 1960s trend to move away from studio-based productions to the realism of location shooting.

Freddie Young, the triple Oscar winning ace cameraman told me "The studio at Boreham Wood was never properly utilised to its full potential and would sometimes have empty stages just in case MGM decided to use it. When you have expensive overheads and hundreds of staff, that can mean a lot of red ink."

By contrast **'The Cuckoo Patrol'** was a low budget comedy about a scout troop featuring Kenneth Connor, a **'Carry On'** regular, John LeMesurier and Freddie and the Dreamers. It started on 10th May and finished on 27th May including shooting on stages 8 and 9.

'The Liquidator' was a secret service comedy starring Rod Taylor, Trevor Howard and Jill St John under the directorship of Jack Cardiff. Shooting took place in Nice from 5th to 24th April and in the UK from 26th April to 25th June.

Trevor Howard told me "Taylor was not popular as he had 'gone Hollywood', turning up with an entourage, and the film was not a big success."

The film's distribution was held up when MGM, who had advanced £600,000 to finance the film, unsuccessfully took the Producer to the High Court to gain possession of the film in an argument over distribution rights.

'Where The Spies Are' was filmed under the working title **'Passport To Oblivion'** with the shoot commencing in the Lebanon on 30th November 1964 and a return to the studio for interiors commencing 28th December. The film starred David Niven and shooting had to be suspended from 11th March 1965 to 22nd March while he was away filming **'Lady L'**.

MGM veteran Terry Clegg worked on the film and recalled for me an amusing problem that arose while filming at the studio. "There was a scene involving a jet aircraft crashed on a frozen lake. We placed the aircraft in the middle of the backlot surrounded by foam masquerading as snow. It was freezing cold weather. One night it snowed for real, very heavily, and we were left in the ridiculous situation with the aircraft surrounded by yellowy dirty foam but real snow wherever else you looked."

Director Val Guest read the novel 'Passport To Oblivion' and ten weeks later was shooting this film version. Wolf Mankovitz spent twelve hours a day, seven days a week to get the script ready. Kine Weekly described it as 'An excellent general attraction.'

'Return From The Ashes' directed by J Lee Thompson starred Maximilian Schell and was shot on the cheap, much to the disgust of the Director who wanted to use locations in Paris. Instead, from 18th January to 19th March they utilised sound stage space at MGM and spent a week on the backlot. The film was designed to star Gina Lollobrigida but she walked over a row about perks in addition to her salary; the film flopped as her replacement Ingrid Thulin was not a big enough star.

Cashing in on the popularity of Australian singer Frank Ifield, the studio produced a bargain basement musical entitled **'Up Jumped A Swagman'** which required an eight week shoot on stages 2 and 4. Kine Weekly felt 'A lot of clever thought has been put into this picture as well as a number of pleasant songs professionally put over by Ifield. It's not a pop picture but it could have wide appeal.'

The studio was used for casting tests for the forthcoming film version of **'Camelot'** and actor Simon Ward told me "I remember going to MGM for the test but did not get the part. However, I still recall the smell of fear as we all had to wear the same costume."

'The Eye Of The Devil' which was known during production as **'13'** and **'Day Of The Arrow'** proved to be a challenging shoot. Filming started on 13th September and moved into the studio on 12th October, but filming was suspended on 25th November and not restarted until 13th December.

The official reason was that the lead actress Kim Novak fell off a horse, but it was also rumoured that she had fallen out with the Producer. The company decided to recast with Deborah Kerr. This had different effects on her two male co-stars. David Hemmings recalled "We had to reshoot most of the film. As a young actor I was not worried as it meant twice the pay."

By contrast David Niven told me "It was lovely to work with my old friend Deborah but when you find yourself reshooting scenes the spontaneity has gone and your performance suffers. It was also a sad film as we had a young actress named Sharon Tate in the cast and a couple of years later she was brutally murdered while pregnant by Manson in Hollywood. That's when you started to see big fences going up around stars estates in Hollywood."

Director J Lee Thompson remembered "We had completed about 80% of the film when Kim fell off the horse and left the film. The insurance company had to pay out £600,000 and after a break we restarted. MGM got cold feet about the devil worshipping theme and it was only when Hemmings and Tate became rising young stars that MGM decided to release it. The result was it was greeted by laughter and derision from the critics, especially seeing Niven playing a Frenchman."

Flora Robson was in the supporting cast and the veteran actress told me "We filmed a key scene at a Roman Catholic church in London. The priest gave permission without seeing the script. He got bored watching the filming over the days and wandered off. He came back to find Donald Pleasance conducting what he assumed was Mass. The priest came over and told Donald he was not saying the correct words without realising in the scene they were celebrating a demonic Mass!"

In November **'Cast A Giant Shadow'** used stage 5 for just two days to shoot an additional scene.

In August Producers Anatole and Dimitri de Grunwald announced they were at an advanced stage of negotiating a £20 million British production programme with MGM over the next three or four years, covering about 12 films.

1966 found the studio dominated by one particular film and a cult TV series. George Catt resigned as the studio manager, having joined the studio as the estates manager in 1946 and being appointed studio manager in 1963. He retired to Australia and died in 1986.

'One Eyed Jacks Are Wild' was a television pilot directed by Franklin Schaffner and starring George Grizzard, Ann Bell and Edward Woodward who went on TV fame in the series **'Callan'**.

'The Biggest Bundle Of Them All' was a comedy crime film shot mainly on location in Italy starring Robert Wagner, Raquel Welch and Edward G Robinson.

'Far From The Madding Crowd' starring Julie Christie and Terence Stamp was another production mainly shot on location but filmed at MGM for one week in December.

The crime drama **'Stranger In The House'** started on 19th September starring James Mason, Bobby Darin and Geraldine Chaplin. Location work was undertaken in London and Southampton.

Kine Weekly commented 'Geraldine Chaplin confirms the good impression previously made and newcomer Ian Ogilvy is notable. However, Bobby Darin plays the part of evil Barney with over-enthusiasm worthy of Lyceum days which is a pity.'

'Grand Prix' was a racing car story starring James Garner mainly shot on race tracks around the globe including locations in the USA, Belgium, France, Monaco and Brands Hatch in England. The racing sequences have since been credited as the finest of their era. Kine Weekly described it as 'A certain big screen winner'.

'Casino Royale' was a massive James Bond spoof filmed at several studios but spent time at MGM between 6th July to 9th September. The super flying saucer was constructed on stage one for scenes with David Niven and Woody Allen.

Dave Prowse, later to become famous at Elstree Studios as Darth Vader in **'Star Wars'**, told me, "I remember being very excited about appearing in a scene with Niven even though my role was basically a walk-on part dressed as the Frankenstein monster."

Veteran actor Bernard Cribbens recalled for me "I like to say I worked at MGM but in reality it was pretty brief. I had one night time scene on the backlot in **'Casino Royale'** in which I played a London cab driver."

'The Prisoner' TV series has whole books dedicated to it so we will not duplicate those very detailed and excellent publications. The series generally used stage 6 at the studio and the backlot with, of course, the famous locations in Portmeiron. It has been reported that each episode cost £50,000 with an episode completed every two weeks. The series, backed by Lew Grade of ATV, was the pet project of Patrick McGoohan who nearly drove himself to a nervous breakdown starring in and producing the show.

Fans of the series for years identified the backlot tree still standing in the Toby Carvery car park as the one featured in the episode entitled 'Living In Harmony' set in the Wild West but recent investigations have decided the actual tree was destroyed when the nearby houses were built.

Patrick Cargill, who once guest-starred in an episode, told me "The fans of the show are very dedicated and I often get asked very detailed and analytical questions. The problem for jobbing actors like myself is that it was just two weeks work many years ago and I never even went to Portmeirion as they used a double to save money."

Peter Graham Scott directed one episode entitled 'The General' and told me, "Patrick phoned me and asked if I could come down and direct an episode but I said I was busy setting up an ATV TV series called **'The Troubleshooters'**. He persuaded my boss I could be spared. He sent the script and I thought it was a con as I could not make sense of it and then I got it. I was promised the script for the Wednesday but got it on the Friday for shooting on the Monday and only half the casting had been done. It was ridiculous really.

I talked to the story editor George Markstein and we both agreed McGoohan felt trapped by his own success but he could not give it up because its money and its success. I did a bit of work on the script and got the actor playing 'number six' changed. I cast John Castle who was a good actor with a kind of lurking presence rather than just a straight young man and he did it very well. When directing I played it by ear rather than detailing every scene in advance as there is a danger of overthinking things."

Actor Kenneth Grifiths commented "Patrick had an enormous dynamic presence on screen but in private life was a very private person which I guess the public would find odd when someone is in the public eye as a chosen career. He had a remarkable talent."

Actor Peter Bowles later recounted that when he turned up to guest star in an episode he was warned that McGoohan had 'changed' since the old days. Apparently McGoohan said the Director was rubbish and encouraged him to improvise the scene with him. Peter thought the rehearsal was successful but then McGoohan suddenly turned nasty on him and said he was not just the star but the Producer and to do it the way the Director wanted, leaving Peter bemused.

Ernie Morris remembered "I first used McGoohan when he was a £7 a day extra in the 1950s. I directed loads of TV episodes and second features for the Danzigers, but in a way that ruined my career as their name became associated with the words 'cheap' and 'bad'.

By the mid 1960s I had dropped back to assistant Director and McGoohan employed me to do an episode of **'The Prisoner'** entitled 'Many Happy Returns' because I could help shoot fast but well. He would get me to sing for some reason and would be charming in the mornings, but after a liquid lunch it could be a different matter."

'The Bells Of Hell Go Ting A Ling A Ling' was a film that never was. It began on 4th July on location in Switzerland starring Gregory Peck. Due to extremely bad weather, the film was abandoned with the idea of restarting the following year but this never happened. Cameraman Arthur Ibbetson told me "We did six weeks in Switzerland but the constant rain put us so far behind it became a lost cause."

It had a 60 strong unit and was expected to spend 10 weeks in Switzerland and Austria returning for 6 weeks of interiors at the studio. Ian McKellan recalls "It was to have been my screen debut. After the first two weeks, the film was already one week behind schedule. When it was cancelled I still got paid and I believe Gregory Peck got his full salary."

'The Vampire Killers' started on 26th February with a proposed completion date of 26th May but eventually finished on 29th July. Filming began on location in the Tyrol and then moved to the backlot of MGM for one week before relocating to the nearby Elstree Studios due to the amount of stage space being taken up at MGM by **'2001'**.

Roman Polanski later commented, "The unions were very strong and would not be flexible about working long hours. Due to weather delays on location, we ran behind time so after a period at MGM we moved down the road to Elstree. The last scene we shot at Elstree before moving on to Pinewood was the ballroom scene. We had to film it in five days and we had an agreement that the crew would work two hours overtime each day. Then two of the crew would not work due to a dispute with the Elstree management so the rest of the crew refused to work the overtime even though we still had to pay them!"

Polanski's comments highlight the then problems with restrictive work practices and the 'gravy train' attitude that within a few short years would derail massively . Under the title **'Dance Of The Vampires'** the film had a premiere at the Ritz Cinema, Leicester Square on 5th December in aid of the Grand Order of Water Rats with tickets priced at 2, 5 and 10 guineas each.

The evening was entitled 'First Ghoulish Gathering' with many British comedians in attendance including Peter Sellers, Jimmy Logan, Charlie Chester, Max Bygraves and Mike and Bernie Winters, all of whom adjourned after the premiere to the Eccentric Club for a night of laughter and dancing. In the USA it was known as **'The Fearless Vampire Killers'**. Kine Weekly described it as 'A mixture of comedy, burlesque and slapstick as light relief for chiller fans.'

■ ■ ■ ■

'The Dirty Dozen' *started on 25th April with the intention of finishing on 13th August but was finally completed in October.*

One of its stars, Ernest Borgnine, recalled "Making the film was a dream and great fun, one of my best memories in making movies. Lee Marvin was a good pal but sadly was drinking heavily. He and Jim Brown did not get along."

The cast all chose to stay in various parts of London. Robert Webber, Robert Ryan and Charles Bronson stayed at Carlton Tower and Telly Savalas at the Cumberland Hotel. The others preferred to be in rented homes. Lee Marvin went for Old Barrack Road, SW1, Ernest Borgnine for Balfour Place W1 and Jim Brown to Portman Street W1. Trini Lopez was in Piccadilly, Clint Walker in Eaton Place SW1 and John Cassavettes in Church Street SW7.

Lee Marvin was drinking heavily throughout the production, although he always managed to do his scenes. On one occasion for a night time shoot on the backlot he was nowhere to be seen. A production staff member rushed off and found him drunk in the Star Tavern in Belgravia. He was driven back to Boreham Wood complete with a flask of black coffee. In the scene he had to drive a vehicle across a bridge but managed to do it. Apparently Charles Bronson was furious with his drinking and late arrival, considering it very unprofessional. Bronson later commented "It had a great cast, good Director but poor script. I admired Aldrich for what was his greatest success as a Director but not his best film."

There were apparently five versions of the script over a period of time and John Wayne was originally going to star but decided against. Trini Lopez left the film early, due to insistence from Frank Sinatra to fulfill an engagement in America, so his character is killed off in one of the scenes and his lines reallocated to other actors. The actor-singer celebrated his 29th birthday bash at the Sportsman's Hotel in Chorleywood and told the 50 strong press corps that he had given up $250,000 worth of night club appearance fees to do the film.

The film used a crew of 85 and constructed impressive sets on the backlot. A river 600 feet long was dug, 200 tons of earth moved and 600,000 square feet of timber used. The studio provided 11,500 square yards of turf, 5,400 square yards of flowers like heather and lilac , 400 ferns, 450 shrubs, 35 thirty feet tall trees and 6 fully grown willow trees. American records of production costs revealed that the cost of the landscaping of the chateau grounds totaled $5,000.

The main French chateau set in addition to its timber required 70 tons of cement, 100 tons of plaster, 8,000 cobblestones and 30,000 feet of scaffolding. The interior set for the chateau cost £14,000 to create.

MGM claimed they used one of Herman Goering's Mercedes cars and they bought six American Stewart tanks found in a Portsmouth scrap yard. They were apparently reconditioned by the studio at a cost of $10,000; they appeared on screen for less than a minute and were then sold for scrap.

I certainly remember the complaints from local residents. Night time explosions were filmed on the backlot, although generally these things were better tolerated then in what was essentially a film and television town with thousands of people employed at the three studios operating in Boreham Wood. The local

Council certainly got a number of complaints on Tuesday 3rd September when half the town was rocked by the sounds of violent explosions!

Studio publicist Julian Senior told me "I found Lee Marvin a slightly bitter man. He had been taken on to do instruct the other actors to handle six-guns, etc on **'Cat Ballou'** but a few days before filming began they had still not got a leading man so they offered the role to him. He went on to win the Academy Award but he was very bitter about that in many ways, because his whole career had taken off simply because there was nobody else.

He was a brilliant man and liked a drink or two or twelve. I had to take him to do the Eamonn Andrews late night talk show but anything late at night was dangerous with Lee. In fact anything after 10am was dangerous as he was usually well-oiled at <u>that</u> stage. We went to the studio at Twickenham and Lee had drunk more than enough, so I asked the floor manager who else was on the show.

It was Richard Harris and that was like running into an explosives store with a lighted match. They met one another, took an instant dislike, and within five minutes were rolling on the green room floor thumping each other while I stood mesmerised against the wall. When the call came to go on Lee simply got up, with one eye closing, adjusted his tie and walked on and did the show.

On another occasion I went to see him at the flat he was renting one evening. He was well gone and he asked the time and I said about five to nine so he got up and walked outside. After a few minutes I went outside and found him leaning against the wall like a cigar store Indian. I asked what he was doing and he said the studio had promised to send a car at nine. I had to point out that was 9am in the morning!"

'2001: A Space Odyssey' according to studio records started shooting at Shepperton on 29th December 1965 and finished the main shoot at MGM on 1st July 1966 although the original planned completion date was 27th May. The original title was **'Journey Beyond The Stars'**. During its tenure at MGM this film occupied most of the complex. The budget spiraled from $4,500,000 to $10,500,000.

Without doubt this was Stanley Kubrick's masterpiece and the space sequences were superb, achieved in an era long before CGI.

In his autobiography Michael Caine claims that Kubrick got the idea of the classical music score from borrowing record albums from the Boreham Wood library. For a number of years Kubrick lived in Barnet Lane, just a couple of miles from the studio.

Props man Mick Brady recalled "Kubrick took over all 10 stages and he had that big wheel on stage 6 that went from the floor to the ceiling. It actually turned and the middle of the floor opened and the camera shot through that. Then when it went past the camera, the door would shut again so it looked like the floor was solid.

After three or four months there seemed to be no end to the film. The obelisks were made and painted, repainted and painted again because Kubrick was a perfectionist. The first obelisk was a kind of see-through plastic. It came in rough, so props had to plane it down, rub it down and on and on. Then Kubrick would come along and say

> In 1996 Variety, the main industry trade magazine, produced a list of the all-time 'rental champs' in America, that being the money paid to the exhibitor from cinema showings. In first place was **'E.T'** with $228,168,939 released in 1982 and in third place the Elstree-made **'Star Wars'** with $193,777,000 released in 1977. **'2001'** released in 1968 totaled $25,521,917 and only just beat Spencer Tracy's last film released the same year which raised $25,500,000.
>
> Those figures were not adjusted for inflation or the increase of ticket prices over the years so make comparisons difficult and do not reflect the number of seats sold. In 1998 Variety did a similar exercise, this time adjusting the figures for inflation and this time **'Gone With The Wind'** released in 1939 topped the poll with income of $1,299,400,000 and **'Snow White And The 7 Dwarfs'** released in 1937 taking $1,034,300,000 knocking **'Star Wars'** into third place and **'E.T'** into fourth.
>
> Since then **'Titanic'** and other films have grossed a fortune but are unlikely to beat **'GWTW'** when time differences taken into account.
>
> It is interesting to note that the five main stars of **'Gone With The Wind'** all worked in Boreham Wood during their careers; Thomas Mitchell, Vivien Leigh and Leslie Howard filmed at Elstree Studios and Clark Gable and Olivia de Havilland at MGM.

he didn't like it. 'Try something else.' and it went on for weeks. When filming was over we scrapped all the sets; it took weeks to dismantle the wheel."

The wheel apparently measured 12 metres in diameter and 2 metres wide, costing $750,000 to construct. ABC Television expressed an interest in buying the sets and models used in the film for a proposed science fiction TV series but were told they had been scrapped.

Post production veteran John Grover recalls " **'2001'** and Kubrick were a challenge for me as sound editor. For instance he wanted the sound of someone breathing in an astronaut's helmet so I spent ages recording myself doing just that. When I played it to him. he simply replied it was not right without telling me what he wanted."

Robert Watts is best known for his work with Lucasfilm at Elstree Studios on the **'Star Wars'** and **'Indiana Jones'** films. However, he also recalls working on **'2001'**. "The film was on schedule until the centrifuge scenes. They were supposed to take 10 days but ended up taking 10 weeks!

Kubrick was OK if you were 'one of his people'. Years later I was interviewed to work on **'Star Wars'** and later found out that Kubrick had put in a good word for me, which was a nice surprise."

It has been said that the MGM management got very nervous about the budget overrun and announced a visit to Boreham Wood. In order to allay their concerns Kubrick is reported to have ordered the conference room be decked out with official-looking charts and graphics that looked impressive but were meaningless.

Joan Feldwick, manager of the studio's printing department recalled "Kubrick was very naughty, always altering the script. Sometimes he would call me in on a Saturday to run off some scripts and the studio would send a car. Sometimes it was only 30 minutes work but being called in on a Saturday meant fantastic pay as I was paid for a full day and time and a half, or in other words for 12 hours."

Veteran actor Robert Beatty had a small role in the film and told me "Kubrick was a very intelligent man but not an actor's Director as he seemed more interested in the technical aspects of a scene. He always seemed to carry a camera around with him. We did a scene where we were all in space suits and miked up but they could not get it to work so they cut out the dialogue. The art department added so many little details in the film that was really just a waste as the camera never picked them up. He did say to me after the film was released that he wished he had used my voice for the computer."

In his autobiography, a copy of which he kindly signed for me ('2001 Memories – An Actor's Odyssey' published by Cowboy Press 2001) Gary Lockwood recalled "On either side of this huge giant wheel that was 60 feet high were TV screens that were supposed to be computer screens showing various readouts. We couldn't simply use TV screens and images though, because the lines of resolution would be visible on screen. So we used 16mm projectors located behind every one of those 'computer' screens."

Gary commented that certain scenes took ages to shoot although they represented only seconds on screen. Also, Kubrick played the voice of the computer Hal during filming. "Principal photography took about 13 months … it's a completely unusual picture, nothing had ever been done like it before and maybe never

> At this point the MGM British Studios was the fourth largest in the UK with 10 stages totaling 91,260 square feet. In first place was Shepperton with 13 stages and 124,502 square feet, followed by Pinewood with 10 stages and 120,583 square feet. In third place was Elstree Studios who had just built 3 small stages bringing their total to 9 and 96,950 square feet.
>
> MGM did, however, enjoy a vast backlot and the studio's construction supervisor recalled "In about 1967 we built what we called the European street set up to a height of 15 feet. The main street was 250 feet long built both sides leading into a square 60 feet by 120 feet. Four streets led off Main Street and they were 186 feet, 80 feet, 40 feet (cobbled and on a ramp) and 31 feet. At the other end of Main Street was another 60 feet long street and a complete Georgian brick frontage house with room to build more.
>
> The sets were available to outside productions and in 1968 Elstree Studios hired it to shoot scenes for the Roger Moore film **'Crossplot'** over a couple of days.'

will again."

Although the film got a mixed reception on release, it went on to amass a reported $31,000,000 box office gross worldwide within the first four years, making it the most successful film to be made at the MGM Studio.

'Blow Up' started on 25th April and finished on 13th August, later than the planned completion date of 15th July. The film, about a photographer who accidentally photographs a murder, launched David Hemmings as a star under the directorship of Michaelangelo Antonioni.

Roy Parkinson recalled "We were going to shoot a nightclub scene in Windsor but there was a two week lay-off while Antonioni assembled a rough cut of the film. It was then decided to build the set at MGM. Antonioni was a bit of a cold fish and it was difficult to work out the schedule as he presented me with a script of just 76 pages and said that was it. He would usually film scenes with two or three cameras. It meant an enormous amount of rushes. David Hemmings was in his wild days and would roll up in the mornings in his Land Rover usually looking like he had enjoyed a hectic night."

■ ■ ■ ■

1967 saw production beginning to slow down and no really big films but some quite entertaining ones.

In February a Green Shield Stamps commercial was shot on stage 10. Sadly I have been unable to locate details of any other commercials shot at MGM as the studio hire records presumably were lost or destroyed.

'Dark Of The Sun' or if you prefer, **'The Mercenaries',** started on 16th January and included location work in Jamaica. The film starred Rod Taylor and making a guest appearance was 1950s British star Kenneth More. He recalled "It was really a nothing role and just a case of remembering my lines and playing drunk as required by the script. However, it was all I was being offered after my fall out with Rank. My lines were actually cut and I remember friction between Taylor and his co-star Jim Brown. The Director was Jack Cardiff, and his casual approach affected the film."

More had fallen out with the head of the Rank Organisation, John Davis, when having imbibed a bit too much, he heckled Davis during a speech at an industry function. Not a man to forgive, Davis blocked More appearing in **'The Guns Of Navarone'**.

The train used on the location was a 1902 locomotive originally made in England but had been mothballed. In one scene Rod Taylor and Jim Brown were protected on the sound stage by bullet proof glass as the action was set in a bar in the Congo being shot up by sub machine guns.

The next film in was the Hammer production **'Quatermass And The Pit'** which started on 27th February and went on until 25th April. The film was originally due to have been shot at Elstree Studios but they were too busy to house it.

Roy Ward Baker was the Director and he was not the most popular member of the crew. He told me "I enjoyed working at MGM as we had that great studio to ourselves. We cast Andrew Keir as Quatermass but I was very surprised to hear years later he felt I had ignored him during filming as he thought I had wanted someone like Kenneth More in the role."

At the time Elstree Studios had consultants reviewing their operations and I have probably the only surviving copy of their extensive report. Part of the exercise was to make a comparison of what **'Quatermass And The Pit'** had cost to make at MGM. It noted that a construction manager was earning about £3,380 a year, a master carpenter £2,340, a master painter £2,180 and a property clerk about £1,190 a year.

The budget for the film totaled £275,000. The budget included £7,700 for the story and script, £28,688 for the cast and £13,998 for the Director. Hiring the facilities at MGM came to £36,907 with an extra £45,771 for the crew and £11,304 for prop hire and set dressing. Film stock, labs and editing came to £27,781, make-up and hair dressing £6,173, music £2,978, publicity and stills £2,255, various costs £27,245 and overheads of £22,760.

The entrance to a London underground station was constructed at the end of the street set and the interior was built on stage 2. It has been reported that Hammer originally intended the film to be directed by Val Guest and to star Peter Cushing who had more box office potential but schedules clashed.

The writer of Quatermass, Nigel Kneale, thoughts the effects used in the film were poor but liked Andrew Keir as the Professor. By contrast, he hated the performance of Brian Donlevy in the role in two earlier films. Barbara Shelley co-starred and told me "I thought Andrew was a great actor and a lovely man."

Props man Mick Brady recalled "I always remember Hobbs End. We built the entrance on the backlot and built the pit. We dug this great big hole and then had to dress it so it looked like a crater. We were up there with Wellingtons on, cutting lumps of clay and sticking them here, sticking them there and it was quite a dirty job."

Actor Julian Glover told me "It was a fast shoot and I did my own stunts but it was a very straightforward role. The Director was quite prickly and was not popular with the crew."

Andrew Keir remembered "The Director had wanted Kenneth More with whom he had made **'A Night To Remember'**, so it was a very unhappy shoot for me and really 7 weeks of hell. It had an excellent cast and script but overall, not a happy memory. I had not seen the previous **'Quatermass'** films before I took on the role and

> The stage rentals at MGM, although subject to negotiation, were as follows. Stage one at 11,500 square feet was £1,730 per week. Stage two at 7,100 square feet was £1,155 and stage three at 18,500 square feet was £2,310. This was considered the second largest stage in Europe and unlike the larger one at Shepperton, it was sound-proofed. Stage four and stage six were 11,500 square feet and 11,100 square feet were both £1,730 and stage five was 7,100 square feet at £1,155.
>
> Stage seven was 7,100 square feet at £1,155 per week, stage eight was 3,650 square week at £462 as was stage nine at 3,750 square feet with finally stage ten at 10,200 square feet at £1,730.

have only seen my film a couple of times since we made it.'

'Battle Beneath The Earth' was a strange 'B movie' that centred around Chinese military try to bore their way underground to America, starred Kerwin Matthews and in a bit part, silent screen star Bessie Love.

It was basically schoolboy adventure material and would form part of a double bill. Character actor Peter Arne recalled "I overacted terribly in that film but Kerwin was a wonderful actor and it was a happy production." Sadly, Arne was murdered in 1983 when he picked up a man who battered him to death. The murderer committed suicide a few days later and his body was found in the Thames. I recall seeing the crime scene photographs when I visited the Metropolitan Police's Black Museum in the 1980s.

'Decline And Fall' was another odd film, this time a comedy starring Robin Phillips, Donald Wolfit and Colin Blakely.

It utilised stages 2, 8 and 9 plus a wide range of locations including Ritz Hotel, Royal Pinner School, Hatch End, Pembroke College, High Street Woburn Sands, West Heath Road Hampstead and the crematorium at West Wycombe Park. A.D Peters, who was the literary agent for the late Evelyn Waugh commented, "Mr. Waugh was especially sensitive about film versions of his novels but he would have approved of this. He had worked on the script with the Producer and had approved it, which was rare. He didn't go to see the film version of 'The Loved One' having read what the critics said about it and there was an abortive attempt to film 'Brideshead Revisited' but he never approved the script and eventually MGM's option lapsed."

Kine Weekly described the film as 'Bright, boisterous and a slightly black laughter-spinner handsomely mounted.'

The next production was a return to 'daring do' set in the Second World War and tells the story of a Canadian officer leading a commando raid on the French coast against a naval base. Entitled **'Attack On The Iron Coast'** it starred Hollywood import Lloyd Bridges and home-grown talent Andrew Keir and Mark Eden. It is interesting in the night raid scenes to see parts of the studio doubling up as the naval dockyard.

The Director was Paul Wendkos (1922-2009) who spent most of his career in television with occasional films such as this and such movies as

> One important issue was agreed with the unions in 1967. It was decided that tea breaks would be 10am to 10.15am and 3.15pm to 3.30pm.

> As 1968 loomed the studio had only a couple more years to live, but that was in the future and as yet nobody had seen the writing on the wall. The management applied to the local council to clad the exteriors of the eight Romney huts used as workshops, extend the cutting rooms and the outdoor water tank.
>
> As late as February 1970, the Council gave approval for a new sports and social club building.

'Guns Of The Magnificent Seven'. The film started on 15th May with location work for action sequences at the West India and St Katharine Docks in London. During the eight week schedule other locations were planned. Gaddesden House would double as Admiralty Headquarters and apparently a school in Pinner awaiting demolition would stand in for the German headquarters.

'Submarine X1' started on 16th July with a schedule that included six weeks on stages 1 and 2 and the outdoor tank plus two weeks at Loch Ness. The tank was used for the Norwegian fjord sequence.

The story revolved a mini sub raid in World War Two on a German ship in Norway and starred a young James Caan a few years before his Hollywood stardom kicked in. Kine Weekly were a touch scathing of the finished product by commenting 'James Caan seems to have been determined to extend that Royal Navy stiff upper lip to his whole face. It is a monosyllabic script.'

■ ■ ■ ■

After the relative QUIET *of 1967, the following year saw the creation of two iconic films, both concerned with exploits during the Second World War. Meanwhile financial storm clouds were gathering.*

1968 started with **'Hammerhead'**, a crime drama starring Vince Edwards, Judy Geeson, who enjoyed a short period of stardom during the 1960s and Diana Dors who in her early career was cast as 'Britain's Marilyn Monroe' but later developed into an excellent character actress.

Six weeks were spent on location in Portugal then three days at MGM before time at the Round House in Chalk Farm, then returning to MGM for a few days prior to moving into Elstree Studios to film the bulk of the interior shots.

1968 saw the backlot street set hired for a scene from **'Don't Raise The Bridge, Lower The Water'** starring Jerry Lewis and Terry Thomas.

'Where Eagles Dare' was the studio's last major blockbuster, and starred Richard Burton and TV cowboy actor Clint Eastwood, who would go on to become a highly successful big screen star and Director.

Burton is reported to have signed for a fee of $1 million plus a percentage of the box office and $40,000 living expenses. It has been said that including his original fee this deal earned him a staggering £8 million over the next five years.

The schedule called for location work in Salzburg and ten weeks at MGM which included shooting on the standing street set and constructing a scaled-down mountain on the backlot.

Producer Elliott Kastner explained "I phoned Alistair MacLean and asked if he would write me an original story for the screen. I gave him £10,000 of my own money and the promise of $100,000 when I arranged finance. Later I gave him 10% of the profits which was a big mistake as I have to write a cheque every February all these years later."

Kastner whittled the script down from 170 to 130 pages but did not like the title. Then "I remembered a line from Richard III 'where eagles dare to perch' and went for that."

During filming Richard Burton often invited fellow cast members for lunch and long drinks

As the table reveals, the parent company in America (Loew's Inc./MGM) had shown a significant profit in most years during the whole time it owned MGM British Studios. Note: all amounts are shown at their current levels and are NOT adjusted for inflation.

1944	$14.5 million	1957	$ 0.05 deficit
1945	$12.9	1958	$ 0.8
1946	$17.9	1959	$ 7.7 (cinemas hived off)
1947	$10.5	1960	$ 9.6
1948	$ 4.2	1961	$12.7
1949	$ 6.0	1962	$ 2.6
1950	n/a	1963	$17.5 deficit
1951	$ 7.8	1964	$ 7.4
1952	$ 4.6	1965	$ 7.8
1953	$ 1.5	1966	$10.2
1954	$ 6.3	1967	$14.0
1955	$ 5.0	1968	$ 8.5
1956	$ 4.6		

However, the crisis came when in 1969 a loss of $35 million was registered followed by a $8.2 million loss the next year. A sale of assets resulted in a profit of $7.8 million in 1971 after the MGM British Studio had closed. The studio sold six acres of their front field bordering Elstree Way which had only ever been used for their sheep to safely graze. It was sold to Hunting Surveys and their building was sunk into the natural slope of the land, although MGM did request that they restrict it to one storey.

In 2012 planning permission was granted to erect 130 homes on the site and the value of the development was quoted as worth £34,702,000 ! It begs the question what would have been the value for the entire studio site if MGM had only remained there for a few more decades.

at the nearby Thatched Barn hotel (demolished 1989), sometimes joined by visitors Peter O'Toole and Robert Shaw.

Peter Barkworth, who was in the supporting cast, remembered "It was a happy shoot although the weather on location sometimes caused delays. There was a jump from a cable car but the snow had gone by the time we were ready, so the crew had to spend three days putting down industrial Epsom salts as snow. Then there was a big downpour and it washed away into the river. The cows in the adjoining fields suffered from diarrhea for a week.'

Roger Garrod, who was working in post-production department, told me "I remember they built a complete model village around the outdoor tank."

The Director later said "The film cost about $7,200,000 but took three times that on its initial release alone. I made it as a spoof but in the USA they took it seriously. I gave one German officer so many medals that our German adviser said he would have to had spent 60 years in the army. We included a helicopter, but how many of them were around in 1943? We had them flying from London to middle of Germany in 90 minutes which probably would have taken ten hours. I recall Clint Eastwood kept fit by running around the giant MGM lot."

Props man Mick Brady remembered "We were on that film for about six months and the big set was on stage 3 where they made two cable cars that travelled up from the tank bottom to the top of the stage. I always got the impression Burton was not happy with heights.

Clint Eastwood was always very nice and would say hello to everyone. There was one young girl who used to bring the tea round each morning. She used to stand there looking at him almost drooling. He heard about this and on the last day of shooting he went up to her and said he was leaving and would she mind if he gave her a little kiss. It was a lovely gesture that made her day, if not her year!"

Carpenter Jim Hedges remembered "We had to take up the studio floor for that picture and I built my greenhouse out of some of the wood. We built this big set that went from the top of the stage down into the tank for the cable car scenes. I was at the top with Richard Burton. He had to cross over part of the set and he was not happy with heights. I had to put a barrier over the sloping roof so it did not look so far down. I put about a half inch thick piece of Perspex and dressed it with snow. He would say 'Get that down as soon as you can as it makes me look a fool.'

On some occasions I acted as the chargehand and you would be allocated six or seven men and everyone clamored to get the best chaps as you knew they would do the best work. I used to be content to do the best I could with what I got, as I did in the army, and I found it paid out very well as I made a lot of friends by that method."

Rigger Alf Newvell told me, "Richard Burton was one of the best. He had a pint glass of liquid on the stage and I tested it and it was neat brandy! Clint Eastwood was a bit remote."

A comedy drama **'Hot Millions'** followed, with Peter Ustinov, Maggie Smith, Karl Malden and Robert Morley. A sequence filmed on the backlot required building a fairground. The interior set of a bistro cost £1,890. Unit publicist Julian Senior told me "Ustinov was a quite extraordinary man. He would mimic the crew and got their voices to such an extent there was a photographer who worked with me and I thought I was talking to him, he was hidden from view behind scenery, but it was Ustinov."

They say remakes are usually a mistake, and MGM remaking **'Goodbye Mr. Chips'**, especially as a musical, was probably not the best idea. The original version made at Denham in the 1930s made a star of Robert Donat and told the story of a beloved teacher at a public school before the First World War. This time MGM allocated a 23 week schedule and a budget of $8.3 million. The role of 'Chips' was given to

Peter O'Toole.

This version shot on location for 14 weeks including a period at Sherborne in Dorset where a 40-strong crew had moved to build sets for three months prior to shooting starting on 16th July. They altered the school's façade, built an 80 feet high camera tower and a Victorian sports pavilion.

Camera grip Dennis Fraser MBE recalls "One of the most difficult assignments I had was the opening shot when we had to do a 100 feet tracking shot, pulling up the tracks as we went, then going up in a lift 80 feet to show the whole of Sherborne and finally zoom into a classroom to a boy sitting at his desk and I think we did it in a couple of takes."

Sets built at the studio included the school's assembly hall, the Savoy Hotel ballroom as it would have been in 1924 and an old variety theatre. Before filming completed in December, a 125 strong crew had worked for 107 days on 50 different sets.

It was reported that Petula Clark signed for £75,000 but Lee Remick later sued MGM for £416,000 claiming they had originally signed her to play opposite Rex Harrison.

MGM British Studio's penultimate venture into television was with the production of **'Journey Into The Unknown'** which comprised of 17 episodes each 60 minutes in length. The budget was a reported £70,000 an episode and the cast was a mix of imported Hollywood and home grown stars including Joseph Cotton, Robert Reed, Patrick Allen, Vera Miles, Stephanie Powers, Edward Fox, Bernard Lee, Michael Gough, Dennis Waterman, Julie Harris, Barbara Bel Geddes, Roddy McDowall, Barry Evans, John Fraser and Brandon De Wilde.

Robert Mintz, the post production consultant on the series found shooting in England great for locations but MGM British Studios was not always cooperative during production. He found the dubbing facilities as good as in Hollywood but thought the crew worked slower and their work practices caused some episodes to go over schedule and budget.

The production utilised the outdoor street set for the episode 'Eve'. At the time it was hailed as the most expensive TV series shot in England, with each episode costing $175,000 although this was still 10% cheaper than filming in Hollywood. Two episodes were produced every 10 days, with filming taking place between 24th May to 27th November.

The Producers had grown weary of Peter Sellers' difficult personality so Alan Arkin was cast as the famous policeman in **'Inspector Clouseau'** with support from Patrick Cargill, Beryl Reid and Frank Finlay. This film utilised a number of standing sets in scenes filmed on the backlot.

The production also hired the exterior tank at the nearby Elstree Studios at a cost of £1,500. That tank had been constructed for the Gregory Peck movie **'Moby Dick'** and was in use up until **'Indiana Jones And The Last Crusade'**. When part of that studio was sold to Tesco, the reservoir tank was filled in but the effects tank itself remained and was used as the base for the **'Big Brother'** television reality show.

Sadly the film was not that funny and proved the role was now 'owned' by Sellers.

The backlot street set proved a draw to outside productions and several scenes for **'Assassination Bureau'**, a comedy crime story starring Oliver Reed, Diana Rigg, Telly Savalas and Curt Jurgens were shot on it although the film was based at Pinewood.

'Mosquito Squadron' was the studio's final visit to World War Two and covered much of the ground featured in **'633 Squadron'** . The film starred that **'Man From Uncle'**, David McCallum. With a limited budget it used scenes filmed around the studio lot including the oil tanks and Nissen huts. The crew also visited Tykes Water in Elstree, whose bridge later featured in the opening sequence of the Linda Thorson episodes of **'The Avengers'**. They used the nearby Edgwarebury Country Club which had recently featured in the Elstree-made **'The Devil Rides Out'**.

Nicky Henson co-starred in the film and told me "To save money they used a lot of aerial shots from **'633 Squadron'**. George Chakiris was the star of that film, so you could say he appeared in our film more than some of us did. They counted up the words in my original script , tore up my contract and put me on a daily rate to save money." 1968 ended with **'Alfred The Great'**, now a forgotten historical drama mainly filmed in Ireland but crewed by MGM personnel. It starred David Hemmings and Michael York, with Clive Donner at the helm.

MGM used a 60 acre field at Eskershanore, 20 miles outside Galway. They even constructed a temporary shooting stage 120 feet by 100 feet and a further 16,000 square feet of workshops and offices. Battle sequences were filmed at Castle Hackett and Ross Lake.

In 1968 for **'It's A Knockout'** David Vine and Eddie Waring shot a three minute BBC promo film on the exterior western set, dressed as cowboys.

Several years later, in 1971 the nearby ATV Studios also utilised the set for a sketch for the Marty Feldman TV series they were filming.

■ ■ ■ ■

1969 dawned and MGM in America hit the skids, accumulating huge losses which were bound to affect their overseas operations.

Originally it was expected that Stanley Kubrick would keep the studio busy with his production of **'Napoleon'**, Fred Zinnemann would be shooting **'Man's Fate'** at Shepperton (later relocated to Boreham Wood after the collapse of **'Napoleon'**) and on location and that Michael Anderson would be directing **'TaiPan'** starring Patrick McGoohan.

The first to bite the dust was **'Napoleon'**, no doubt a bitter blow to Kubrick but one wonders if MGM were also nervous of him after their experiences with **'2001'** just a couple of years earlier. The plug was pulled on the project in December 1968.

It was obvious MGM were getting nervous about **'Napoleon'** back in the summer of 1968 and it provoked Kubrick to write to the Head of MGM Robert O'Brien (died 1997, aged 93) stating "For anyone to say that our film of the life of Napoleon is copying **'Waterloo'** (Author's note – a reference to the large scale production starring Rod Steiger) should, I think, be regarded only as an uninformed impertinence."

On 30th September 1968 O'Brien had sent a telegram to Kubrick stating "Am concerned at the mounting expenditure as well as projected commitments discussed with Griff. We must read and consider full treatment before any increase in current expenditure or addition of any kind including staff and surveys. Eagerly awaiting receipt of your treatment. Please advise when we can expect it.'

Kubrick was looking at a start date of July 1969 and anticipated a film running 180 minutes. He predicted a 150 day schedule averaging one to three minutes of screen time filmed each day plus allowing ten days for travel. Locations were planned for Yugoslavia and Italy with interiors at MGM.

As usual with his style of preparation, it was nothing if not thorough. A picture file was gathered of 15,000 Napoleonic subjects . Costume designs were made and samples made of military uniforms. Extensive location photos were taken in Italy, France and Yugoslavia. A master biography file of 50 principal characters was compiled, a library of 500 books gathered and Professor Felix Markham hired as history adviser along with the rights to his book.

It was interesting to note how Kubrick had estimated possible costs. A UK costumed extra would be $19.20 compared with a similar person in Spain at $14.28, in Italy at $24 and in France $24.30. Romania offered up to 3,000 troops at a cost of $2 a day compared with Yugoslavia at a cost of $5 a man.

For making uniforms for crowd scenes, an American company quoted $1 to $4 a man. Uniforms for front line troops more prominent on screen would cost $200 each in the UK but only $40 each if made in Eastern Europe.

Kubrick estimated the cost of building the palaces at between $3 million to $6 million although actual palaces could be rented for $350 to $750 a day.

On 2nd December 1968 O'Brien had written to Kubrick at his office at MGM Boreham Wood, stating "All of us were very much impressed with the presentation of your Napoleonic venture that Louis Blau was kind enough to stage for us on Wednesday morning. The work which you and your associates have put into the project is not only impressive but shows a rare dedication. Over the weekend we all read the treatment and discussed it the first thing this morning. Again we were impressed with the thoroughness of your preparation, but felt after reading your material that I was facing one of the most difficult decisions of my career. You know how much I admire you and how much faith and confidence I have in your great talents.

At the same time I must frankly confess to you try as I might, based upon this treatment, I can't quite see what your point of view or approach to Napoleon's life would be. Furthermore, again judging from your material, it seems quite evident that the most challenging aspects of his life and career are concentrated in the last 15 years of his life. At least this is where I see shape and focus as far as a film is concerned and, of course, this is exactly the same span of time which De Laurentis also plans to exploit in his film, which I understand is to go before the camera in the spring.

In short Stanley, though this is a decision I make with a great deal of regret, I honestly cannot recommend that MGM go ahead with the development of your project. If I did not know how deeply you were committed to the film based upon Napoleon's life, I would urge that you think of another theme, not necessarily abandoning the Napoleonic one but at least postponing it. Should you be willing to consider such a course, I would be more than happy to discuss any other venture you found challenging."

It was obvious MGM were wary of entering into a film which might exceed its budget in the present economic situation and certainly not one that would be up against another film dealing with much of the same subject and leading character. For MGM Boreham Wood this meant a loss of work for the second half of 1969.

Five months later, in May 1969 Robert O'Brien resigned as Chairman of MGM two years before the end of his term and was replaced by 39 year old Louis Polk who had no previous experience in the film business. He announced "Our men running Boreham Wood are first rate. I will shortly appoint a new man to run our production there and set up picture-making deals.'

He lasted only a few months. 18 films planned by the old regime were cancelled, including seven which might have been made in England including **'Rosencrantz and Guildenstern Are Dead'**, **'Canterbury Tales'**, **'Half Way Up A Tree'** and a musical called **'Baker Street'**.

A surprise production into the studio was **'The Private Life Of Sherlock Holmes'** starring Robert Stephens as the great detective, Colin Blakely as Watson, Irene Handl as Mrs. Watson and Christopher Lee as Mycroft.

The film was based at Pinewood and they originally intended to film the monster at Loch Ness but the model sunk to the bottom of the loch. Instead they rented stage 3 at MGM for a week, tarred the floor and put up a huge backing around three sides of it . They filmed various models of the monster from full size to one eighth scale, using almost every 'brute lamp' in the studio for the enormous lighting requirements.

'Bushbabies', released as **'Bushbaby'**, was a family drama about a young girl and was set in Tanzania starring Donald Houston and Lou Gossett Jr. The subject setting required the film to be shot on location, and three weeks of interiors were planned for the studio.

'Captain Nemo And The Underwater City' was good family entertainment starring Robert Ryan, Chuck Connors and Nanette Newman. Apparently Ryan felt the role was a step back after **'The Wild Bunch'** in acting terms and took the role mainly for the money.

A model Nautilus submarine used in the film sold at a Los Angeles auction in 2011 for $14,000.

Roger Garrod told me, "I was working overtime in theatre 3 awaiting rushes when a crew member rushed in and asked for volunteers to jump into the tank for the sinking scene as they were short of extras, which was no surprise as it was freezing!"

Filming on location required eight weeks in Malta where eleven sets were dropped under the sea ranging from a 13 ton replica of the city gates to 4,000 square feet of a fish farm, followed by two weeks at the Red Sea shooting sea life and sharks.

Oscar winning special effects expert George Gibbs told me "Sadly the model submarines were corroded by the sea water in Malta. At one point we created a special effect with what might have been considered a dangerous chemical. The riggers complained it might kill us all so we negotiated a special £2 a day hazard payment and everybody was happy and lived."

Focus puller Brian Harris recalled like at the Studios. "It was very unionised and I will give you a couple of examples of 'the gravy train'. When I was working on **'Captain Nemo'** I was required for only the morning but still got a day's pay. They then asked me to pop over to **'Goodbye Mr. Chips'** in the afternoon. That triggered another full day's pay, even though they never used me!

On another occasion a small fire broke out on a stage and the MGM fire brigade was called out with their 1930's-looking fire engine. Meanwhile a props man had used an extinguisher and put out the fire. So they went on strike."

'The Walking Stick' starred 'flavour of the decade' David Hemmings with Samantha Eggar, supported by Phyllis Calvert and Emyln Williams in a story about a crippled girl deceived into helping out with a robbery.

'One More Time' brought together 1940s MGM star Peter Lawford with actor and singer Sammy Davis Jr under the directorship of comedy actor Jerry Lewis.

The film shot between June to September and included cameo appearances from Peter Cushing and Christopher Lee. This was filmed in July over a few hours and Cushing was sent 12 bottles of champagne and a colour television by Sammy Davis who was a big fan of Hammer Films.

A row developed in July when the film crew arrived at the local lawn cemetery and erected fake headstones for a sequence to be filmed over two days. Naturally those residents who have loved ones interred in the real graves, including the one containing my 16 year old brother, were none too happy to see the crew walking over the graves and the headstones. The crew withdrew; why they could not have shot the scene on the MGM backlot remains a mystery.

Ironically the film's two stars were not to enjoy eternal rest either once they had left for 'the big studio in the sky'. Peter Lawford died broke from drink and drug abuse and his ashes were interred near to Marilyn Monroe's in Los Angeles. As his estate had not paid for the burial, four years later his ashes were disinterred and scattered at sea.

Sammy Davis Jr died after a long fight against cancer. His widow buried him wearing a reported $70,000 worth of jewelry. However, it was discovered that he had died heavily in debt, including government taxes, so it is alleged he was dug up so the jewelry could be recovered and used by his widow towards the debt repayments.

Lewis wanted it to be an open set so there were many visitors and in the end perhaps too much partying which, coupled with a poor release, ensured the film was not a success.

'My Lover My Son' was filmed under the working title **'Hushabye Murder'** with a 12 week schedule. Dennis Waterman starred with Romy Schneider playing his mother; it is alleged they enjoyed an affair although during production. Waterman later commented about the film "I was shocked at what they had done to the picture in the editing but luckily nobody saw it."

The Producer Wilbur Stark recalled "If we found a location or a shot could be done at MGM or locally we would alter the script accordingly without damaging the story. That way we completed it in seven weeks with 130,000 feet of film without rushing anything. On one day alone we shot 16 minutes screen time on location, and these were careful shots set up accordingly. I thought the Brit crew was great."

The final all star production to go before the cameras was **'Julius Caesar'** directed by Stuart Burge and featuring Charlton Heston, Richard Chamberlain, Diana Rigg, John Gielgud, Jason Robards and Richard Johnson. The film started on 28th May and the seven week schedule included locations in Spain. The cast gathered a week before filming started for a rehearsal. The film returned from location to film at the studio on 9th June where sets of ancient Rome had been erected.

Heston later recalled "I loved shooting in England, especially in the summer. I was in awe of Gielgud but I did not think the Director was the best choice and Robards was miscast as Brutus and proved not very good." In his autobiography 'Robert Vaughn, A Fortunate Life' (JR Books 2009) Vaughan comments "We had our first reading and blocking rehearsal in a typical low-end London building that looked more like a squatters residence than a legit theatre rehearsal space. During the table read-through I noticed two things. One was that Jason, whom I had first met that morning, was either seriously jet-lagged or terribly hungover and somewhat out of his element in tangling with Shakespeare's words.

What's worse, our putative star, 'Chuckles' Heston (as Jason called him, though never to his face) didn't seem any more at ease with his interpretation of Anthony than Robards did with Brutus. The air seemed heavy with potential catastrophe."

Vaughn went on to say that a duplicate of the Coliseum was built at MGM but scaled down due to financial reasons and joked that Heston padded his already broad shoulders requiring him to walk sideways through some of the reduced sets. He also recalled that the film was being financed by the Playboy empire, and in a scene with John Gielgud addressing the crowd as Caesar, they shot the crowd scene separate from his oration and added some topless beauties . Overall, Vaughn felt the film was a disaster.

The last production to complete shooting at MGM was a television series created by Gerry Anderson entitled **'UFO'** which started shooting after five months planning in April on stages 6 and 7 with each episode taking an average of nine days.

The series contains shots taken of the sets on the backlot and features the Neptune House office block at the nearby ATV Studios (now BBC Elstree Centre). 'Exposed', 'A Question Of Priorities', 'The Responsibility Seat', 'Confetti' and 'Court Martial' show backlot sets and 'ESP' features theatre 3 and the car park. 17 episodes were shot at a reported cost of £100,000 each.

As with much of Anderson's work, this series still has a cult following and even has a book by Chris Bentley ('The Complete Book of Gerry Anderson's UFO' published by Reynolds & Hearn Ltd 2003 & 2006) dedicated to it for further reading. Sadly most of the main actors in the show are no longer with us. The final episode filmed at MGM, entitled 'Sub Smash' completed on 28th November 1969.

Away on location went David Lean's **'Ryan's Daughter'** to Ireland but manned by a crew from Boreham Wood. Although it proved to be a long drawn-out production, Lean was able to avoid cuts in its budget, but the critical reaction to the film on its release almost put paid to his distinguished career.

'Man's Fate' and **'Taipan'** were two big budget movies that should have occupied much of the studio during the latter part of 1969 and into 1970.

'Taipan' was a film to be produced by Carlo Ponti with Michael Anderson directing and Patrick McGoohan starring, but during pre-production it was cancelled by MGM. It was due to have started in February 1970.

However, the *cause celebre* of MGM's history was the cancellation of **'Man's Fate'** and the way it happened. This was explained to me by the film's Director, Oscar winner Fred Zinnemann and his Associate Producer, Andrew Mitchell.

Fred was already a distinguished Director, with such classics as **'High Noon'**, **'From Here To Eternity'** and **'A Man For All Seasons'** under his belt. He was to return to Borehamwood seven years later to direct another classic, **'Julia'**, with Jane Fonda and Vanessa Redgrave at Elstree Studios.

By a twist of fate, by then his old friend Andrew Mitchell was the Managing Director of Elstree Studios. He had introduced the 'four wall system' that, given time, might have saved the MGM Studios.

In 1966 Carlo Ponti owned the rights to the novel and in October 1966 asked Zinnemann if he would direct it. They met the MGM hierarchy in New York in November and at the meeting it was agreed to assign the rights to MGM if they financed the production with the profits shared between the three parties.

Zinnemann agreed he would be paid $500,000 plus 25% of the net profits and if the project did not proceed would get $166,667.

In July 1968 pre-production began at Shepperton and key staff were employed. In August 1968 MGM announced filming would start on location in January 1969 but in November it was agreed to postpone until November 1969.

With the cancellation of **'Napoleon'** and with space now available, it was agreed in January 1969 to move production to MGM British Studios. A provisional budget of $8,700,000 was set.

In July and August Liv Ullman, David Niven and Max Von Sydow were signed to star, and by October the rest of the cast were engaged, costumes made and sets built at the studio and on location in Singapore. On 10th November the cast were assembled and rehearsals began, and on 15th November some music was pre-recorded.

Then the unthinkable happened, when the new top dog of MGM, James 'smiling cobra' Aubrey, under orders to cut costs by the new owner of MGM, Kirk Kerkorian, sent a telegram cancelling the film. This took place on 19th November and on 2nd December Aubrey cabled that Ponti and Zinnemann were responsible for all outstanding commitments.

David Niven later told me "I knew the old Hollywood had died that day when 'the Tiffany of studios' would behave in such a manner."

Back in July the then president of MGM, Luis Polk, had telexed Zinnemann "News reports about MGM need in no way concern you. We look forward to the successful completion of what may be your finest motion picture and which could be a major factor for our future success." Zinnemann had requested the now maximum budget of $10,000,000 be increased by $85,000 but was told that would require new Board approval and the Directors were in a turmoil.

MGM had spent £500,000 on pre-production but were now insisting that as the film was being made by a company created by Ponti and Zinnemann, they were responsible for all the cancellation costs. Zinnemann argued correctly that MGM well knew their company had been set up just for the film, for tax and other reasons. That was common practice but in reality it was an MGM movie and so MGM were liable as they were cancelling it.

The costs at issue were the actors' fees totalling £342,694 including £135,417 for Peter Finch, £125,000 for David Niven and £62,499 for Max Von Sydow. In addition there were the crew costs of £37,110, building costs in Singapore of £27,000 and costumes produced by Berman & Nathans costing £84,713. In total Ponti and Zinnemann faced a bill of £557,210 which is a lot of money today, let alone in 1969.

Their response was to sue MGM for the money, not claiming for themselves but in effect acting on behalf of all those owed money. The case dragged on but just before the hearing was due to start on 25th June 1973 MGM settled out of court. MGM agreed to pay half the £30,000 legal fees incurred by Ponti and Zinnemann.

It was further agreed that MGM would settle all claims at their discretion and indemnify the two men against any liabilities. It was decided that if the claims of Finch, Niven, Sydow and Clive Revill and Shepperton were not settled by January 1974 they could proceed with their own claims against MGM.

In July 1973 the film crew union ACTT accepted a settlement of 20% of their claim. Andrew Mitchell told me "It was cancelled after rehearsals had completed and just 3 days before principal photography was due to start. The way MGM behaved was unbelievable. Zinnemann never believed they would try shift all the responsibility onto his £100 company just set up at their request to obtain the Eady Money benefits. They were taking the stance that they had simply loaned him the budget!"

Terry Clegg was the location manager and told me "I was out in Singapore with the construction manager, an accountant and 32 MGM crew. Nine days before shooting was due to commence we were all at the Intercontinental Hotel when Andrew Mitchell suggested we go somewhere private and broke the news that the film had been cancelled.

MGM's attitude was that it was up to Zinnemann to deal with the crew which left us stranded. I persuaded a local travel firm to pay for the crew to be flown back, saying that it was only postponed and we were leaving equipment and the sets standing ready to return, but I knew that was highly unlikely. I arranged the return of myself, Bill Welsh the construction manager and the accountant by selling back early a car I had purchased locally as I had expected to be there a year.

We did not seem very welcome upon our return and I ended up in Fred's office without pay for three months wrapping up the film. We certainly left a number of bad debts and ill feeling in Singapore and the sets were still standing on the MGM backlot."

In the end, the four actors settled for £335,816 compensation between them but Niven lamented "It robbed me of the best film role I was ever offered." Nathans settled for £65,000 and in the end MGM spent £557,000 settling 200 claims including the money owed in Singapore.

James Aubrey later defended his actions by saying that when he was offered the job to run MGM, he had no idea the studio had no money and was awash in red ink.

The International Years – The 1960s

Director Anthony Asquith shows First Assistant Director Frank Hollands and lighting cameraman Jack Hildyard exactly what he wants on 'The Millionairess'

The incomparable Sophia Loren draws deeply on her acting skills to appear pleased to receive the attentions of Peter Sellers

A Norwegian Barn in the depths of Hertfordshire where Sophia Loren had her jewels stolen

WARNING! This man is dangerous!

Patrick McGoohan, this time playing 'The Prisoner', loads his plate at a studio buffet

Mystery solved! Meet Agatha Christie, keeping a vigilant eye on the filming of 'Murder She Said'

Olivia de Havilland and Rossano Brazzi, stars of 'Light in the Piazza' look relaxed, while George Hamilton looks ever so slightly uncomfortable that Miss de Havilland's daughter Giselle Galante is resisting his charm.

William Holden relaxes on the set of 'The Devil Never Sleeps'

The International Years – The 1960s

Clifton Webb charms Hedda Hopper during filming of 'The Devil Never Sleeps'

Radlett railway station is the real star of 'The Password is Courage', while Maria Perschy and Dirk Bogarde argue over who has the tickets

Dirk Bogarde and co-star Maria Perschy are STILL having trouble with their tickets, this time at London Bridge railway station. Yes, really

Dolores Hart invites you to 'Come Fly With Me'

Can you spot Orson Welles in 'The VIPs'?

Poster for 'Impact'

Cliff Robertson displaying his full range of emotions in '633 Squadron'

The children plus their teacher at MGM during 'Children of the Damned'

The International Years – The 1960s

During a break in 'Murder Most Foul' Margaret Rutherford plants a maple tree to celebrate her 72nd birthday

Sean Connery is definitely not over 'The Hill'

We'll never know what Rex Harrison has just said to Jeanne Moreau on the set of 'The Yellow Rolls Royce'

On the set of 'The Yellow Rolls-Royce'; can you spot the ladder, light and rigging?

George Peppard welcomes his (current) girlfriend actress Elizabeth Ashley to MGM during 'Operation Crossbow'

Sophia Loren and George Peppard compare notes on the quality of room service

Michael Anderson, Director of 'Around the World in 80 Days' and 'The Wreck of the Mary Deare' as well as another local film, 'The Dam Busters'

Maximilian Schell and friends explore MGM during filming of "Return From The Ashes"

PHYSICIAN'S REPORT

PART I.
STUDIO: M-G-M
PRODUCTION: Operation Crossbow
NAME: George Peppard
NATIONALITY: Am   AGE 35 YEARS

DATE: July 1—1964
HOUR: 2:00 P.M.
LOCATION: Beverly Hills, Calif
SEX: Male

IT IS IMPORTANT THAT EXAMINED PARTY ANSWERS THE FOLLOWING QUESTIONS:
Have you during the past 3 years, to the best of your knowledge and belief, been prevented by sickness or accident from taking part or continuing to take part in a film or theatrical production? If so, give details: no

1. Upon commencement of your work in production for which examination is now being made, will you be working in any other production? ... no
2. Do you contemplate working in any other production before completion of your part in the one for which you are being examined? ... no

Comments by Doctor on above if answered in affirmative.   SIGNED George Peppard
(TO BE SIGNED BY PARTY EXAMINED)

PART II. TO BE COMPLETED BY PHYSICIAN.

1. (a) Height: 6 ft. — inches.   (b) Weight: 170 pounds
2. Blood Pressure:
   Systolic 124 mm.   78 Diastolic (Phase V)   mm.
3. After careful inquiry and physical examination, do you find any evidence of past or present diseases or disorders of: DETAILS
   (a) Brain, Nervous System? (Test Reflexes and Co-ordination).   (a) no
   (b) Ears, Nose, Eyes, Throat, Teeth or gums   (b) no
   (c) Thyroid or Lymph Glands?   (c) no
   (d) Heart, Blood Vessels? (If you find any abnormality of heart, size, rhythm or sounds, please complete Question No. 6)   (d) Normal Heart sounds + rhythm, no enlargement or any other Pathology.
   (e) Lungs?   (e) normal
   (f) Stomach or Abdominal organs?   (f) no
   (g) Genito-Urinary System?   (g) no
   (h) Skin or Extremities?   (h) no
4. (a) Is there a hernia (if so, describe it)   (a) no
   (b) Is there any evidence of varicose veins or ulcers   (b) no
5. Urinalysis:
   Are you satisfied that the specimen is authentic?
   Specific Gravity   Reaction   Albumin   Sugar
6. To be completed if Question 3D is answered "Yes."
   (a) Is there a history of Rheumatic fever, chorea, Scarlet fever, diptheria, recurrent tonsilitis, syphilis? ...
   (b) Is there a Murmur?
   Timing   Intensity   Quality
   Systolic: Faint: Soft:
   Presystolic: Moderate: Blowing:
   Diastolic: Loud: Rough:
   (c) Is the murmur constant or inconstant?
   (d) On exercise, does the murmur
   Intensify?   Decrease?   Disappear?

EXAMINATION WAS MADE IN PRIVATE AT:
On this 1 day of July, 1964, at 2:00 a.m./p.m.

RESULTS OF EXAMINATION:
RISK: Excellent/Very Good/Good/Average/Below Average.

Physicians Recommendations
1. Full Cover.
2. Full Cover be granted subject to the following restrictions by excluding:
3. Accident Risks only.
4. Rejected.

Signature of Examining Doctor: ...
Address: ...
FORM NO. ST 1

George Peppard's medical report before filming on 'Operation Crossbow'

While filming '13' or 'The Eye of the Devil' David Niven poses with Kim Novak

Stanley Kubrick takes Arthur C. Clarke on a tour of MGM, home of '2001: A Space Odyssey' But who is wearing cricket whites? And why?

Film crews setting up for night shooting at 'the chateau'

Lee Marvin takes a break from winning World War II with some help from 'The Dirty Dozen'

The International Years – The 1960s

Sets created on the sound stage for '2001'

Sets created on the sound stage for '2001'

Another birthday, and this time it's Andrew Keir, during filming of 'Quatermass and the Pit' with Barbara Shelley

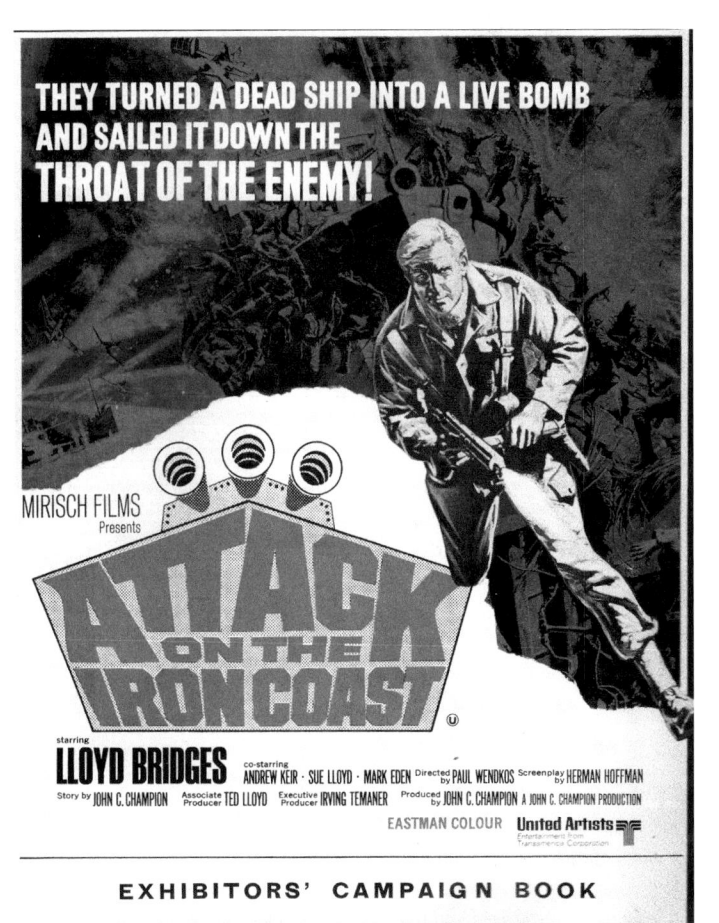

Poster for 'Attack on the Iron Coast'

— 141 —

Clint Eastwood keeps a straight face when confronted by Ingrid Pitt, while Mary Ure and Richard Burton can scarcely contain their excitement on the set of 'Where Eagles Dare'

Filming at Sherborne railway station for 'Goodbye Mr. Chips' Photo courtesy of Dennis Fraser.

David Hemmings is pointing at something of interest on the set of 'The Walking Stick'

Photo courtesy of Dennis Fraser.

Robert Ryan is starring in 'Captain Nemo and the Underwater City'; the two young ladies in authentic costume play "salesgirls trying to interest him in some gold trinkets"   But those were the 60's!

The International Years – The 1960s

Poster for 'One More Time'

Jerry Lewis directing his first film, 'One More Time'

Francesca Anderson, the rich wife of an older millionaire, can't cope with the death of her lover, who is the father of her only son, James. Confused? Romy Schneider starred with a young Dennis Waterman in 'My Lover, My Son'

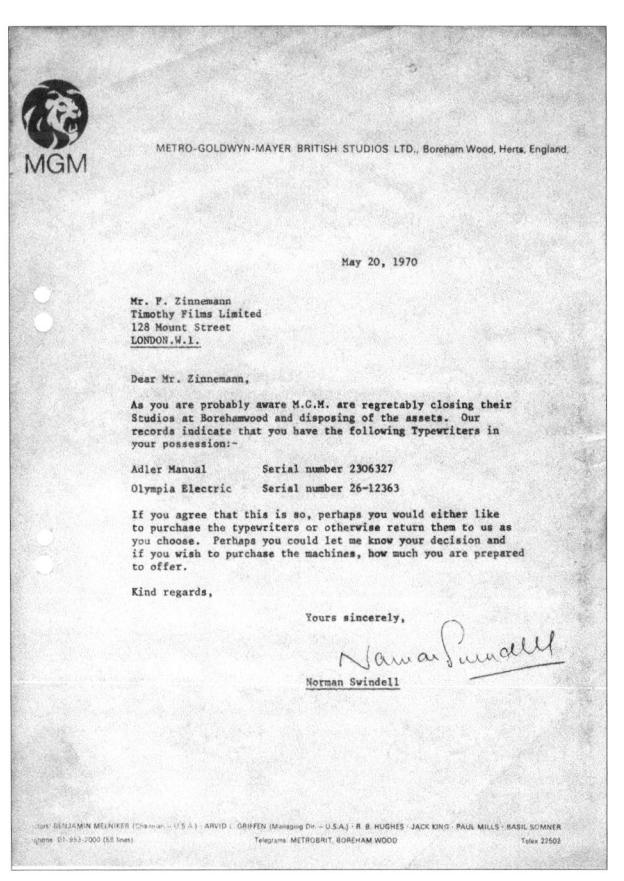

We wonder whether legendary Director Fred Zinnemann accepted this generous offer after MGM pulled the plug on 'Man's Fate'

– 143 –

MGM British Studios

Cast and crew of 'Man's Fate'... did they suspect their fate?

An urgent FAX to Steven Spielberg from Stanley Kubrick during filming the maze for 'The Shining' on the deserted MGM backlot

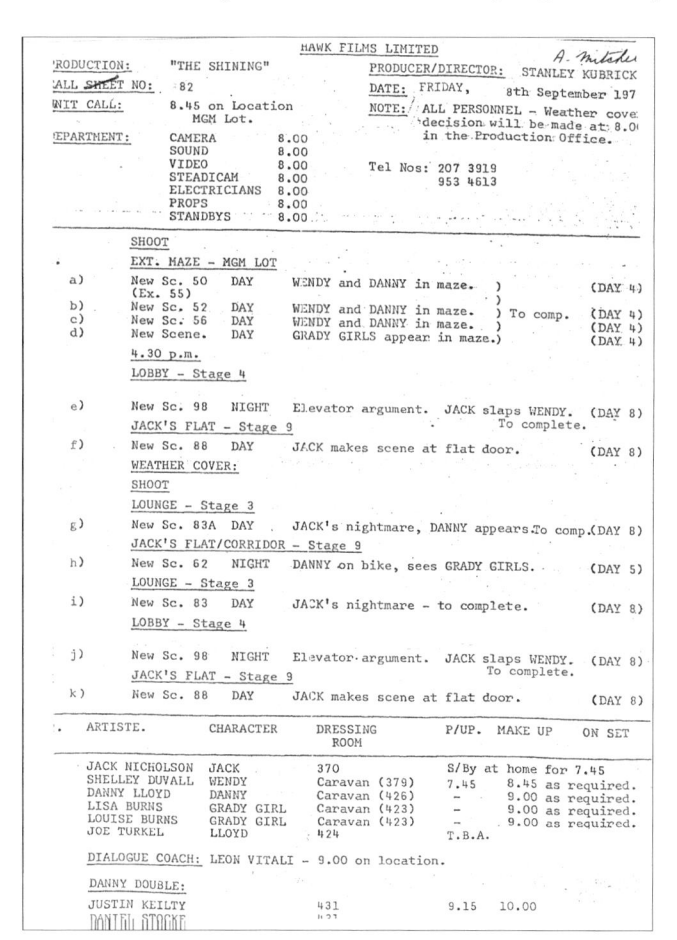

A call sheet for filming for 'The Shining' at MGM

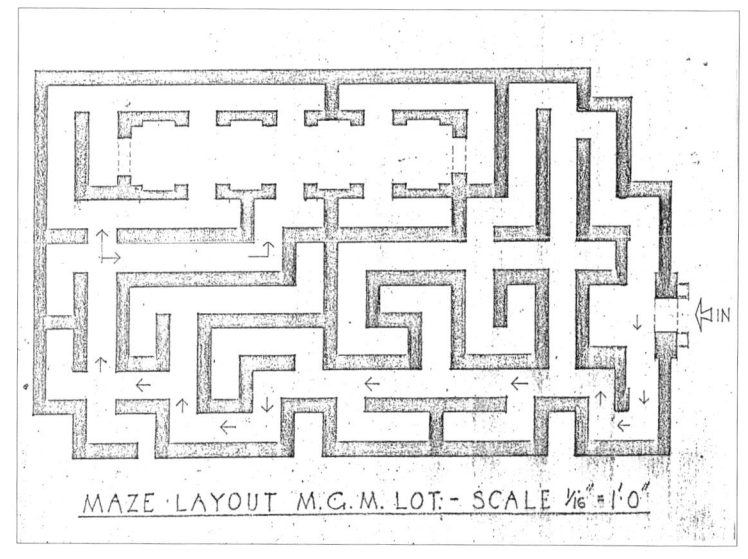

This would be handy if you ever enter the maze of 'The Shining'...

— 144 —

The 1970s and Beyond

As 1970 arrived, the end was in sight. In January James Aubrey told MGM stockholders at the annual meeting in New York that the studio in Boreham Wood was being closely examined for reductions but would be kept busy with plans for 10 or 12 films a year, starting with **'No Blade Of Grass'** *and that the European distribution office would move from Paris to London.*

SOUND EDITOR JOHN Grover recalls "The last time I was at MGM was to do postproduction work on a film called **'Soldier Blue'**. We were booked in but then told we must leave as the Studio was closing and we had to relocate." Then the **'UFO'** TV series were told to look elsewhere and decamped to Pinewood.

'No Blade Of Grass' did start production with actor turned Director Cornel Wilde at the helm, but although they did do some filming on the backlot street set, this was planned to be mainly a location movie. Unit publicist Brian Doyle told me "Cornel was very easy to work with and always put on a bad Hollywood-style cockney accent whenever he saw me. The studio was first class."

Cornel Wilde recalled "I came across the idea for the film when I bought the book in Foyles in London. I thought it would make a good film so I approached MGM as I heard they had the screen rights. I remember the child birth scene caused quite a stir. We shot an actual birth at a nearby hospital and paid all the expenses of the mother."

Actress Wendy Richard who achieved TV stardom in **'Are You Being Served'** and **'East Enders'** recalled: "Appearing in **'No Blade of Grass'** was an enjoyable experience, especially the location work done in the Lake District. Cornel Wilde was not that popular with the crew and was a real keep fit fanatic."

Props master Peter Hancock told me, "I was on location with the film but I returned to an empty studio and was told to deposit the two truckloads of props in stage 8. It was a shock to see the studio then compared with when I had left it. All the beautiful props, the antique furniture, fabulous bookcases filled with period books, all gone. I eventually went freelance and retired in 1994 after I was the first English props master to get a screen credit and the only English props master nominated for an Oscar for **'Casualties Of War'** so I had a good career."

'Zeppelin' starring Michael York was

set-building and in pre-production with a 64 day schedule but were asked to leave. Producer Owen Crump commented "We scouted six studios throughout Europe before deciding on MGM. A week before we were due to start shooting, they told us we would have to get out. The sets were built and everything was ready. We eventually filmed at Pinewood.'

Veteran MGM production manager, Roy Parkinson, who by now was freelancing, told me "I had first worked at the studio in 1946 so I was there at the beginning and at the end. I was working for Producer Raymond Stross on his film **'I Want What I Want'** starring Anne Heywood.

We had been to MGM on 7th April to discuss offices and moved in on 13th April. We were then informed on the 23rd that MGM British Studio was closing on the 28th and so we moved to Twickenham. It was very sad and a bit of a shock as I had worked on 21 films made at the studio."

In February, Jack King had been appointed as Director of Operations and Paul Mills as Director of Administration. Basil Somner took over the duties of the Managing Director Arvid Griffen who had resigned.

The studio was bleeding money with expensive overheads not matched by income. In 1968 the local rates (tax) bill alone had amounted to £148,000.

Back in November 1969, a total of 124 employees had already been made redundant. That still left 780, but by February 1970 that would be down to 192. Eventually 40 of those staff were employed by Elstree Studios.

Chief shop steward Harry Downing recalled "I negotiated the redundancy packages and then stayed on until July to oversee the removal of equipment and dismantling of sets. I then went freelance and retired after working on the TV series **'The Sweeney'** in the 1970s."

In March MGM announced further redundancies to reduce the annual wage bill of £500,000 for the studio to £138,000. Each craft department would be reduced to one supervisor with staff recruited as and when needed. In effect the studio was moving towards a 'four wall' operation later adopted by all film studios in the UK. If time had permitted, this policy could possibly have saved the studio as it did with nearby Elstree Studios in 1973.

The ACTT union favoured the idea of Elstree becoming a television production centre and film production moved to MGM. Their General Secretary Alan Sapper commented at the time "We tried to get Elstree to move to MGM and we suggested Elstree be converted into a TV film production centre. Our proposal was put to the Minister of Technology and the companies concerned but they said it was unrealistic."

At a press conference in July, Elstree Studios Managing Director Bryan Forbes rejected the idea, citing that Elstree had more production space than MGM and company Chairman Bernard Delfont commented that he had not seen one feasible suggestion that would suit everyone.

At a meeting of 1,000 union members at the Apollo Theatre in London, Alan Sapper described MGM as standing for 'My God Murder' in that they were murdering Boreham Wood and closing 20% of the studio space in Britain.

Tommy McComb was a gateman at the studio from 1947 to 1970 when it closed and remembered for me "The last 200 employees were due to be made redundant but only 61 received their notice due to a hitch. The problem was that the crew attached to **'Zeppelin'** were told they would transfer to Elstree but it went elsewhere."

Roger Garrod still remembers how he found out about the closure. "I remember they built sets for **'Man's Fate'** and changed the **'Dirty Dozen'** chateau to resemble an Asian mansion. Sadly, I remember that MGM had a strict policy forbidding visitors and employees from taking photographs around the studio. I took most of mine on a smuggled-in small Kodak Instamatic wrapped up in a brown bag disguised as sandwiches. I got them developed in a chemists but he lost the negatives.

I was the first member of staff other than the management to hear of the closure. I eavesdropped on a conversation in theatre 3 after a screening and heard them discussing a timeline. I repeated it to our union representative and it spread like wildfire before it was made official two days later. The facilities were dated but worked well.

I was looking forward to **'Man's Fate'** as I had spent many hours showing 16mm footage of Japanese atrocities in China to Fred Zinnemann and his crew of costume designers and art Directors.

I had a wonderful time at MGM and was probably the best job I ever had. After being made redundant I got a job as a projectionist on board the SS Himalaya cruising to Australia where I met my future wife and settled in Queensland although I am now living on the Gold Coast."

Damian Cluskey recalled he replied to an advert on the Evening Standard and joined MGM as a carpenter on £50 a week when the

---

In 1946 when MGM began refurbishing their studio, British cinemas attracted 1,635 million attendances at 4,709 cinemas. The year after MGM closed that had slumped to 176 million attendances in 1971 at just 1,482 cinemas.

The net box office admissions in 1946 had been £76 million and in 1971 that was £56 million which, after adjusting for inflation, was a 75% drop.

In September 1948, the year MGM made its first film in Boreham Wood, there were 25 studios in operation and 27 films being made. On the same date in 1972 only 14 studios were operating and 6 of those were being used for commercials.

In 1948 film production was healthy in the UK. British film registration shows 68 films over 72 minutes , 101 films between 33 to 72 minutes and 266 short films under 33 minutes. By 1970 those figures were 85, 11 and 108 respectively, showing the death of the support feature.

It is against this background that the MGM British Studios was doomed.

average wage outside was about £12. Damian was only 25 years old and remembered the social life involved, a lot of drinking and some drug-taking among younger staff. This was 'the Swinging 60s'.

He added that "There was little 'Health and Safety' then so you might be asked climb up a three storey set with your hammer rather than use a cherry picker." Damian was very sad when the Studio closed but, in his words, 'made a fortune' by leaking the story of its demise to the Press.

MGM's print room Manager Joan Feldwick recalled "Paul Mills was in tears when he addressed all us staff on the sound stage announcing the closure as it was a big shock. I took the big face of Neptune from **'Captain Nemo'** as a souvenir.'

Alan Kelly worked in the stills department and recalls "We had some marvelous large framed photos of the stars. We knocked out a window and simply threw them out into a skip positioned below. It was so sad."

Props man Mick Brady remembers "At the end when people were made redundant and the studio was to close, some of the staff would turn up in vans, slip the security £10 and help themselves."

In July the Board of Trade ruled that the National Film Finance Corporation had no powers to buy the studio and on 6th August members of the Federation of Film Unions visited the now closed facility. In August actress Honor Blackman led a march of 300 film workers in London at the same time that 50 members of the crew on **'Get Carter'** filming on location in Newcastle went on a one day strike. It was all too little, too late.

■ ■ ■

How did the CLOSURE *of the MGM British Studios happen, and why?*

It has often been speculated on in other publications, but luckily I was able to conduct a series of interviews in the early 1990s that clarified the true story.

The story was told to me by the executives in charge of EMI and Elstree Studios and the executives in charge of the MGM British Studio. Of the seven individuals concerned, sadly none of them is still alive so this is a unique record of the events.

The management started to implement cuts at the MGM Studio in 1969 and were moving towards 'four wall' operation that a few years later was the standard format for UK studios.

However, the owners of MGM in America were in dire financial straits in 1970 and large banks loans were becoming due. They needed to embark on what became virtually a fire sale.

In 1969 James Aubrey, a TV executive who had been sacked as head of NBC in 1965 and was known as 'the smiling cobra', was appointed by the new owner Kirk Kirkorian. Aubrey quickly realised they had no money to finance the intended programme of films, resulting in the cancellation of **'Man's Fate'** and **'Taipan'** at short notice.

In January 1970 it was announced that MGM had lost $35,000,000 in the previous year. At their historic studio in Culver City, the backlots were sold off to a developer, resulting in the demolition of many famous standing exterior sets. Debbie Reynolds told me "I got together some friends and offered to buy the backlots and open them up as a tourist attraction but they were simply unwilling to discuss the matter and turned their backs on potentially millions of dollars income as it could have rivalled the Universal tour."

The famous Thalberg administration building, named after the legendary 1930s head of production Irving Thalberg, had its name removed to break the link with 'nostalgic views' of the past.

The famous wardrobe and props departments were put up for sale in an auction. By today's standards the items went for a pittance. Spencer Tracy's morning suit from **'Father Of The Bride'** went for $125 and Clark Gable's trench coat used in several films fetched $1,250. From **'The Wizard Of Oz'** the Witch's hat got $450, the Cowardly Lions costume $2,400 and a pair of ruby slippers went for $15,000. By comparison just one pair of the red slippers made for Judy Garland recently sold for $2,000,000 !

Thousands of costumes unsold often were consigned to charity shops or sold retail for a few dollars each, while filing cabinets full of unwanted paperwork were sent to a landfill site. When Kirkorian opened a Las Vegas hotel, staff were sent to scour the studio for any remaining items for the gift shop and it was later reported that Director William Wyler's personal annotated script for the Oscar winning **'Mrs. Miniver'** film was purchased for $12. Animation cells for **'Tom and Gerry'** cartoons were consigned to oil drums and burnt.

MGM was not alone in disposing of assets during the 1960s and 1970s. For instance 20th Century Fox sold its 260 acre studio and then leased back 80 acres to maintain film production. It meant the backlot was developed and the whole deal was worth about $43 million.

Had 20th Century Fox management been more forward thinking, they would have taken a percentage deal in the development of Century City that replaced the backlot. It might have netted them a huge amount. Then again, it was reported that they junked all of their special effects movie photographs and plans in three skips!

I visited the MGM Culver City studio in 1988 and 1997 and on the first visit found it much unchanged except minus the backlots. It was then owned by a television company called Lorimar who were still finding old MGM files and consigning them to skips. I got to travel in what had been Louis B Mayer's private oak paneled lift and to stand on the side entrance of the commissary steps where Katie Hepburn first met Spencer Tracy in the 1940s.

Against that background James Aubrey and his lieutenant Douglas Netter flew to London to decide on the future of the MGM British Studio. It appears that at the beginning the proposal was to suggest EMI close their nearby Elstree Studios and move to the MGM facility.

It is an interesting footnote to history that in 1968 when EMI began a hostile takeover of ABPC (owners of Elstree Studios and the ABC cinemas) it was revealed that they had considered mounting a bid for MGM in America but decided against this. Had that gone ahead it

MGM British Studios

While MGM British Studios was awash in red ink, Elstree Studios was enjoying a rare profitable period. During the 15 month period ending 30th June 1969, the Studio earned £466,478 from hiring its facilities to television productions – **'The Saint'** (£49,508), **'The Avengers'** (£200,655), **'Dept. S'** (£109,212) and **'Randall And Hopkirk'** (£107,103).

Feature films generated a further £159,026 from **'Crossplot'** (£40,315), **'Secret Ceremony'** (£14,200), **'Frankenstein Must Be Destroyed'** (£20,205), **'Moon Zero Two'** (£45,594), **'Crescendo'** (£1,512) **and 'Some Will Some Won't'** (£37,200).

The overall sound stage occupancy over the 65 weeks had totaled 88% bringing a total revenue of £625,504. Other studio income raised that to £805,572. When running costs are deducted, the profit was £215,082 which in some minds strengthened the case to retain Elstree. The studio employed 674 personnel.

In 1971 an internal studio memo stated that Elstree had serviced 15 feature films, 4 television series and 4 commercials. It further stated that they had been associated with 5 of the top 10 box office hits of the year and were the only studio fully equipped to service 16mm television productions, giving Elstree a virtual monopoly on such productions.

Ironically Elstree's profits suddenly descended rapidly. Figures given to the studio board in 1974 indicated the studio lost £364,000 in 1969/70, then £517,000 in 1970/71 with only 27% stage occupancy and after a contribution of £135,000 from MGM.

It 'improved' in 1971/72 to a loss of only £128,000 after receiving £175,000 from MGM and then experienced a massive loss of £550,000 in 1972/3 after receiving £100,000 from MGM.

Elstree never came closer to being redeveloped, but that is a story for another book.

By 1979 the Studio profits had risen to £324,000, having gone 'four wall' and by 1985 that had increased to £1,386,000. Three years later Elstree was again threatened with closure and saved only after an 8 year campaign, which I had the pleasure to Chair, albeit on reduced acreage.

would have presented EMI with the interesting dilemma of owning both studios in Boreham Wood.

Here then are the memories of those involved in those discussions, minus those of James Aubrey who sadly died just two days after I wrote to him to get his point of view.

Sir John Read was the Managing Director of

EMI, the parent company that owned Elstree Studios. In 1994 he told me "It is difficult to remember after 24 years but as I recall, when MGM first contacted us they thought EMI just owned a studio and wanted to talk about a merger, takeover or other options.

However, they had not researched our company and soon realised how big we were. So the discussions were referred to our film division which was controlled by Bernard Delfont. It was very clear at the time that one of the two studios had to close. I cannot recall the details of the discussion other than it resulted in MGM closing their studio and that they would invest in Elstree.

In general I was always supportive of Elstree and later negotiated the 'four wall staffing system' with the unions to keep it open. Bryan Forbes was a likeable and talented individual but I do think there was a rivalry between him and Nat Cohen. The films Bryan chose to make did not seem to make us much profit and at the time he had made enemies on the film division board, especially amongst the old guard who simply wanted to boost cinema attendances. I feel the company supported him as much as the times permitted."

Bryan Forbes, who had recently been appointed the Managing Director of Elstree Studios, told me "I had the unhappy task of crossing the road and telling the entire MGM staff they would be given a fortnight's notice. (Author's note – this was denied in my interviews with the MGM executives, who asked why they would ask an EMI employee to talk to MGM staff.)

I think of that occasion as one of the unhappiest episodes of my entire career. It was something that I fought against, but ultimately my advice was ignored and the decision went against me. Aubrey came to England with the express purpose of closing the Boreham Wood studios which at that time were one of the best-equipped in Europe. For reasons I could neither comprehend or acquiesce with, the board of EMI entered into discussions with Aubrey with a view to a quasi-merger.

Together with Sir Joseph Lockwood, Bernard Delfont, Nat Cohen and legal officers of EMI, we had prolonged discussions with Aubrey and his sidekick Douglas Netter at Manchester Square. Realising everyone present except me was intent on closing MGM, I argued vehemently that if a merger was to take place and one of the two studios had to go, then it made sense to close my own studio and move across the road to MGM.

I maintained that if MGM/EMI agreed to plough the profits of such a sell-back into production then I had a reasonable chance of selling the deal to the unions, and with voluntary redundancy could go some way to allaying the inevitable distress. I argued that with its enormous backlot and much more modern facilities, MGM was the obvious answer.

Elstree at that time was incredibly run down; although I had asked for capital expenditure of some £800,000 in the event I was only given £80,000 which was just about enough to repaint it. It was a shabby and cynical exercise, and I was overruled and given the unhappy task of communicating the decision to the MGM staff. I was then made Chief Executive of the merged company and the benefit to EMI was miniscule.

The MGM studio was immediately stripped and the assets sold off. The enormous props department, for example, went for £5,000. It was a shameful episode and as subsequent events have proved, it meant the total demise of feature film production in that neck of the woods. A high street site properly negotiated would obviously have produced an enormous sum of money when sold.

The infinitely superior MGM would still be a major studio on a par with Pinewood. Aubrey acted in a most cynical manner and the board of EMI went along with it."

Forbes left his position early as head of production at Elstree Studios in April 1972, disenchanted with lack of support and because EMI failed to give the film **'The Raging Moon'** which he wrote and directed, a general release. At the time he was quoted as saying "I was only head of the production arm and had no say in exhibition and distribution, which was vital. I differ from Nat Cohen in that I would not make such films as **'On The Buses'** to the exclusion of all others."

Bernard Delfont told me "There was merit in the idea of closing Elstree and moving to MGM but I could see a real problem. It would have meant redundancies, as jobs would have been duplicated and if MGM were run as a 'four wall' operation it would have needed much smaller staffing levels. I could envisage strikes at Elstree which would have impacted on our film programme and it could have spread to our ABC cinema chain. It was simpler to have MGM close and contribute towards our operating losses at Elstree."

Ian Scott had started at Elstree Studios in 1962, rising to becoming company secretary and Director of admin and finance. He would eventually become Managing Director when Bryan Forbes resigned. Scott told me "Jack King and Oscar Beuselinck of MGM came to see me at my home when I was ill with flu (Author's note – both King and Beuselinck denied such a meeting ever took place or that Scott was directly involved in the decisions).

They said Delfont had agreed that Elstree would close and move to MGM. I was totally opposed and wrote a lengthy memo to the EMI board members who were persuaded to reverse the decision. My reasons were that I preferred we were masters of our own fate by remaining at Elstree which we owned. The value of the Elstree site for any future development was considered greater than MGM which had planning restrictions. In addition, the unions were very strong and to have attempted to close Elstree could have resulted in industrial affecting the cinemas and everything."

■ ■ ■ ■

It becomes clear that whilst the EMI executives could see the advantages of a merger based at MGM, which was the better studio plant-wise, they also feared the repercussions more than the MGM decision makers whose backs were against the wall 6,000 miles away and out of harm's way.

However, what was the MGM view of these discussions? In 1994 I asked the three top executives of the MGM British Studio and MGM's lawyer in the UK, the renowned Oscar Beuselinck.

Jack King was Director of operations at the studio and he recalled "We had been losing embarrassing amounts of money in previous years, so from Christmas 1969 we negotiated staff redundancies with the unions. People accepted the situation and we were moving towards a four wall facility operation as we had maintained the studio well. We were going to sell off the camera department and in all departments employ people on a freelance basis when needed.

Then independently of our efforts, Kirkorian decided to reduce costs and to close the studio immediately. James Aubrey came to London but did not visit the studio. They wanted maximum money as quickly as possible. Talks went on at a senior level for some days to close Elstree, but Kirkorian did not believe that was the most profitable solution."

Paul Mills had been at the studio as head of publicity since the early 1950s and was now Director of administration. His memory was "First I was told MGM was going to be kept, then I was told the reverse. I suspect Delfont and the EMI board knew that the Elstree Studio site was ripe for future development due to its location whereas had they closed it and merged with MGM, that option had less development potential due to green belt restrictions.

Kirkorian was not interested in anything but realising money and Aubrey was his hatchet man. When Aubrey had agreed the lesser cost of contributing to the running costs of Elstree, I was left with the task of calling together the MGM staff on one of the sound stages and informing them of the immediate closure. It was a tragedy as the studio was the finest in Europe with excellent facilities and top rate staff."

Mills held many stories about the stars he had worked with over the years but declined offers to commit them to paper and took them to his grave.

The third executive at MGM was Basil Somner, who told me "I recall sitting in on meetings for three days and there appeared to be general interest in closing Elstree and retaining MGM. Then, on the Saturday morning Netter phoned me to say MGM will close as Kirkorian wanted the money from the sale. On the Monday I informed King and Mills and it was agreed that Mills would call the staff together on one of the stages and break the news."

■ ■ ■ ■

The final word came from MGM's top lawyer Oscar Beuselinck who told me the whole story over lunch at the Strand Hotel in London in 1994, just three years before his death.

Beuselinck was England's top showbiz lawyer and a much feared libel barrister who oozed charisma. He arrived in his Rolls Royce, certainly a man at the top of his game. It is reported that he was born to a Belgian sea cook and an English mum, raised in the slums of Hoxton, London and left school at 14 years old.

"I first arrived at Elstree in the early 1930s when I was involved in a court case at Elstree Studios and I was a junior legal assistant. My first job after the war was to take a cheque for £10,000 to the MGM studio as payment for one of the stages.

The meeting about the closure took about a week with Sir John Read, Peter King, Bernard Delfont, James Aubrey, Douglas Netter and myself. Originally we were discussing moving Elstree to MGM but I told Aubrey we could sell MGM which he assumed we could not due to planning restrictions.

Then the discussion reverted to closing our studio. I found a purchaser but I was sorry it went as it was a magnificent studio. Reginald Maudling MP objected to the closure but I told him 'Why don't you and your rich friends buy it if you care so much?' I met Kirkorian at the Hilton and advised him it could be sold. I am not proud of that but it was my duty to my client.

Delfont brought Bryan Forbes in for part of the meeting to appoint him as Managing Director of MGM-EMI but he was never allowed to do the job and is entitled to feel bitter about the lack of support from the EMI board.

Ian Scott never featured prominently in the discussions. Nat Cohen became involved and he virtually saved MGM from nicking EMI's film business as Delfont was really a theatre man and Read knew little about the Industry. Cohen prevented his side from being taken to the cleaners.

I did all the talking for MGM at the meetings. I asked Netter if I was saying the right things as Aubrey wasn't saying much and he replied 'If you are not, he will get rid of you'.

Jack King had nothing to do with the discussions with EMI. He was in the running for being MD of MGM-EMI but that went to Forbes. Basil Somner was not involved nor was Ian Scott. Paul Mills was a good 'meeter and greeter' publicity man but also not involved. Kirkorian was a quiet man but a genius who had come from nothing to being a billionaire.

I found MGM a purchaser and had to negotiate a golden handshake for the staff. The studio was handicapped by having to keep stages empty in case they were needed by MGM productions. The Council never seemed to assist over the years and seemed to resist any development. If the Council had permitted the sale of some of the enormous backlot it might have saved the studio.

In regard to **'Man's Fate'** we settled eventually by MGM agreeing to settle at 20% of what was being asked which was good as it represented only 5% interest on the principal sum which we had delayed for four years. Zinnemann came out with the best behaviour as he was honourable and stuck up for his principles. Zinnemann and Ponti had sued MGM but we disputed there ever had been an agreement with their company to produce **'Man's Fate'**. In reality I think there was, but we fought it and came out ahead financially."

After our meeting, Beuselinck, whose son Paul Nicholas became a well known actor and musical performer, wrote me a letter stating "The agreement for the sale of the MGM studio was signed in my office at 10 Soho Square on 10th December 1970. The legal formalities were completed a few weeks after Christmas. Regarding the comments made in Bryan Forbes'autobiography about this subject, it suffers from the disadvantage of being nearly right. He knows little or nothing about the contractual matters relating to **'Man's Fate'** and **'Taipan'**. I do. I was involved in the cases arising out of them and my instructions when Aubrey decided to cancel these projects was that we have just 'got to be pricks', that is in the American sense of the words which means difficult swines as distinct from the British which normally means stupid.

I do not know where Mr Forbes purports to get all his information but I have written to him today to tell him as regards the studios and the planning permission he was quite wrong and that what he says reflects on myself. Like most people, and I suppose I am no exception, he has been inclined to top up his own role in this matter. He was not, as I recall, present at any of the meetings of the main MGM/EMI board of which I was a member, with Peter King, at which production decisions were and were not taken. Unfortunately for him he, as he rightly says, had to finish a job without the appropriate tools."

So we have it from first hand sources how the fate of the MGM British Studios was decided, allowing for the frailities of the human memory after 24 years. However, I do have the original copies of the agreement that was drawn up in 1970.

The heads of agreement drawn up at the meetings included the following clauses:

1. a company shall be provided by EMI the name of which shall be EMI/MGM Elstree Studios Ltd. The company shall have an issued capital of £100 in £1 ordinary shares.

2. the shares of the company shall be held 51% EMI and 49% MGM.

3. MGM shall give to EMI a first option to purchase any or all the equipment, plant and chattels located at MGM Studios of Boreham Wood at current market prices for the time being in force.

4. so long as MGM owns its Boreham Wood site it shall make locations available subject only to its being paid current market prices for them and being indemnified against all loss and expense in respect of such use.

5. this agreement shall terminate on 30 June 1977 unless terminated earlier by either party giving to the other at any time at least 6 months prior notice. MGM shall pay EMI in respect of the period ending 30 June 1971 the sum of £135,000 payable in 4 equal quarterly instalments. MGM shall pay EMI as from 1 July 1971 the annual sum of £175,000 in 4 equal quarterly instalments.

6. Both parties undertake to use their best endeavours to bring into Elstree Studios all their UK productions and in addition all post production on films financed by them but made outside the UK whenever possible. If MGM successfully conclude their current negotiations with AIP then MGM undertake to ensure the benefits which would have flowed to Boreham Wood studios shall be transferred to Elstree Studios.

In the end Elstree Studios purchased equipment from the MGM Studio to the value of £76,000. Both studios contributed equally

(£76,000) to the redundancy costs.

EMI and MGM also agreed to set up a distribution company (launched 1st September) and to co-finance films made in the UK. This meant they shared equally the budget of **'Get Carter'** which was £508,815 and **'The Go Between'** which cost £482,840.

The success of those two films resulted in the formation of EMI-MGM Productions Ltd in April 1971. The first film under this agreement was **'The Boyfriend'** and two other films were announced, those being a comedy version of Trilby and Svengali directed by Blake Edwards with Julie Andrews and Jack Lemmon and **'Trader Horn'** to be directed by Alan Sharp. Neither project materialised.

On the 20th June 1972 MGM wrote to EMI giving 6 months notice to terminate the agreement. That required a payment of £87,500 but it was agreed instead that MGM would pay £50,000 in September 1972 and £50,000 in June 1973. This had a serious effect on Elstree Studios and in November 1973 it was announced that the studio was now running at a £200,000 a year loss resulting in the staff being cut from 479 to 256.

In February 1973 another planned series of **'UFO'** to be shot at Elstree was cancelled and in June the TV series **'Space 1999'** booked three stages for a year but this too was cancelled when the production moved to Pinewood as they feared Elstree might close suddenly.

An internal studio memo revealed the frustration of running a movie factory by citing two films. **'Murder On The Orient Express'** had a seven figure budget but Elstree received only £30,000 for use of the facilities. **'On The Buses'** cost £98,000 to make, only a fraction of which went to the studio in stage rental fees. The film was an enormous success and took £2,500,000. Of that £2,100,000 went to the cinemas and distributors. Of the remaining £400,000 EMI took 35% as the financial backers, then the cost of prints, bank interest and publicity were deducted leaving the little remaining to the Producers.

Further reductions were implemented and by April 1975 the permanent staff were reduced to 48. EMI mothballed six of the nine stages and a housing plan for 335 dwellings was considered for the backlot. Sir James Carreras was asked to investigate the idea of converting two large sound stages into a studio tour or exhibition but the report indicated the idea was not feasible. Luckily in 1976 Producer Gary Kurtz was looking for a large empty studio and selected Elstree even though it was under threat of closure. The film was **'Star Wars'** and that triggered 12 profitable years for Elstree, but the rest of that history is for another book at another time.

■ ■ ■ ■

The MGM studio was sold to Sterling Homes Ltd for a basic £1,800,000 but depending on planning permissions would allow for up to a total £4,000,000. That company merged and became part of Allied London Properties PLC. They surveyed the site and described it as comprising of existing buildings covering 300,000 square feet spread of 27 acres which were zoned for industrial use. An additional 88 acres of backlot might be suitable for future development subject to planning permission. I am told that Allied London still own the freehold of the two office blocks constructed called Elstree Tower and Elstree House.

However, in 1972 Christian Salvesen, cold storage specialists, purchased 14.18 acres roughly where the sound stages stood, for £1,592,330. They subsequently sold their cold store plant to Sainsburys. After that plant closed it was demolished in 2019 for alternative industrial use. See Appendix A-14 (The Site Today)

Hertsmere Borough Council acquired most of the backlot area totalling 80 acres in 1976 for the purchase price of £2,857,000.

When the last MGM personnel left in 1970 the Studio stood empty until demolition began in 1972. Before the demolition crews arrived, as a young fan of film I approached the new owners and asked for permission to visit the studio complex and was granted access for three days. It was a marvellous but disturbing experience, as I have described it earlier. It is still difficult to express how wonderful and moving it was for a young film buff to find himself with a 115 acre film studio all to himself for three days.

Of course local children would break through the backlot fences and play around the sets and buildings or go looking for tadpoles in the exterior water tank. In 1974 the local fire brigade spent two hours dampening down a fire engulfing the remaining exterior sets on the backlot when they were set alight to by local youngsters.

Occasionally a film buff like Wilf Watters would unofficially gain access to the studio and thank heavens he took along a 16 mm camera and recorded some footage that nobody else achieved. Appendix A-11 (Final Visits) includes some of Wilf's footage.

My last visit was around May 1973 when I returned to photograph the sound stages being demolished. These photos are in Appendix A-12 (Demolition). Also on the site that day was a film crew from Elstree Studios who were shooting a scene for the film **'Holiday On The Buses'**.

Years later I joked with Reg Varney that he was the last actor to work at MGM, but in fact the cameras were to roll once more on the backlot. In August 1978 Stanley Kubrick had a maze constructed for his film **'The Shining'** on part of the backlot now occupied by an industrial park.

On 29th August Shelley Duvall, Danny Lloyd, Lisa and Louise Burns turned up at 9am for rehearsals. Filming took place on 30th and 31st August and the 1st, 4th, 5th, 7th and 8th September. It was ironic that Stanley, who had made perhaps his greatest film **'2001 – A Space Odyssey'** at the studio a decade earlier, should be the last person to film there.

■ ■ ■ ■

So what happened to the buildings and the backlot over the following decades?

At one point the site was in the running to become the National Exhibition Centre but that went to Birmingham. Stage 10 and four of the workshops survived to live another day when they were purchased by Bray Studios in 1972 and the stage remains there today, although

Bray, at the time of writing, is now closed and awaiting demolition.

The famous MGM white clock tower of the administration building was a landmark for several decades, visible from the A1 trunk road to London and dominating Elstree Way which is a main access into Boreham Wood. It was a two storey building standing about 65 feet high. As you entered under the canopy via the front door there was a mail room on the left and a cleaners room on the right.

If you turned right there were six offices (two occupied by the personnel department), a chief shop stewards office, a conference room and two toilets. If you had turned left there was the studio operations secretary's office, the studio operations office, a duplicating room, another mail room, three production offices and two more toilets.

On the second floor were 17 general offices and two toilets. The building was leased for five years by Hertsmere Borough Council in 1974, who also leased the gatehouse which was converted into a print room. A local building company was engaged to refurbish the building and a local resident Mr. Onion told me "I was a carpenter but the builder asked me to hang from a rope from the clock tower roof and dismantle the MGM letters which I let drop to the ground."

When the Council first moved in they found a number of old MGM files which they threw away. I can still remember attending meetings in the building in 1977. A large number of box files containing production files were moved to Elstree Studios and were stored until 1989 when the building concerned was due to be demolished to make way for Tesco. I was then asked to contact MGM and request their removal which they reluctantly did, but I later heard they destroyed them to save storage charges in London.

In October 1983 our local M.P Cecil Parkinson took up my request to try to get the building granted listed protection but on 27th October the Secretary of State for Environment Patrick Jenkin declined the request citing "It is not of significant architectural quality".

In 1984 Christian Salvesen wrote to me saying the building needed a six figure sum spent on renovations including a rewiring and only housed 12 of their employees, making it uneconomical. They decided to demolish the building in September 1986 and replace it with a car park. The clock tower and administration building was just over 150 feet long. The studio frontage (excluding the car park and front fields) was just over 600 feet from one gatehouse to the other, and this can still be traced by the foundations of the brick wall bordering Elstree Way which remain. Appendix A-9 documents the construction of the clock tower and its demolition.

The backlot area purchased by the Council started to be developed and in 1980 it reported that 3.5 acres had been used to build 68 houses that were sold to tenants. A community hall near the Well End footpath was considered but the idea abandoned. Land set aside for a primary school was subsequently sold to make way for the hotel and Toby Carvery that now stand at the top of Studio Way. Appendix A-2 includes site plans which show how the site might have been redeveloped.

The backlot lingered on for three years after the studio buildings were demolished (See Appendix A-15: The Backlot Fades Away) In time the remainder of the backlot was developed for housing and I was keen that all the roads and courts should be named after film stars, Directors and other film studios and for the past several decades I have provided the names. Only one was rejected by the Post Office, which was Howard Close, named after Trevor Howard, as there was already a Howard Drive in Boreham Wood.

The developers had originally wanted to name Studio Way as Hunting Gate and the roads off it as Wolsey Way, Abbey Close, Aragon Way, Mercia Court and Abbots Mead. We adopted a policy of only choosing names of dead stars or Directors in case we picked a live star who subsequently disgraced themselves. The only exception was Dame Anna Neagle and we agreed to name a close after her and one after her late husband, film Director Herbert Wilcox. Dame Anna commented "I am very honoured to be remembered in this way and especially happy Herbert is also remembered; he contributed so much more than me." When the Council purchased the backlot, they found 50 acres were subject to a restrictive covenant from the Wrotham Park Estates which meant they had to get permission to build housing. They also discovered a stretch of grass verge needed for access was Metropolitan Common Land and required the Council to seek an Act of Parliament to cross it.

At the time of writing the 17 acres of cold storage plant that has occupied the site of the MGM sound stages and ancillary buildings has been sold for £53 million pounds and new warehouses are to be built. On an adjacent site a current distribution depot is to be demolished to make way for a supermarket. See Appendix A-14: The Site Today.

■ ■ ■ ■

Half a century later, the great MGM British Studios is today but a distant, if not mainly forgotten, memory.

Even a long term local resident aged under 60 is unlikely to be even aware it existed as they would have been only 10 at the time it closed in 1970. Film buffs and fans of **'The Prisoner'** and **'UFO'** recall it but probably have no idea of the range of productions that came from this dream factory.

Metro Goldwyn Mayer itself has changed considerably as a company, and I doubt any of its current employees know their company once owned a studio in England. However, the studio lives on in the memories of those of us who remember it on the screen credits of so many fine productions as 'Made at MGM British Studios, Boreham Wood, England.'

I hope you have enjoyed this walk down memory lane and perhaps it may inspire you to view or find out more about some of the films mentioned. This book is as accurate as my memory, research and what veterans have told me allows and I apologise for any errors or omissions you find. It has been a joy to write and hopefully is a successful companion to my earlier effort 'Elstree Confidential' which records my 60 years of star encounters and memories of the various studios of Elstree and Boreham Wood.

Appendix A

The Studios, from Start to Finish (and Beyond)

Introduction … … … … … … … … … … .. 163
1: Aerial Views … … … … … … … … … … 165
2: Site Plans … … … … … … … … … … .. 169
3: During The War . … … … … … … … … … 183
4: After The War … … … … … … … … … ..201
5: Inside MGM British … … … … … … … …..207
6: Sample Of Correspondence … … … … … ... 217
7: 'Foremost In Europe' … … … … … … … ..227
8: The Backlot … … … … … … … … … ..247
9: The Clock Tower … … … … … … … … . 251
10: The Ivanhoe Castle … … … … … … … … 255
11: Final Visits … … … … … … … … … … .259
12: Demolition … … … … … … … … … ..263
13: The Backlot Fades Away … … … … … … ..265
14: The Site Today .. … … … … … … … … ..271

Appendix A
Introduction

The story of the site of MGM British Studios started in 1936 with the construction on Hertfordshire farm fields of Amalgamated Studios and continues to the present day, with new developments waiting to receive planning permission.

The following sections illustrate this story using photos and drawings from the Author's private collection and not previously published.

Section 1: Aerial Views

Thanks to the once locally-based aerial survey firm Hunting Aerofilms, we have records of the development of the site from 1936 through the 1960s. We appreciate the support of English Heritage, who now own the photo archives of Hunting Aerofilms and have granted Elstree Screen Heritage permission to use these photos.

To these photos we have added aerial views up to the present day.

Section 2: Site Plans

The planned development of the site over the years has been recorded in architectural drawings which the author rescued during the demolition of MGM British. These drawings reveal ambitious intended uses for the site, some of which never took place.

Section 3: During The War

Before Amalgamated Studios was transformed into MGM British Studios, its buildings made a significant contribution to the war effort.

In order to piece together the events of those missing years, the Author needed to find and research primary sources of information. In August 2015 he obtained a reader's ticket to permit him to study files in the National Archives at Kew.

Our selection of extracts from these files charts the extraordinary tug-of-war between the Ministry of Works and Buildings and the Ministry of Aircraft Production in late 1940 and early 1941.

Section 4: After The War

This section charts the transformation of Amalgamated Studios into MGM British.

All of these photos were taken in 1946.

Section 5: Inside MGM British

These photos go behind the scenes to provide glimpses of various departments and the people who worked in them.

We are grateful to Guy Nolan, who shared with us these photos from the days when his grandfather, Sam Nolan, was Head of Catering at MGM.

Section 6: Samples of Correspondence

The Author found many files abandoned at the Studio after its closure; sadly most were subsequently destroyed by disinterested demolition workers. These are some examples of what the Author was able to collect to show day-to-day life at MGM British Studios.

Section 7: 'Foremost In Europe'

Published in October 1962 as a supplement to Kinematograph Weekly, this is a detailed technical description of MGM British.

Section 8: The Backlot

This section shows the backlot when it was just farm fields in the 1940's.

Section 9: The Clock Tower

The iconic clock tower stood for years after MGM British had disappeared.

Section 10: The Ivanhoe Castle

From the architect's models in 1950 to the finished construction in the summer of 1951, this section documents the creation of the famous 'Ivanhoe Castle'.

Section 11: Final Visits

These photos record visits to MGM after it closed in 1970. The first six photos are courtesy of Wilf Watters; the rest were taken by the Author.

Section 12: Demolition

In 1973 the Studio was being used by an 'On The Buses' movie to film the demolition of a building. This provided an opportunity for the Author to record the final days of the studios.

Section 13: The Backlot Fades Away

The sets on the backlot lingered on for three years after the studio buildings were demolished. These photos are courtesy of Roger Garrod and Wilf Watters.

Section 14: The Site Today

The Author was permitted to visit the site once again, as it starts its latest transformation.

APPENDIX A-1
Aerial Views

Thanks to once locally-based aerial survey firm Hunting Aerofilms, we have records of the development of the site from 1936 through the 1960s. We appreciate the support of English Heritage, who now own the photo archives of Hunting Aerofilms and have granted Elstree Screen Heritage permission to use these photos.

To these photos we have added aerial views up to the present day.

18th March   1936

October   1936

Late 1930's
(From the National Archives)

Boreham Wood in the 1940s
(Photo courtesy of Dick Klemensen)

– 165 –

MGM British Studios

1940's

1947

October 1951

1950's

1958 'The Inn of the Sixth Happiness'

*2nd May 1958 'The Inn of the Sixth Happiness'
500,000 square feet (£90,000)*

Appendix A-1: Aerial Views

1964 'Operation Crossbow'

1960's Backlot Sets

The backlot in 1966 during filming of 'The Vampire Killers'
(Photo courtesy of Dick Klemensen)

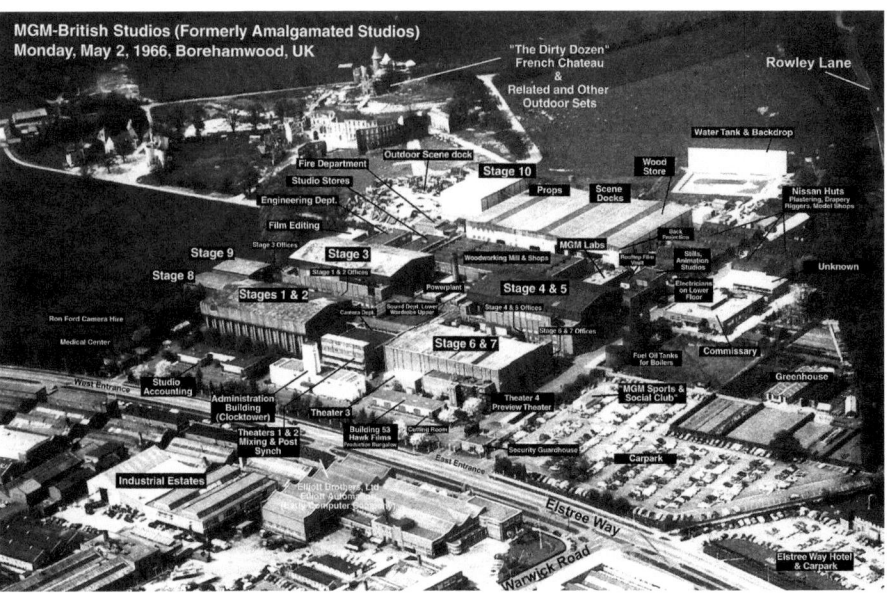

2nd May 1966
(Photo courtesy of Roger Garrod)

MGM British Studios

1973   Christian Salvesen Depot under construction

Circa 2000   The backlot site

Circa 2000   The Studio site

Circa 2000

27th October   2018
Photo courtesy of Nick Wells

Appendix A-2
Site Plans

The planned development of the site over the years has been recorded in architectural drawings which the Author rescued during the demolition of MGM British. These drawings reveal ambitious intended uses for the site, some of which never took place.

Thrift Farm at the centre of the MGM site   Ordnance Survey   1930's
Elstree Way is clearly marked at the bottom of the sheet.

MGM British Studios

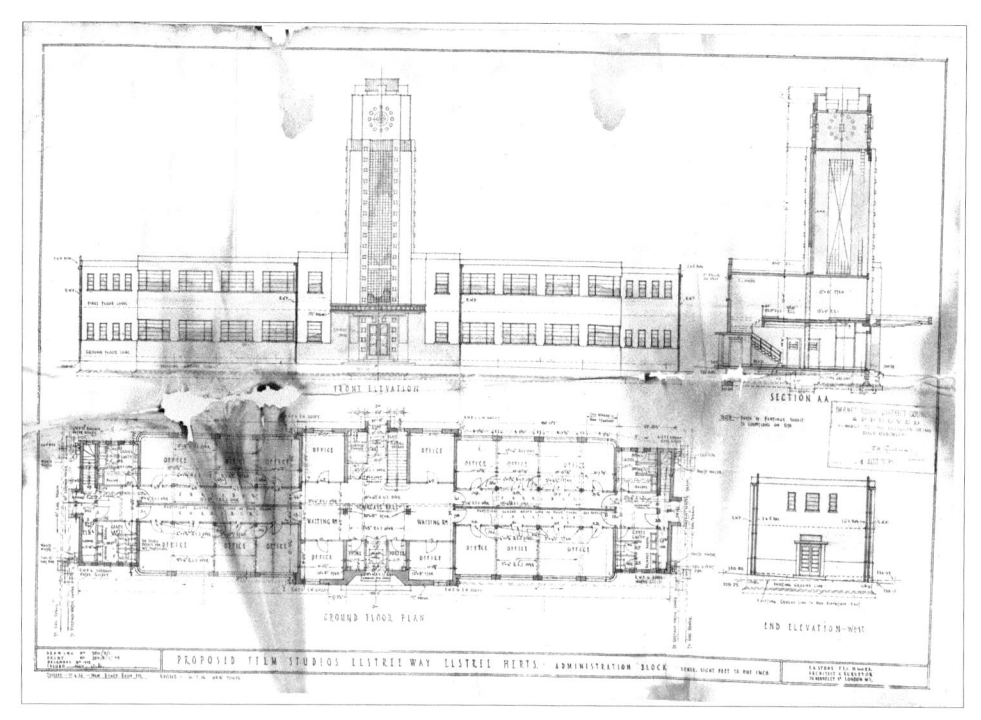

Proposed Film Studios   Elstree Way (Amalgamated)   Front Elevation
8/12/35   Barnet Rural District Council

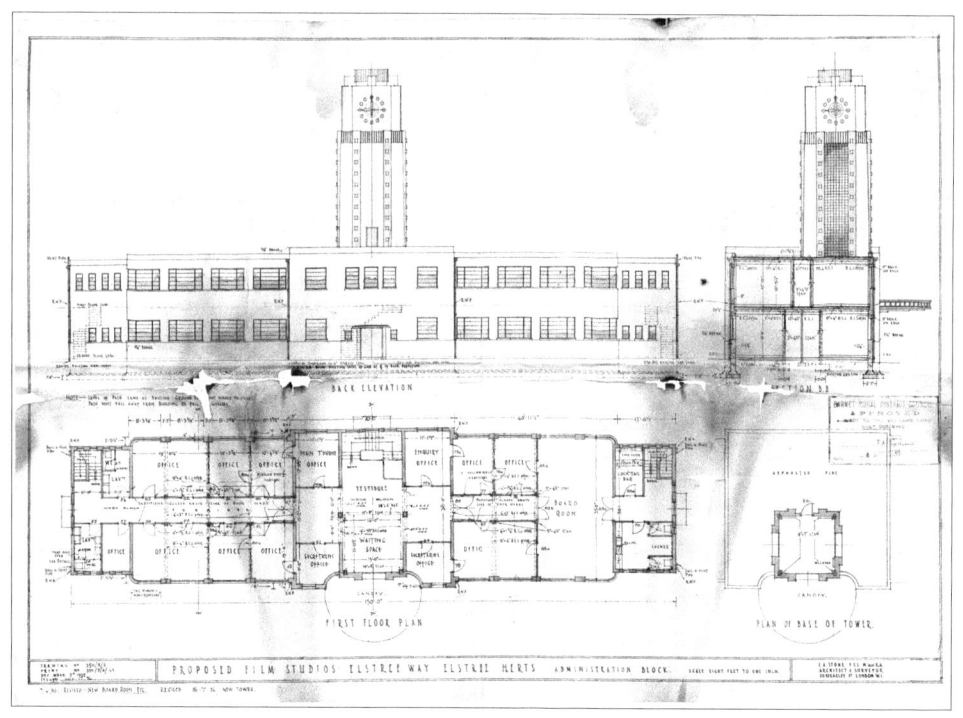

Proposed Film Studios   Elstree Way (Amalgamated)   Back Elevation
7/12/35   Barnet Rural District Council

Appendix A-2: Site Plans

Block Plan   MGM/95
4/9/45   Elstree Rural
District Council

— 171 —

MGM British Studios

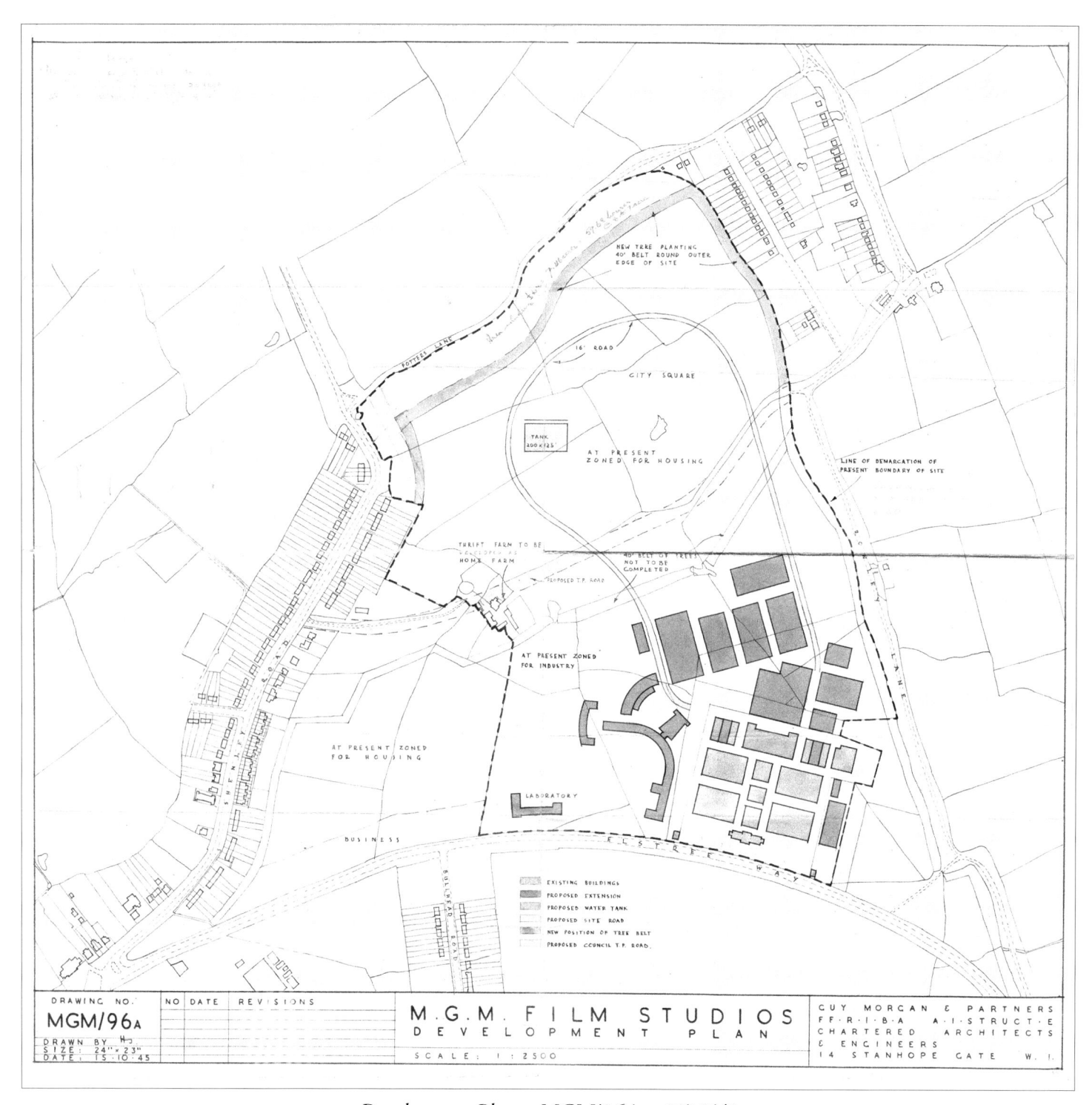

Development Plan   MGM/96A   15/10/45

Appendix A-2: Site Plans

View From Elstree Way   21/11/45

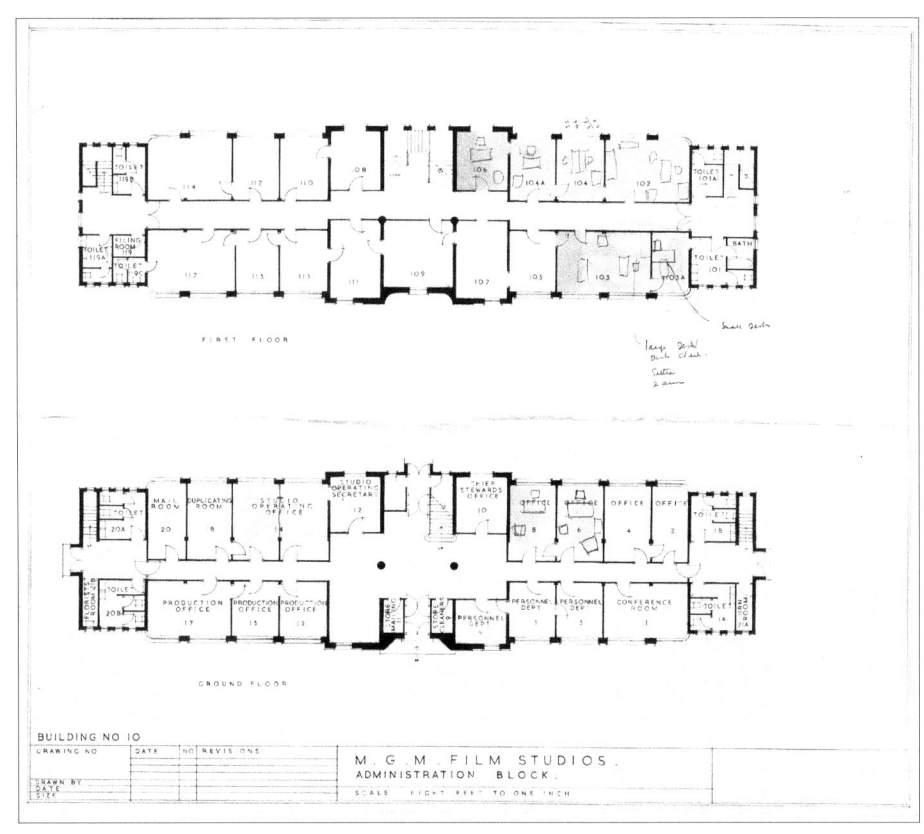

Administration Block   1945

— 173 —

MGM British Studios

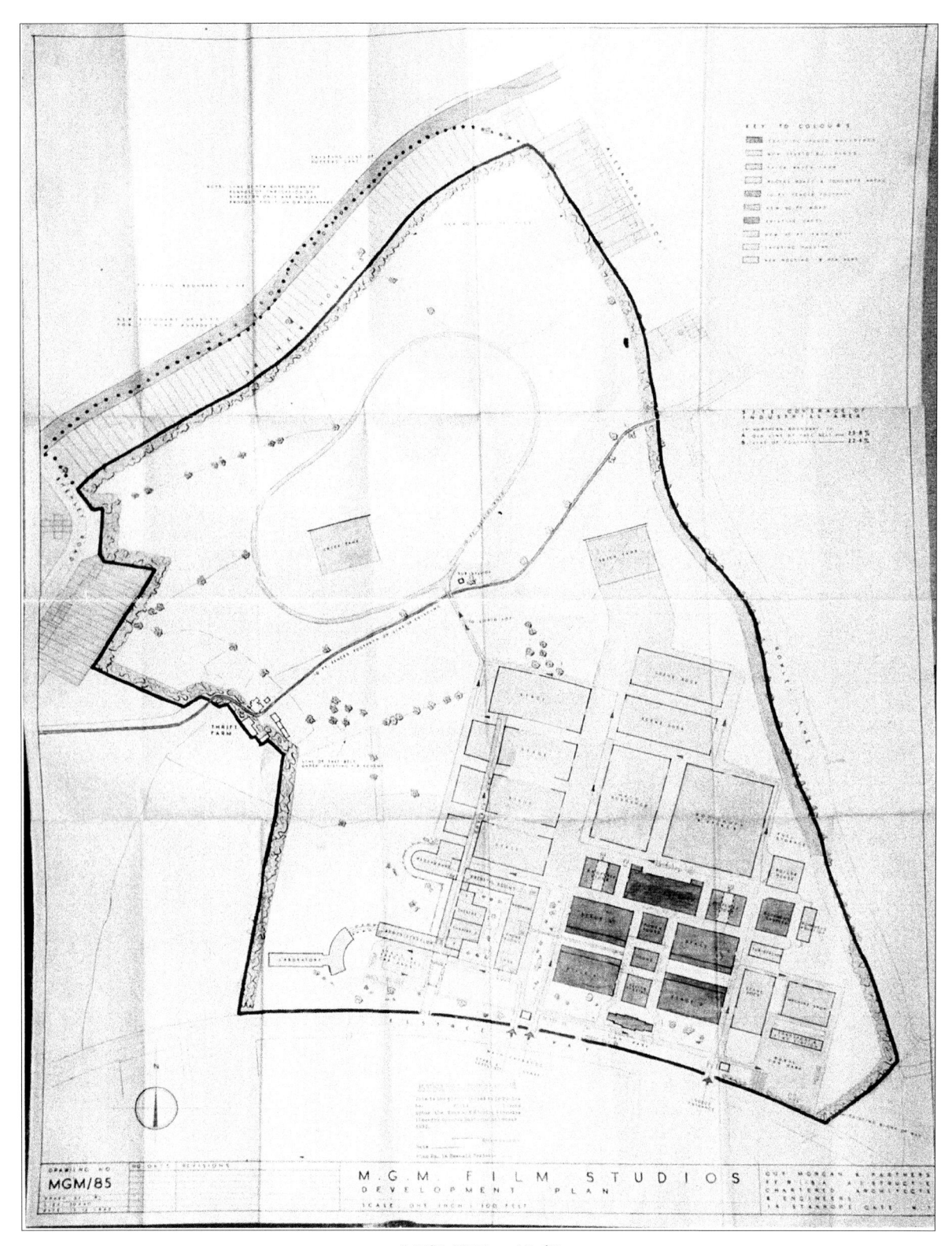

MGM/85   1945

Appendix A-2: Site Plans

Formal development permission granted by Elstree Rural District Council   1st February, 1946

CONDITIONS REFERRED TO:-

1. The land north of the northern boundary of the land which is covered by the Ingram Agreement shall be used only for the erection of temporary sets in connection with and for the purposes of the Film Industry, except for the erection of one permanent trick tank and the erection of small electrical sub-stations.

2. A building depth of not less than 150 ft. fronting on to Potters Lane measured from the widening line as laid down by the County Council of Hertfordshire shall be reserved for the erection of dwellinghouses at a density of 8 houses to the acre.

3. There shall be no access from the industrially used land into Potters Lane.

4. All existing trees of 6 ft. girth or over, measured 2 ft. from ground, situated on that part of the land to be used for temporary sets only shall be preserved and shall only be felled with the permission of the Council.

5. The public footpath which traverses the land covered by the submission shall be enclosed by fencing, to be approved by the Council, shall be maintained in good condition at the owners' expense and shall nowhere have a less width than 10 ft.

6. (a) The owners shall provide, reserve and maintain at their own expense a strip of land 40 ft. in width round the boundary of the estate as marked and coloured green on Plan No. 3264 and such land shall be scheduled in the Council's Town Planning Scheme as a Private Open Space and shall be so kept in perpetuity and shall not be used for any other purpose.

(b) The said strip of land shall within a period of 24 months from the date of the permission and at the expense of the owners be planted with trees so as to form a screen to the adjoining land and the trees shall be planted in two rows in alternate positions on each side of the said strip of land at a distance of not less than 10 ft. from each boundary and not more than 40 ft. apart in each row, so as to give one tree for each 20 ft. of the said Private Open Space. The trees shall be of a species to be approved by the Council and should be permitted to grow to their full heights and shall be maintained alive and replaced as necessary at the expense of the owner.

(c) In the event of the failure of the owners to carry out the works specified in these conditions within the times specified, the Council shall be entitled to carry out and complete all such works in accordance with the terms of these conditions and to recover the cost thereof from the owners.

Clerk of the Elstree Rural District Council.

1st February, 1946.

Formal development permission granted by Elstree Rural District Council   1st February, 1946

Appendix A-2: Site Plans

MGM/87   25/8/48   Elstree Rural District Council

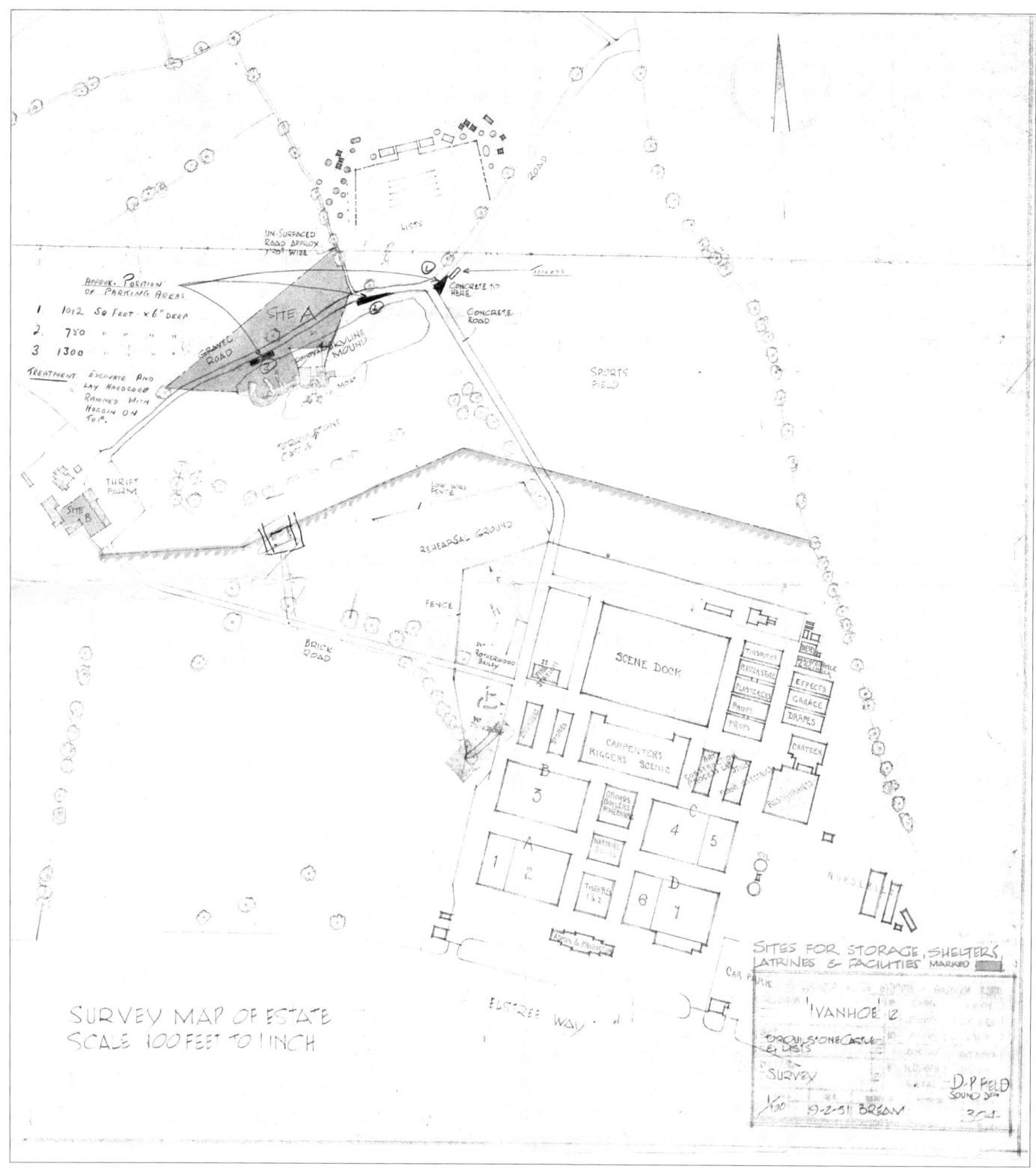

Exterior sets for 'Ivanhoe'   1951

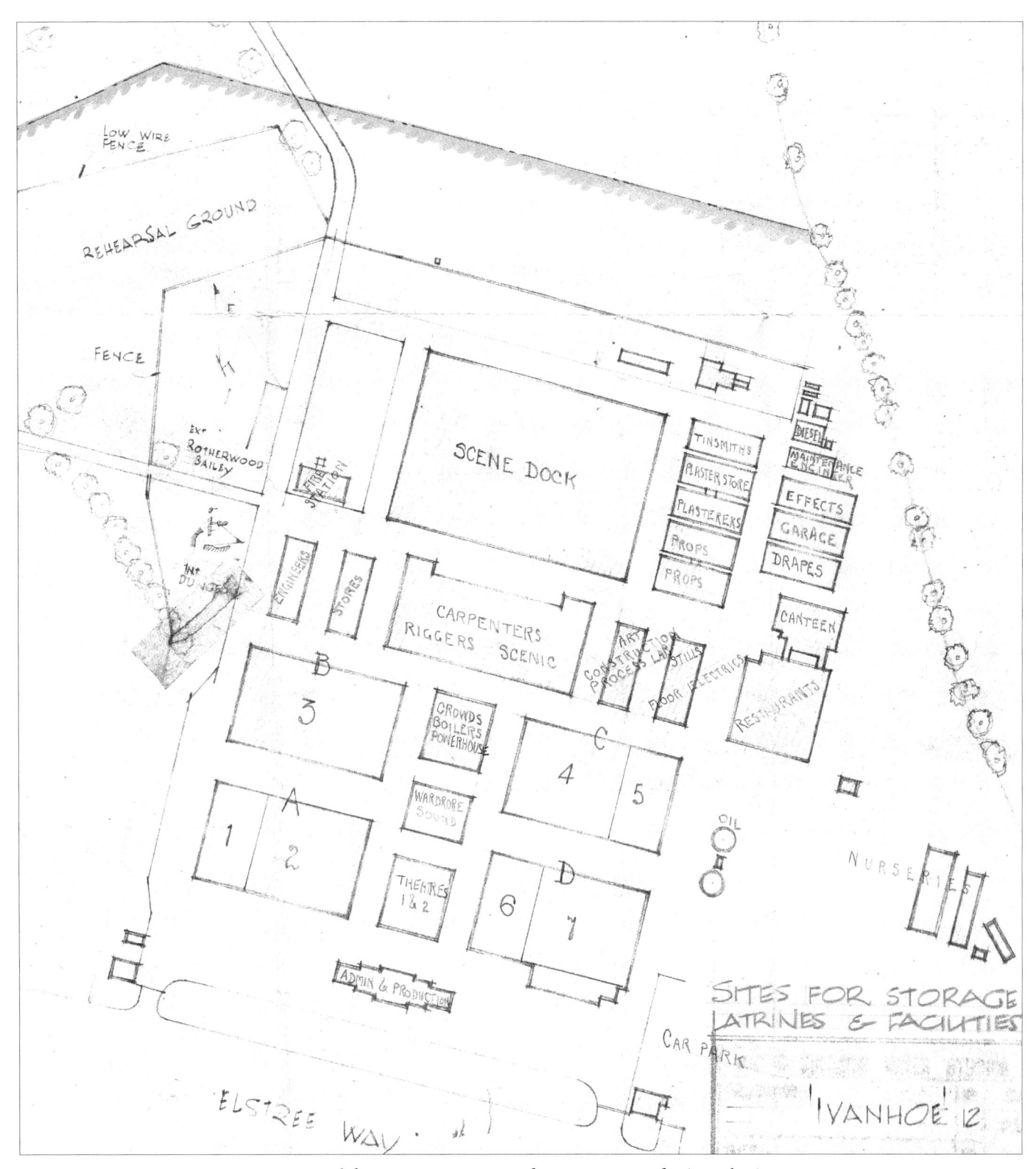

Appendix A-2: Site Plans

Detail from 1951 Drawing for exterior sets for 'Ivanhoe'

MGM British Studios

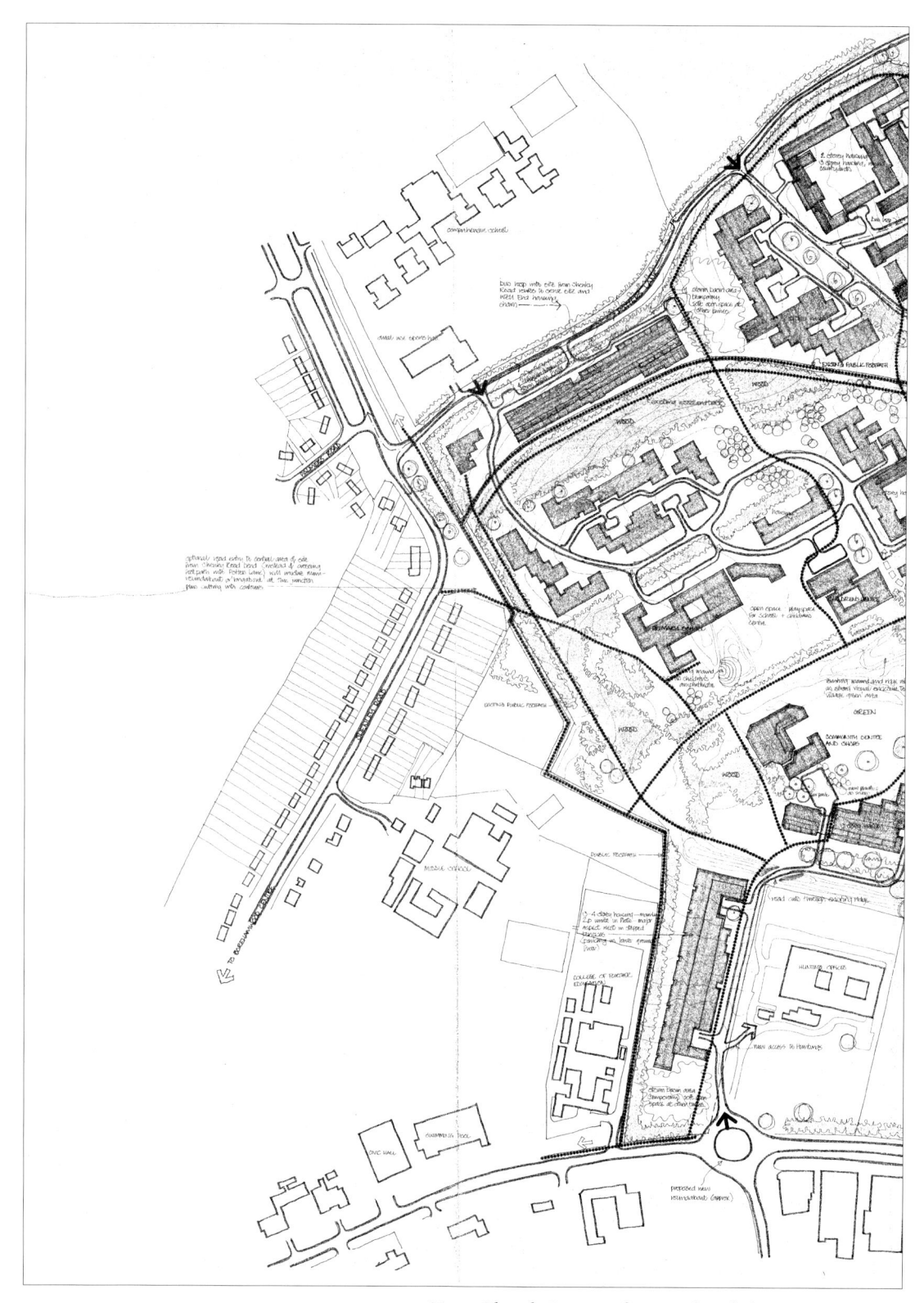

First Sketch Layout from a feasibility study carried

Appendix A-2: Site Plans

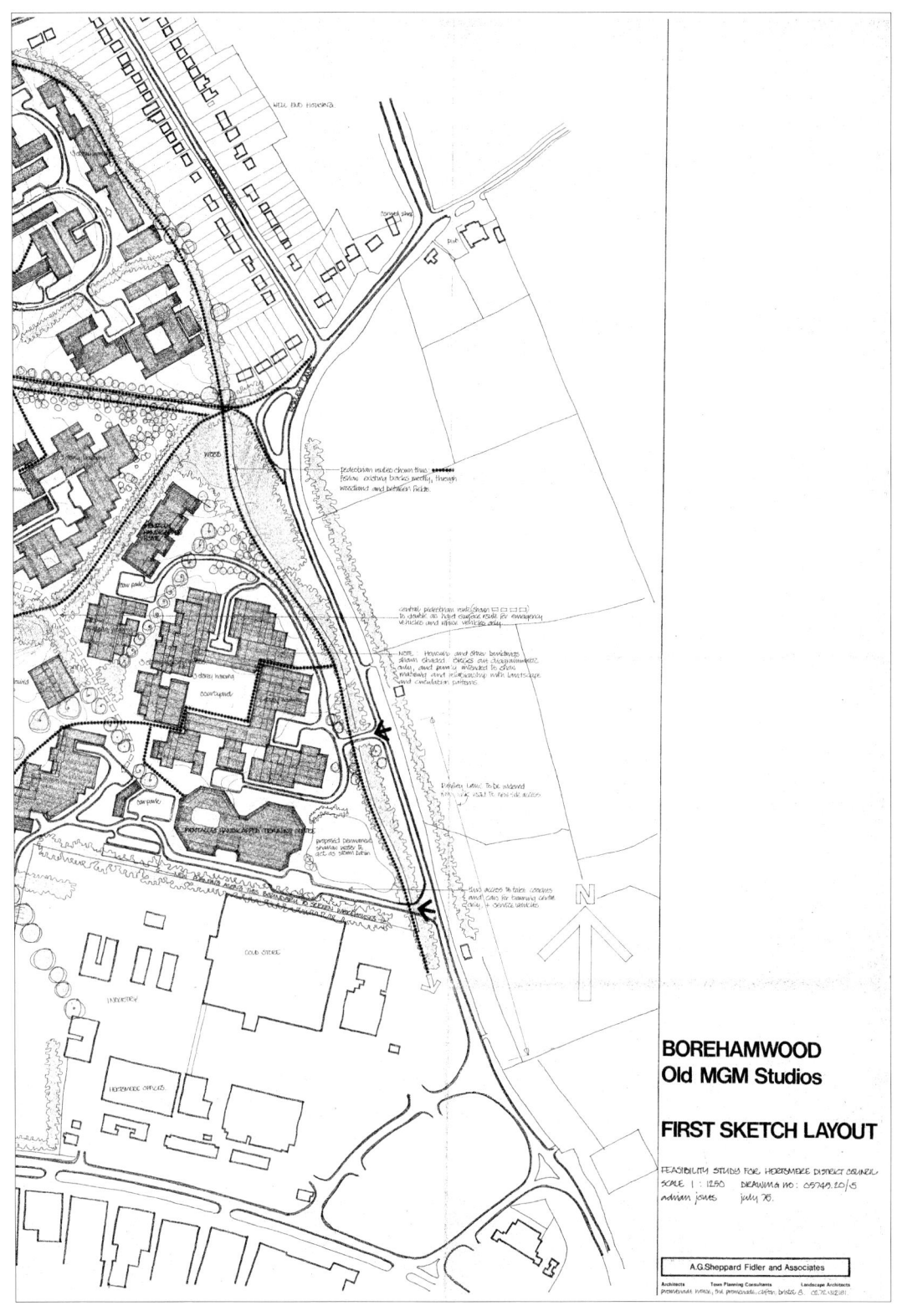

out for Hertsmere (sic) District Council   July 1975

Appendix A-3

During the War

Before Amalgamated Studios was transformed into MGM British Studios, the buildings made a significant contribution to the war effort.

In order to piece together the events of those missing years, the Author needed to find and research primary sources of information. In August 2015 he obtained a reader's ticket to permit him to study files in the National Archives at Kew.

The role of the National Archives is to preserve and provide access to the nation's records. Free-of-charge to the public, it contains over 11 million historical government and public records.

Among all of these records the Author wanted to find the file covering the decisions as to how the buildings of Amalgamated would be used in the 1940s. In a file entitled 'Elstree Studios (sic) Storage of Records Proposed use of premises for aircraft factory' he found exactly what he was hunting.

The following selection of extracts charts the extraordinary tug-of-war between the Ministry of Works and Buildings and the Ministry of Aircraft Production in late 1940 and early 1941.

TREASURY — G.S. & E.P. Division

File No. T162/1001

38,003 / 01

Subject: Elstree Studios — Storage of Records — Proposed use of Premises for Aircraft Factory.

CLOSED — NO FURTHER ACTION TO BE TAKEN IN THIS FILE

1941

DESTROYED

PHOTOGRAPHS RECEIVED

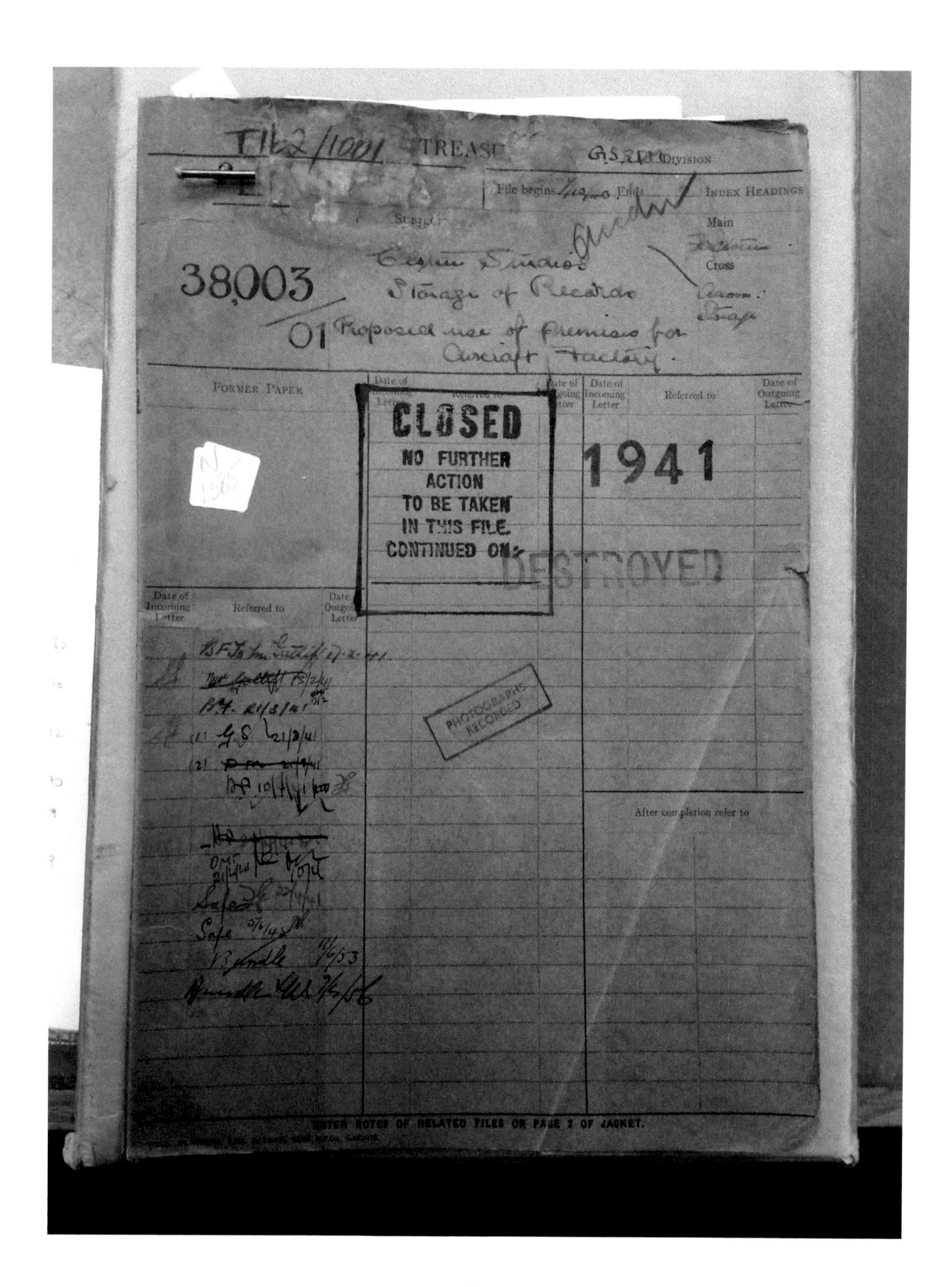

MINISTRY OF AIRCRAFT PRODUCTION,
MILLBANK,
S.W.1.

7th October, 1940

Dear Sir Horace,

There are at Elstree some film studios which it is necessary to obtain in connection with aircraft dispersal.

A photograph of these studios is attached. Each of the four large buildings shown in the photograph with white roofs has an area of 20,000 sq. ft. and is 40 ft. high. They are, in consequence, particularly suitable for aircraft work. The large building at the back has an area of 24,000 sq. ft. and is 20 ft. high. The total area of the large buildings is thus 104,000 sq. ft. and when the other buildings are added in the total area is of the order of 150,000 sq. ft.

The bulk of this area is taken up with the storage of records for a number of Government departments, and it is understood that many of these records are old and little referred to. Some of them were so dirty when transferred there that they had to be specially cleaned. One of the buildings contains bedding for A.R.P. work.

In connection with the Handley Page dispersal from Cricklewood, it is essential to obtain an area of about 60,000 sq. ft. at these studios at once. Other possibilities have been exhausted as Handley Page needs more than 200,000 sq. ft in all and only about 100,000 sq. ft. has been found up to now. Later we shall probably want to obtain the whole of these Elstree buildings, but the 60,000 sq. ft. is urgent.

/You

You know only too well the importance of this work. Bombs have already been within 50 feet of Handley Page's.

To remove all the records and place them in racks as at present would be a very difficult proposition and take a long time. The Office of Works appears to be in favour of disposing of them or dumping them in some other buildings, but in this event it would certainly be difficult, if not impossible, to refer to them for the duration of the war, except such as might be specially important.

Can you help as by obtaining an immediate decision either to get rid of these records for good or dump them for the duration? I cannot believe it to be right that these important buildings should be used for storing papers at times like these.

Yours sincerely,

C Bruce-Gardner

P.S. My reason for writing to you is that so many Gov. departments are involved. D.L.A. Office of Works can give full information as to what is stored in these buildings.

CBG.

Sir Horace Wilson, G.C.M.G., G.C.B., C.B.E.,
    Secretary of the Treasury,
        Whitehall,
            S.W.1.

Appendix A-3: During the War

9.x.40

Discussion with representatives of the
Office of Works and Ministry of Health
with regard to the proposed evacuation
of the Elstree buildings in order that
they may be turned over to Aircraft
Production.

The premises consist of five main buildings of 20,000 square feet each and seven smaller buildings. Of the main buildings, four are used for storage of documents and one for the storage of Medical supplies. Of the smaller buildings, six are used for storing documents and one for accommodating the local staff.

It is the Ministry of Health who occupy most of the premises (almost 60%) and as the major tenants they have been put in actual charge of the whole premises. The next biggest users are the Board of Trade and Ministry of Shipping. After that, the users are the Land Registry, Home Office, Colonial Office, Department of Overseas Trade, Ministry of Transport, the Cabinet Offices and Law Courts. The Cabinet papers and Legal papers are housed in the smaller building No. 9 and are of first-class importance from the point of view of protection and preservation.

The Ministry of Health papers consist for the main part of Local Government records. There is also a very large quantity of papers, such as billeting and pension orders, receipt and insurance cards (which cards are under present practice kept for $2\frac{1}{2}$ years). These documents can hardly be pulped or otherwise destroyed. Indeed, some of them are in current use for accounting, etc. purposes in the day-to-day functions of the Ministry.

It is possible to clear Building "A", which contains the Medical supplies. This is used as an in and out store, according to day-to-day demands, and it is suggested that the 'in' demands can be stopped and the 'out' demands accelerated, until the building is emptied.

The papers of special importants, e.g. Cabinet papers and documents of legal title, must it seems be removed and put in some other safe place. This is a considerable problem, having regard to the difficulties of transport and finding accommodation anywhere in the Country for weighty contents. Ordinary buildings can only be put to this use to the extent of the ground floor. It would be an idle task to attempt to house this weighty stuff in ordinary houses.

As regards the great bulk of documents, which represents many thousands of tons, it must be admitted that there are no present means for removing and housing them. The only thing to do, if the Elstree premises are to be turned over rapidly to Aircraft Production, is to remove this quantity of stuff to open spaces in the neighbourhood, put in on some sort of foundation, if available, and cover it with tarpaulins. It must be left to a later date to decide what should ultimately be done.

We shall no doubt meet with strong opposition to treating these documents in the manner in which it will be apparently necessary if the object in view is to be achieved. From what Mr. Adams, the representative of the Ministry of Health, told me, I think we can rely on the Ministry of Health to do their best to co-operate. It is far from clear that we shall get the ready concurrence from other Departments.

/I have

I have asked the office of Works and Ministry of Health to let us have some general information as to the cubic contents and weight of the documents and stores in question, some description of them and their Departmental owners. We can then attempt to form an opinion as to the size of the problem and the comparative importance of the contents for the purpose of deciding their future destination or fate.

/MLT.

7th October 1940.

Appendix A-3: During the War

Summary showing the accommodation and the approximate weights of records, etc., stored at Government Buildings Boreham Wood.

Department	Accommodation cu. ft. (In Thousands)	Approximate Weights (Tons) Records	Racks	Total	Remarks
Board of Control	78	143	28	171	
Board of Trade	89	368	73	441	
Cabinet (Historical Section)	11	260	52	312	
Colonial Office	35	136	27	163	
Committee of Imperial Defence	50	150	30	180	
Customs and Excise	34	145	29	174	
Dept. of Overseas Trade	11	20	4	24	
Government Actuary	7	16	3	19	
H.M.O. Works.	30	50	10	60	
House of Commons (Library)	3	9	1	10	
Land Registry	11	60	12	72	
Law Courts	33	97	19	116	
Ministry of Health	818	1502	317	1819	
Ministry of Home Security	67	320	64	384	
Ministry of Mines	1	3	—	3	
Ministry of Shipping	34	160	32	192	
Ministry of Transport	48	41	8	49	
Official Receiver in Bankruptcy	7	45	9	54	
Passport Office	55	150	30	180	
Paymaster General	11	35	7	42	
Registrar of Shipping	49	250	50	300	
Treasury Solicitor	7	25	5	30	
Totals	1489,000 cubic ft	3985	810	4795	

The figures exclude accommodation for staff (150) and their equipment (10 tons approximately). No account has been taken of the Medical Stores at present in Buildings A and B.

11.10.40.

E.G.

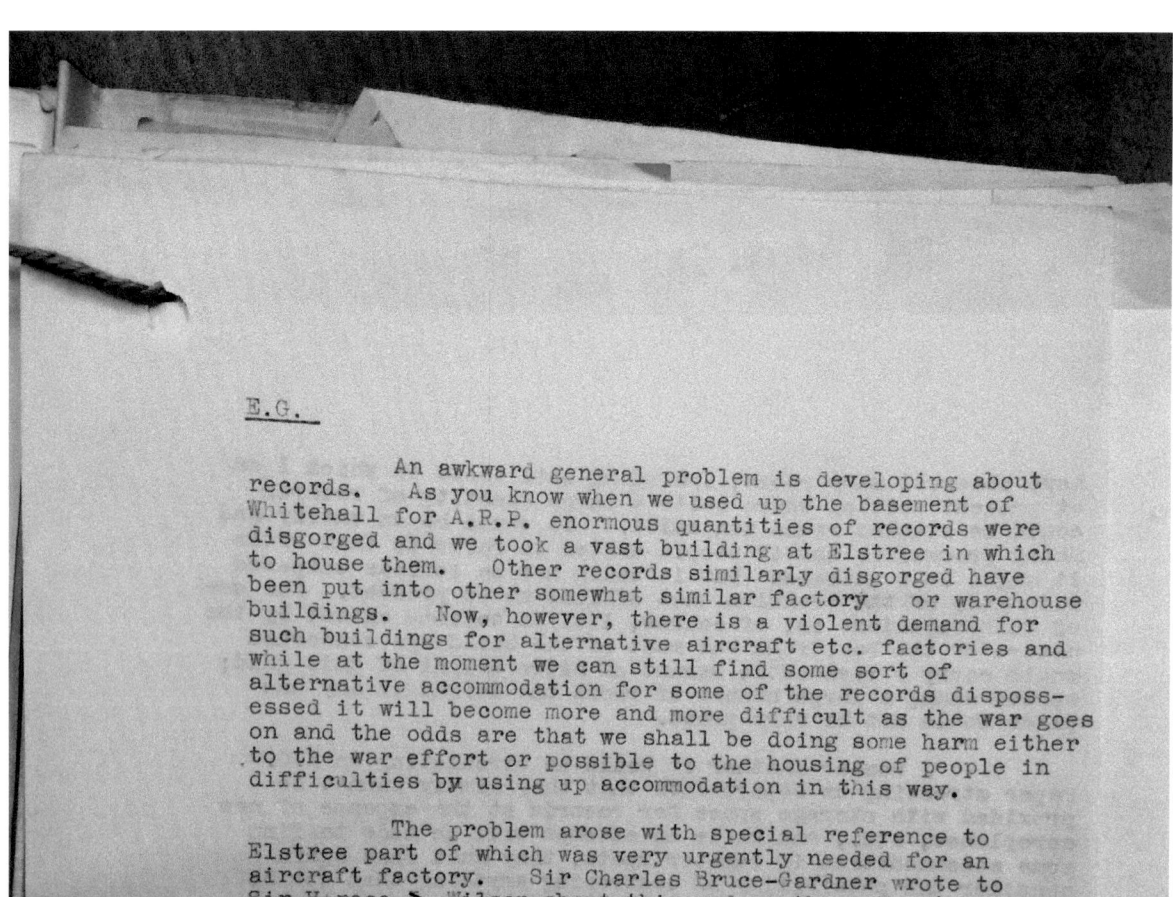

An awkward general problem is developing about records. As you know when we used up the basement of Whitehall for A.R.P. enormous quantities of records were disgorged and we took a vast building at Elstree in which to house them. Other records similarly disgorged have been put into other somewhat similar factory or warehouse buildings. Now, however, there is a violent demand for such buildings for alternative aircraft etc. factories and while at the moment we can still find some sort of alternative accommodation for some of the records dispossessed it will become more and more difficult as the war goes on and the odds are that we shall be doing some harm either to the war effort or possible to the housing of people in difficulties by using up accommodation in this way.

The problem arose with special reference to Elstree part of which was very urgently needed for an aircraft factory. Sir Charles Bruce-Gardner wrote to Sir Horace J. Wilson about this and on the latter's instructions Mr. Trickett and I saw the Office of Works & M Health (as largest occupants) and said that if necessary records must be simply thrown out on the grass and stay there unless and until something less can be done. It looks as if the immediate needs may be met without recourse to such drastic action though the Ministry of Health at any rate were prepared to face it to some extent if necessary but the problem still remains, and while we have told the Office of Works to have a first shot at it we may have to intervene ourselves with one or other of the departments concerned at Elstree; in any case the question may arise elsewhere.

The throwing of records out on the grass, or and under cover of tarpaulins (if they can be found though they cannot always be) may, in itself, have quite a healthy effect, for some will be eventually destroyed and the departments may come to the conclusion that they might as well decide at once to destroy some of them. I do not suppose that any really serious damage would be done if a certain proportion were destroyed unselected by weather, though I am not sure that this is the best way of turning them into new paper. Another alternative they might be offered to departments is to take the stuff back and stack it under dust sheets in working rooms. In my wanderings during the last week I

have

have observed many rooms, including both those in which I am at present sitting where quite a large quantity of records could be stacked round the walls. It would be an untidy and messy proceeding and if people wanted to refer to them often it might be a nuisance but it would not be serious compared with many of the troubles that afflict us at present. The use of this expedient is, of course, limited to some extent by the nature of the buildings but most of the buildings concerned would carry a reasonable amount of extra weight of this kind; spread among a large number of rooms the weight in any one place would not be very great.

    I wonder whether it would be circulating an E.O.C. Paper stressing on Departments that they simply cannot be provided with storage space for records at the expense of new aeroplanes, etc., and while an attempt will be made to find some accommodation in remoter spots, they must once again consider the possibility of destroying anything that can be destroyed, and realising that the alternatives are either to have the records stacked on the floor in working rooms or probably to have them simply thrown out into the open under some kind of waterproof at any rate until they can be despatched to remoter parts of the country.

24th October, 1940.

	Total weight. tons.	Can be destroyed. tons.	Can be dumped. tons.	Must be kept in racks. tons.	Remarks.
Ministry of Health.	1,600	100	700	700	Part of dumped records must be racked later. 100 tons stationery being removed to Whitehall.
Paymaster General.	35	A small part.	One Half.	One Half.	Exact particulars to be given on site.
Treasury Solicitor.	25	Large number.	Balance.		To be kept separate from other Departments' records.
Land Registry.	60	All.	-	-	
Ministry of Shipping.	200	20	30	150	Detailed information not yet available.
Customs & Excise.	145				Detailed information not yet available.
Export Credits.	10	All.			Small quantity of special records removed to H.Q.
Registrar General of Shipping.	250	A few only.	Two-thirds.	One-third. 80 tns	
Government Actuary.	16	None.	Part.	Part.	Precise proportions can only be indicated on site.
Home Office.	320				Detailed information not yet available.
Colonial Office	136	None.	None.	All. 136 tns	
Passport Office.	150	16,000 bundles.	-	Balance.	
Board of Trade.	433		All - for sorting and racking in due course.	433 tns	In the process of weeding which has been going on for some time - destruction takes place periodically.
Lord Chancellor.	97				Detailed information not yet available.
Ministry of Transport	41	None.	Part.	Part.	Proportions to be indicated on site.

	Total weight. tons.	Can be destroyed. tons.	Can be dumped. tons.	Must be kept in racks. tons.	Remarks.
Cabinet Office.		410	None.	None.	410	
Office of Works.	50	A few.	Part.	Part.	Proportions to be indicated on site.

Appendix A-3: During the War

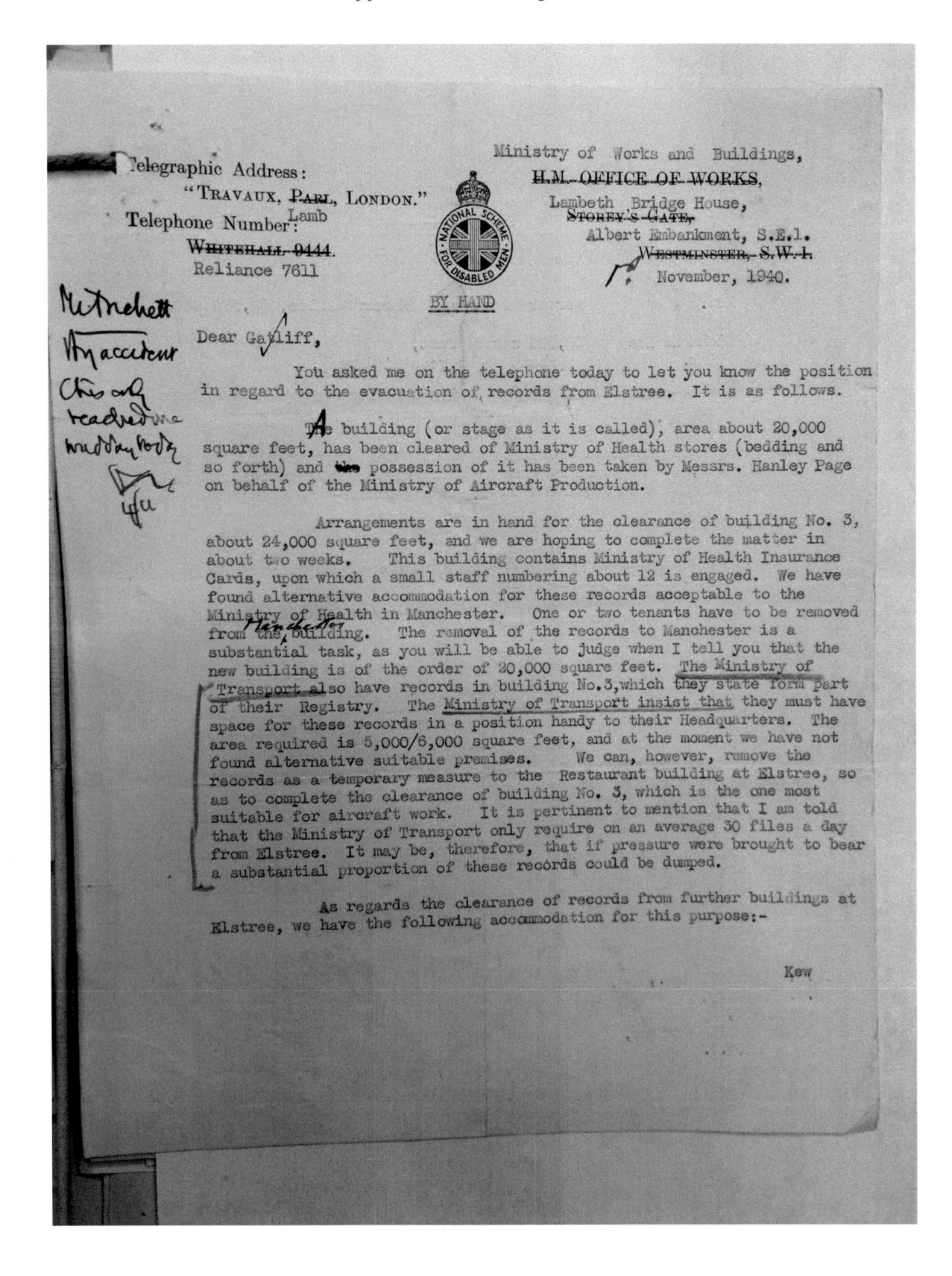

Telegraphic Address:
 "TRAVAUX, ~~PARL~~, LONDON."
Telephone Number: Lamb
 ~~WHITEHALL 9444~~.
 Reliance 7611

Ministry of Works and Buildings,
~~H.M. OFFICE OF WORKS~~,
Lambeth Bridge House,
~~STOREY'S GATE~~,
Albert Embankment, S.E.1.
~~WESTMINSTER, S.W.1.~~
November, 1940.

BY HAND

Dear Gatliff,

You asked me on the telephone today to let you know the position in regard to the evacuation of records from Elstree. It is as follows.

The building (or stage as it is called), area about 20,000 square feet, has been cleared of Ministry of Health stores (bedding and so forth) and ~~the~~ possession of it has been taken by Messrs. Hanley Page on behalf of the Ministry of Aircraft Production.

Arrangements are in hand for the clearance of building No. 3, about 24,000 square feet, and we are hoping to complete the matter in about two weeks. This building contains Ministry of Health Insurance Cards, upon which a small staff numbering about 12 is engaged. We have found alternative accommodation for these records acceptable to the Ministry of Health in Manchester. One or two tenants have to be removed from the building. The removal of the records to Manchester is a substantial task, as you will be able to judge when I tell you that the new building is of the order of 20,000 square feet. The Ministry of Transport also have records in building No.3, which they state form part of their Registry. The Ministry of Transport insist that they must have space for these records in a position handy to their Headquarters. The area required is 5,000/6,000 square feet, and at the moment we have not found alternative suitable premises. We can, however, remove the records as a temporary measure to the Restaurant building at Elstree, so as to complete the clearance of building No. 3, which is the one most suitable for aircraft work. It is pertinent to mention that I am told that the Ministry of Transport only require on an average 30 files a day from Elstree. It may be, therefore, that if pressure were brought to bear a substantial proportion of these records could be dumped.

As regards the clearance of records from further buildings at Elstree, we have the following accommodation for this purpose:-

Kew

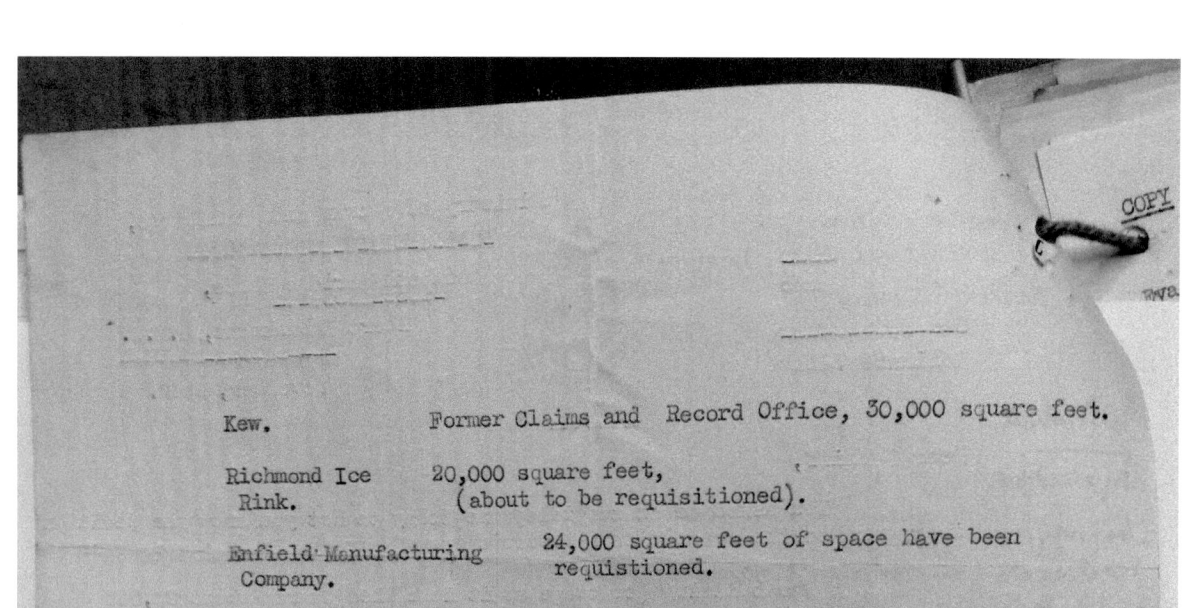

Kew.	Former Claims and Record Office, 30,000 square feet.
Richmond Ice Rink.	20,000 square feet, (about to be requisitioned).
Enfield Manufacturing Company.	24,000 square feet of space have been requisitioned.

The space mentioned above will take a substantial proportion of the records from Elstree, but we shall require a substantially greater area unless Departments will take action on the following lines:-

A. Destroy the maximum possible percentage of their records.

B. Of the remainder agree that they may be dumped without the provision of racking, and

C. Reduce to an absolute minimum the records which must be kept in racks and in sequence.

The Departments concerned have agreed to send representatives to Elstree immediately for the purpose of indicating the various categories of records, and I hope you will be able to bring some pressure on Departments to place the fewest possible records in category C, and as many as possible in category A.

There is some difficulty in the matter of transport. We have a number of vehicles earmarked with the Ministry of Transport for use for emergency purposes, and no doubt these could be called upon, but we should then be faced with the difficulty of providing adequate labour. With a view to getting assistance both in transport and labour we approached the War Office, but without result. I enclose a copy of the correspondence. If you can do anything to persuade the War Office to assist us in this matter it would be very helpful indeed.

Yours sincerely,

E. Balch

H.E.C. Gatliff, Esq.,
H.M. Treasury,
Room 651,
New Public Offices,
S.W.1.

Appendix A-3: During the War

COPY.

D.L. & A. L/7. Ministry of Works and Buildings.

27th January, 1941.

Dear Captain Davies,

Studios - Elstree Way, Boreham Wood.

The above premises are held by this Department for a term of 42 years from March, 1939, at a rent of £7,333 per annum exclusive for the first 21 years and at £9,100 per annum for the remainder of the term.

You will remember that during our conversation on the 4th instant, it was my suggestion that the lease of the above might perhaps be assigned or transferred to the Air Ministry as from a date to be agreed and from which date the Air Ministry would assume all liabilities including maintenance, engineering, etc.

On further consideration, however, it is thought that in view of the length of tenure (i.e. 42 years) assignment now might only result in the necessity for re-assignment at some later date thus causing unnecessary expense and trouble.

I propose, therefore, in place of my original suggestion and subject to your concurrence to recommend the Board to hold the premises and recover from the Air Ministry during their occupation all outgoings under the lease (i.e. rent, rates, taxes, etc.) as from the date to be agreed, leaving all maintenance, engineering services, domestic outgoings, watching and fire watching etc., to be dealt with directly by the Air Ministry.

If this course is adopted we should presumably withdraw our mainteance staff from the building as from the date to be agreed, which I think should be any time now as the premises are more than half cleared and Messrs. Handley Page Ltd. are in possession of the majority.

In view of the special occupation by private firm/firms, upon which I presume you will throw responsibility, it may be deemed necessary to draw up a Schedule of Condition etc., but this detail could, I think, be settled later.

I shall be glad to have your concurrence in principle to this suggestion in order that I may submit the matter to the Board for consideration.

I enclose, as promised at our interview, three copies of a diagramatic plan, one of which has been marked to show the dates upon which Messrs. Handley Page took possession of the portions they now occupy.

Yours sincerely,

(Signed)

Captain R.W. Davies,
    Air Ministry,
        Bush House,
             Kingsway, W.C.2.

Telegraphic Address: Lamb,
"TRAVAUX ~~PARL~~, LONDON."

Telephone Number:
~~WHITEHALL 0444.~~
Reliance 7611.

Ministry of Works and Buildings,
~~H.M. OFFICE OF WORKS,~~
File ~~STOREY'S GATE,~~
~~WESTMINSTER, S.W.1~~

Lambeth Bridge House,
Albert Embankment, S.E.1.

12 February, 1941.

Dear Gatliff,

You spoke to me on the 6th instant about maintenance services at Elstree. I enclose for your information a copy of a letter which we wrote on the 27th January to Captain Davies at the Air Ministry with suggested arrangements; I am sending a copy also to Milward, Sir Charles Bruce-Gardiner's deputy at M. A. P., so that he may be fully informed.

With regard to de Havilland, the position is as follows:-
M. A. P. have agreed to their having 7,000 ft. at once in Building "C" and the rest of it (13,000 ft.) as soon as possible. In addition to this 20,000 ft., they can also have Building 5 (6,000 ft.).

With regard to Handley Page, M. A. P. have agreed that they can have Building 8 for tea-making for their staff. (We understand there was some trouble with the staff, which this arrangement might soothe.)

The position at Elstree is approximately as set out below -

Building.	Area.	
A.B.3. 1 & 2.	77,000 sq.ft.	Handed over to Handley Page (also Building 6 - Canteen, 10,000 sq.ft.).
4.	5,000 sq.ft.	Almost cleared.
5.	6,000 sq.ft.	
D.	20,000 sq.ft.	Were in course of being cleared when ~~they were~~ damaged by bomb. The future home of the records in these buildings - 201/7 City Road - was also damaged by bomb: clearance of these buildings has therefore been delayed.
7.	7,000 sq.ft.	

P.T.O.

Appendix A-3: During the War

Building.	Area.	
C.	20,000 sq.ft.	is being cleared as quickly as possible /In D.H. 7000' already cleared.
9.	7,000 sq.ft.	contains Cabinet papers - some difficulty in finding suitable alternative quarters for confidential documents.
8.	3,000 sq.ft.	boiler and power house with upper floor: the latter offered to Handley Page.

   I send you herewith a copy of my letter to Milward of today's date regarding the above.

                                    Yours sincerely,

                                    A. Toll

H. E. C. Gatliff, Esq.,
H. M. Treasury,
Gt. George Street, S.W.1.

Enclosures.

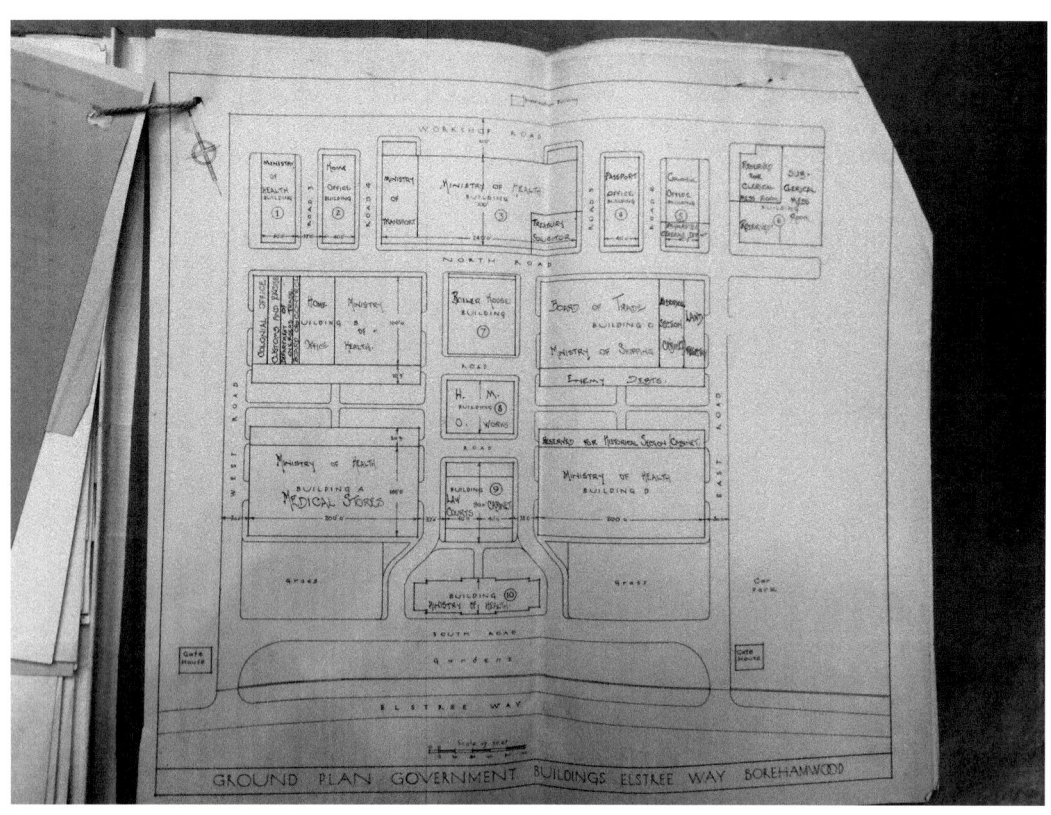

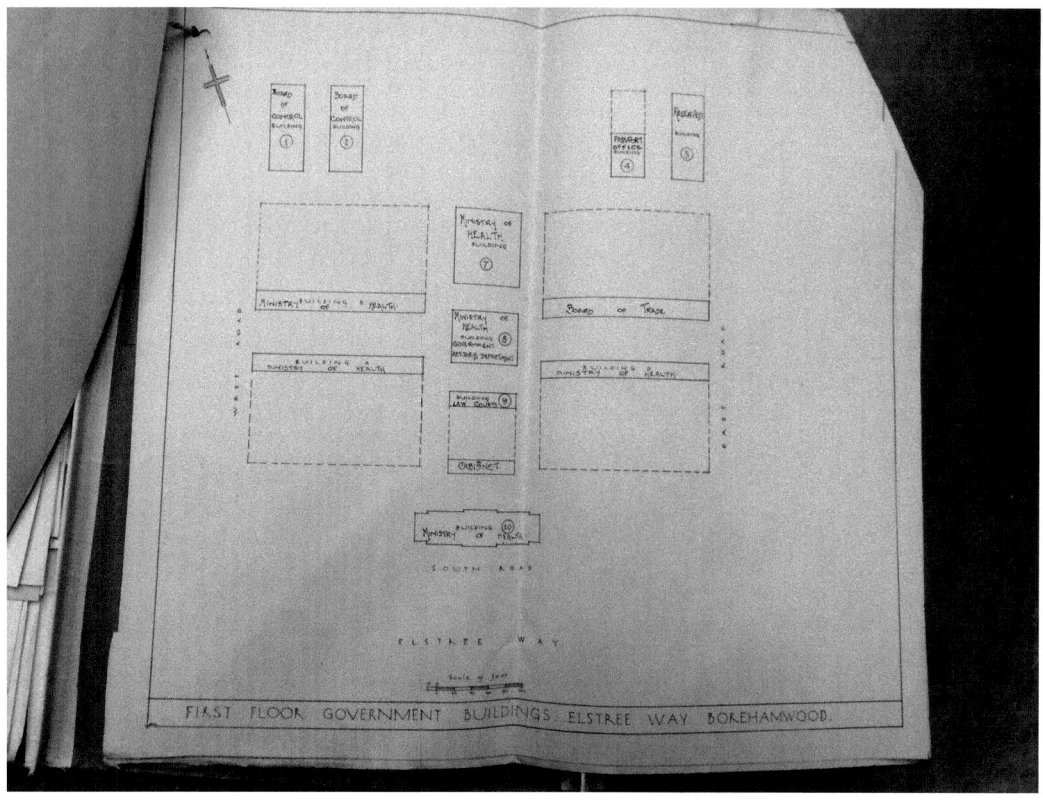

MGM British Studios

– 198 –

Appendix A-3: During the War

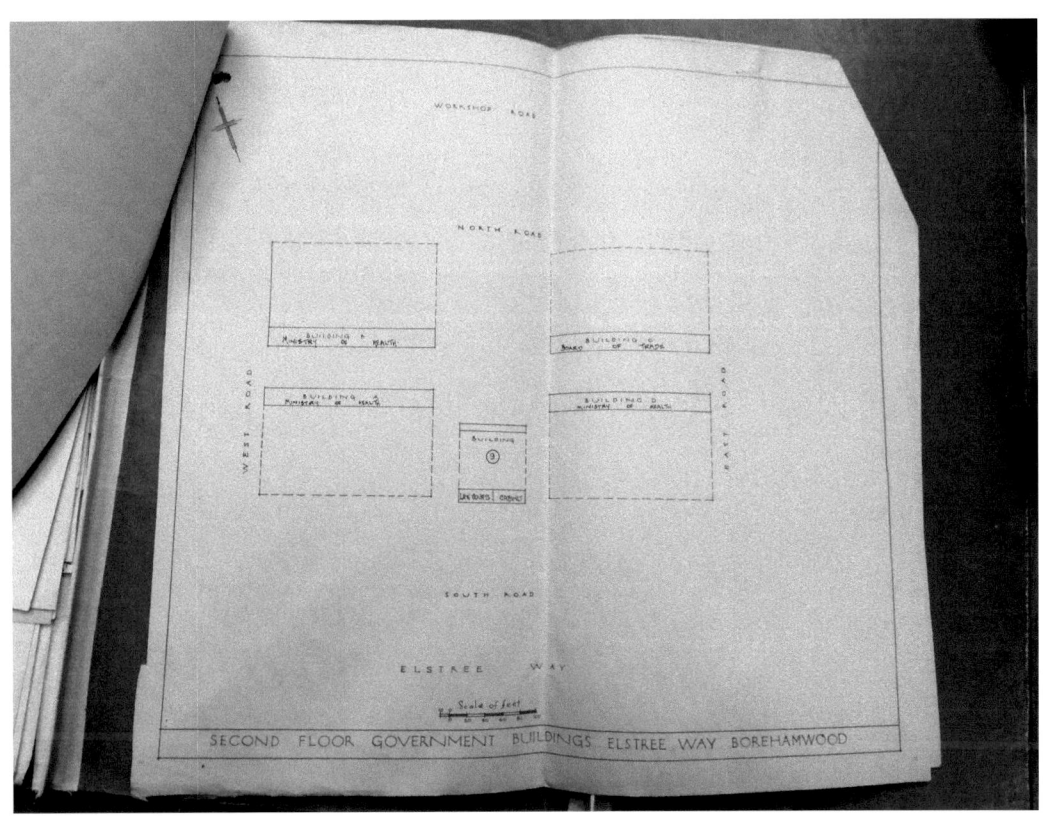

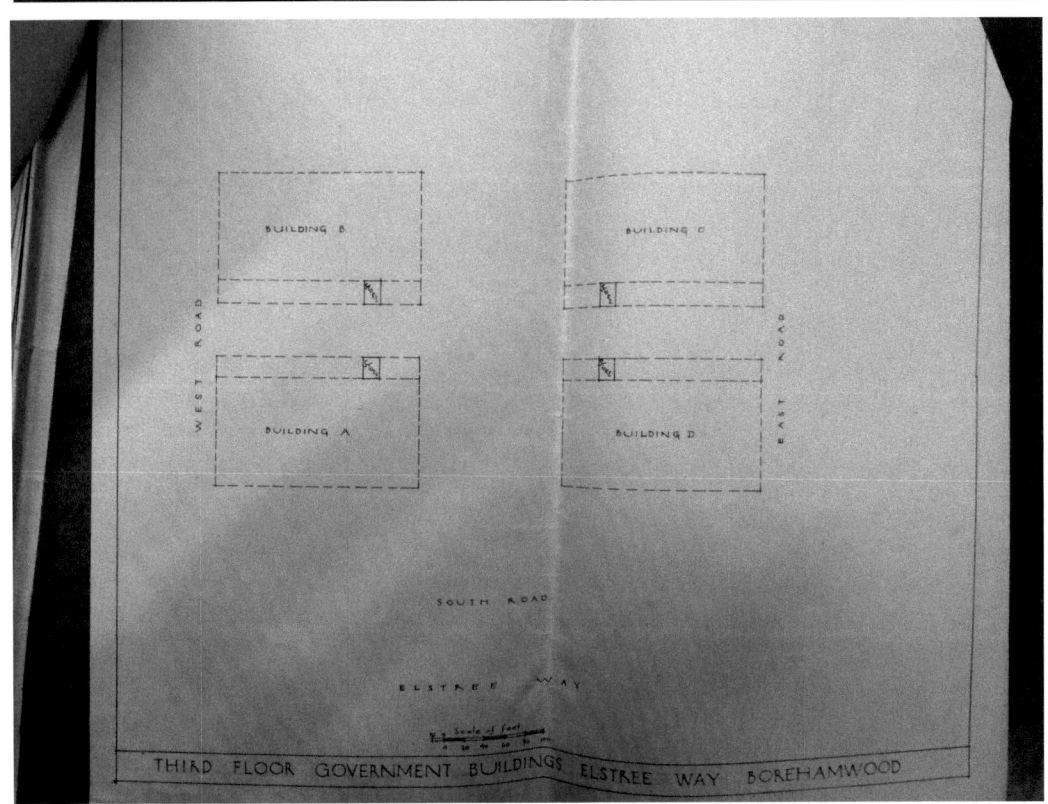

APPENDIX A-4
After the War

This appendix charts the transformation of Amalgamated Studios into MGM British. All of these photos were taken in 1946.

Architect's model

MGM British Studios

Appendix A-4: After the War

MGM British Studios

Appendix A-4: After the War

Appendix A-5
Inside MGM British

These photos go behind the scenes to provide glimpses of various departments and the people who worked in them.

— 207 —

MGM British Studios

Appendix A-5: Inside MGM British

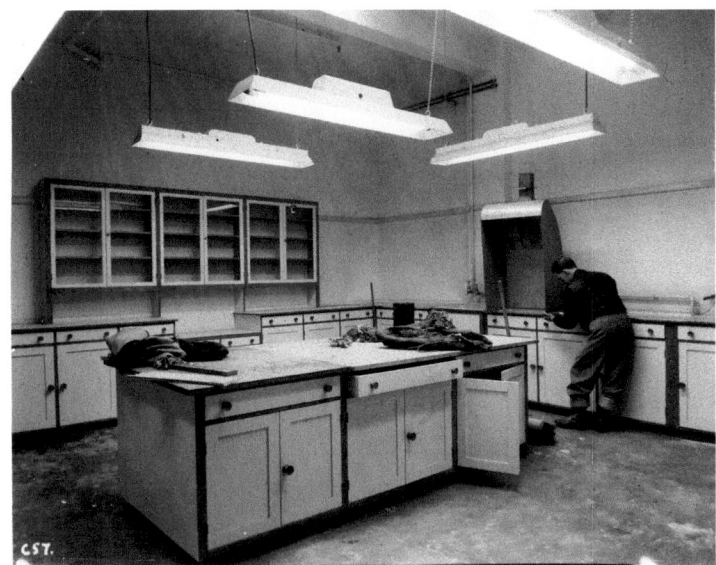

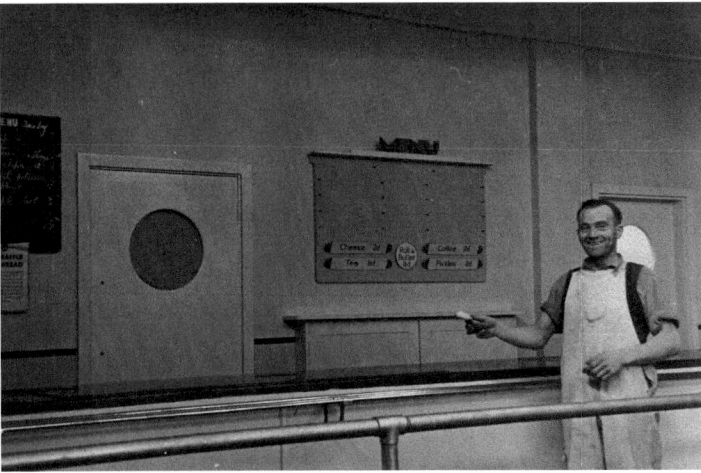

— 209 —

MGM British Studios

Appendix A-5: Inside MGM British

MGM British Studios

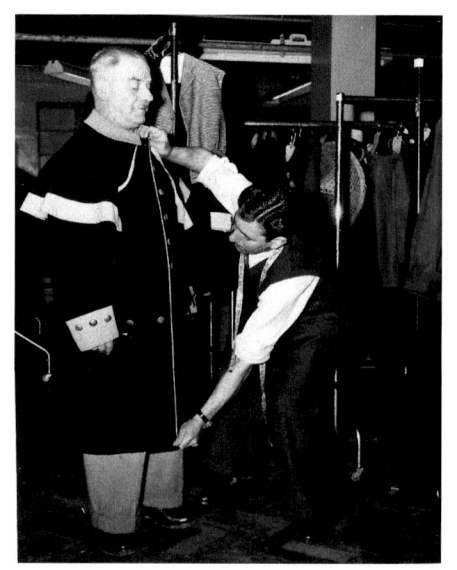

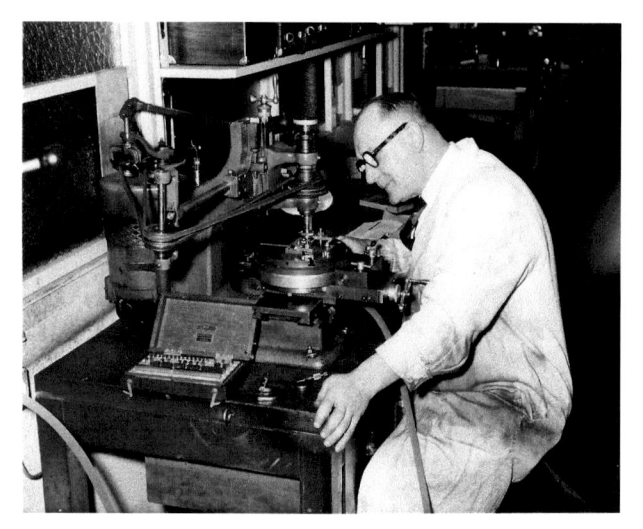

Appendix A-5: Inside MGM British

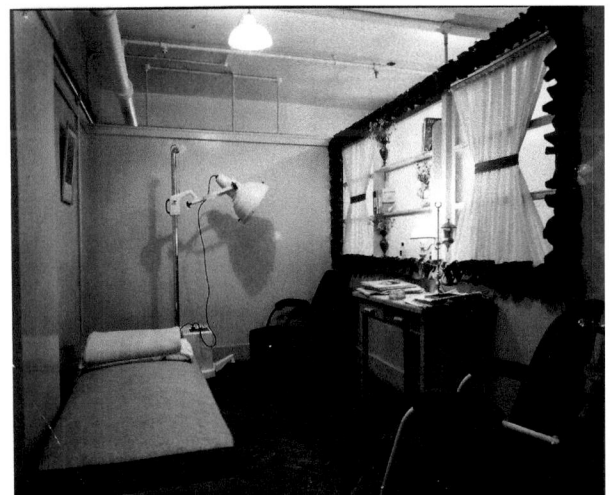

MGM British Studios

Appendix A-5: Inside MGM British

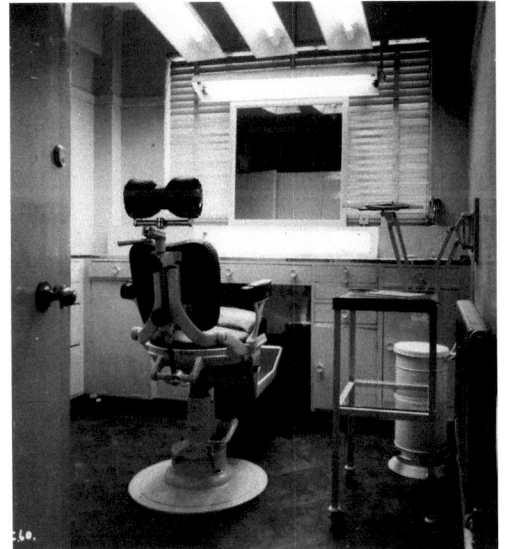

APPENDIX A-6

Samples of Correspondence

The Author found many files abandoned at the Studio after its closure; sadly most were subsequently destroyed by disinterested demolition workers. These are some examples of what the Author was able to collect regarding the day-to-day life at MGM British Studios.

MGM had already sent box files about its productions to Elstree Studios for safekeeping. In 1989 the Author was asked to throw them away as the building was to be demolished. Instead he contacted MGM who reluctantly collected them.

The Author was later told that they were destroyed to avoid storage costs. However, he has recently been informed that they have been saved and now reside at the Academy of Motion Pictures Arts And Sciences in Los Angeles. If so, his actions over 30 years ago were worth it.

```
JH/10th August 1948.


            CONTRACT with IAN HUNTER


Agreement dated          22 June 1948

Production               Edward My Son

Character                The Doctor

Period                   17 days minimum during 9 successive
                         weeks commencing about 14 June 1948.
                         Additional days as reasonably
                         required for re-takes, post sync, etc.
                         Option to Metro to claim first call
                         after period by giving 7 days' notice
                         before expiration of period.

Studios and Locations    Metro's Studios, Elstree Way,
                         Boreham Wood, only.

Concession               Permission to leave early to appear
                         at Theatre Royal, Brighton during
                         week beginning 21 June.

Payment                  £5,000 for minimum period of 17 days
                         by 9 weekly instalments
                         £300 for each additional day payable
                         at end of week
                         £600 minimum payable weekly during
                         "first call" period

Credit                   On screen and in paid advertising:
                         As a feature artist; only stars to
                         be billed in larger type, except that
                         "if really necessary one female artiste
                         may precede the name of the Artist".

Agent                    Connies Limited
```

MGM British Studios

13th June

INCOMING CABLE

Received 22nd May, 1952.

RATE LT TO BEN GOETZ METROBRIT
TELEX BOREHAMWOOD ENGLAND

OFFICE AND DATE OF ORIGIN CIAL Culver City

21st May, 1952

RE GENE TIERNEY SHE WAS BORN BROOKLYN NOVEMBER NINTEENTH NINETEEN TWENTY HAS UNITED STATES PASSPORT NUMBER SIX FOUR FIVE SEVEN ISSUED GENE TIERNEY CASSINI AT WASHINGTON JUNE TWENTY FOURTH NINETEEN FORTY NINE WHICH IS VALID UNTIL JUNE TWENTY THIRD NINETEEN FIFTY THREE OUR DEAL IS LOANOUT FROM TWENTIETH CENTURY FOX UNDER WHICH WE REIMBURSE THEM COST HER REGULAR SALARY OF ONE HUNDRED THOUSAND DOLLARS FOR FOURTEEN WEEKS COMMENCING JUNE FOURTEENTH IN ADDITION WE PAY ROUNDTRIP TRANSPORTATION AND TRAVELING EXPENSES FOR TIERNEY HER YOUNGSTER AND MOTHER PLUS REIMBURSEMENT COST OF LIVING NOT TO EXCEED FIVE HUNDRED DOLLARS PER WEEK COMMENCING ON DATE OF ARRIVAL IN ENGLAND COPY OF CONTRACT WILL BE FORWARDED PLEASE ADVISE WHEN WORK PERMIT GRANTED REGARDS

FLOYD HENDRICKSON

c.c. Mr. Daves
    Mr. Raymond
    Mr. Hudson

Appendix A-6: Samples of Correspondence

```
                                   c.c.   Mr. Goetz
                                          Mr. Davey
```

Mr. Clark Gable,   6th
Dorchester Hotel,   June,
Park Lane,   1952.
LONDON, W.1.

Dear Mr. Gable:

As you know doubt are aware, all visiting artistes to
this country are required to become temporary members of
British Actors' Equity Association in the same way as
British artistes visiting America are required to become
temporary members of American Equity.

In this connection we have received from British Actors'
Equity Association a form for completion by you (in the
space provided at the right hand bottom corner of the form,
between the pencil crosses).

Will you be good enough to sign this and return it to me
in the envelope enclosed and I will see that it is lodged
with "Equity" straight away,

The Studio will, of course, take care of the membership fee.

                                       Yours sincerely,

                                       M. RAYMOND

2 Encls.

MGM British Studios

COPY

        Association of Cinematograph and allied
                       Technicians
          2, Soho Square,
              London, W.1.

     17th July, 1952.

Gene Kelly, Esq.,
M.G.M. Studios,
Boreham Wood,
Herts.

Dear Mr. Kelly,

    Rather belatedly I am dropping you this line to welcome you to this country, and trust that your stay will be enjoyable and the film upon which you are engaged will be a success.

    We are organised, from the trade union point of view, somewhat differently from America, and broadly speaking all film technicians from the Director downwards are organised in our Union.

    Whilst of course, each group works through its own section, we have no separate Guilds as you have in the States.

    It is our policy that visiting Directors should be invited to join this Union for the duration of their stay in this country, and we very much trust that you will complete the enclosed application form for membership and let me have it together with your cheque for eight guineas to cover your Entrance Fee and subscriptions.

    I will probably be at your Studio on Tuesday of next week and hope to have the opportunity to meet you personally.

                          Yours sincerely,

                     (sgd) GEORGE ELVIN

                        General Secretary.

c.c. Mr. Goetz
     Mr. Raymond.

Appendix A-6: Samples of Correspondence

INCOMING CABLE

12th August, 1952

RECE..ED (Date and Time)

OFFICE & DATE OF ORIGIN

RATE AND ADDRESS

GB L ELS1052 CR DG98 ROMA 154 11 1845 1/50

ELT BEN GOETZ METROBRIT TELEX BOREHAMWOOD ENGLAND =

VENICE FILM FESTIVAL COMMITTEE MOST ANXIOUS AMERICAN STARS APPEAR FOR ONE OR TWO DAYS BETWEEN AUGUST 20 AND SEPTEMBER 10 STOP SUGGEST GABLE OR KELLY OR BOTH ATTEND ONE OF THREE WEEK ENDS DURING PERIOD STOP THEY WILL BE GUESTS OF FESTIVAL COMMITTEE STOP WE MOST ANXIOUS COOPERATE AS TOKEN OUR GRATITUDE ITALIAN GOVERNMENT AID QUO VADIS AND THIS YEAR WE ARE RELEASING AMERICAN PARIS DEVIL MAKES THREE WIDE MISSOURI LONE STAR SINGING RAIN STOP PLEASEREALISE ITALY OUR BIGGEST FOREIGN MARKET AFTER ENGLAND AND THEIR APPEARANCE MEANS NOT ONLY GOOD WILL BUT ADDITIONAL REVENUE THEIR FILMS STOP MGM ENTRY THIS FESTIVAL IS YOUR IVANHOE AND FESTIVAL COMMITTEE DELAYING SETTING SCREENING DATES ALL PICTURES TO SYNCHRONIZE IVANHOE DATE WITH MGM STAR APPEARANCE STOP HAVE PERSONALLY CABLED GABLE SUGGESTING COOPERATION STOP CABLE KAMERN METROFILMS ROME DATE STAR WILL BE PRESENT SO IVANHOE SCREENING CAN BE SET =

DAVE LEWIS+++++

c.c. Mr. Raymond
Mr. Paul Mills.

RECEIVED
12 AUG 1952
M. RAYMOND.

MGM British Studios

Keith Cardale, Groves & Co.
SURVEYORS, VALUERS, AUCTIONEERS & ESTATE AGENTS

C. H. GROVES, F.A.L.P.A.
G. LEIGH, F.A.L.P.A.
J. B. WATSON, F.A.I.

MAYFAIR 4631
" 4661

43, NORTH AUDLEY STREET
LONDON, W.1

AM/PG.   12th August, 1952.

Gene Kelly, Esq.,
Metro-Goldwyn-Mayer
British Studios Ltd.,
Boreham Wood,
Elstree,
Herts.

Dear Sir,

    23, Three Kings Yard,
    Mayfair, W.1.

  Further to our Mr. Margo's telephone conversation of even date with your Secretary, we have pleasure in enclosing herewith the Counterpart Agreement in respect of the furnished letting of the above house to you from Friday next, the 15th instant until the 31st October, 1952, at a rental of 30 gns. per week.

  We would appreciate your completing the name of the lessee, signing and initialling the document, where indicated, and returning it to this office together with your remittance in the sum of £371.10.0d. made up as follows:-

Eleven weeks rent at 30 gns. per week. £ 346. 10. 0d.

Deposit against dilapidations, telephone,
electricity, gas, etc... ... . £ 25. 0. 0d.
             £ 371. 10. 0d.

  It is further confirmed that our Inventory Clerk will be attending the premises at 10 a.m. on Friday morning for the purpose of checking the Inventory with your Representative. We understand, however, that you will wish to take possession on Thursday evening and our client has assured us that he will vacate the house not later than 6 p.m. on the 14th instant.

    Yours faithfully,

Enc:

                    1952.

Re: 23 Three Kings Yard, Mayfair, W.1.

  I have requested you to enter into a Tenancy Agreement with Mr. Robert Donat for the letting to you of the above property on a furnished tenancy.

  In consideration of your entering into the said Agreement and paying to Mr. Donat the rent amounting to £346. 10. 0. and also paying to Mr. Donat the further sum of £25. 0. 0. as a deposit against dilapidations, telephone, electricity, gas, etc., I hereby undertake to indemnify you against any actions, proceedings, costs, damages, claims or demands which may arise under the said Agreement or in connection with the said property and I agree that all moneys now paid or in the future to be paid by you in connection with the said letting whether for rent costs or otherwise may be deducted from any amount due to me from you or any parent associated or subsidiary Company of yours.

        Yours faithfully,

TO:
METRO-GOLDWYN-MAYER BRITISH STUDIOS LIMITED.

Appendix A-6: Samples of Correspondence

INCOMING CABLE

RECEIVED (Date and Time) 22nd August, 1952.

OFFICE & DATE OF ORIGIN 325 NEWYORK 57 22 125P

RATE AND ADDRESS BEN GOETZ METROBRIT BOREHAMWOOD

JUST RECEIVED FOLLOWING TELEGRAM QUOTE NOW IS YOUR CHANCE TO SIGN UP QUICK DAVID HUGHES BRITAINS RADIO AND TELEVISION MATINEE IDOL HE HAS THE LUNG POWER OF LANZA SEX ATTRACTION OF SINATRA AND LOOKS OF VALENTINO AIR MAIL LETTER FOLLOWS FRASER WHITE 233 STRAND LONDON UNQUOTE WHAT DO YOU SUGGEST REGARDS

NICHOLAS SCHENCK+++

cc: Mr. Raymond

OUTGOING CABLE

SENT (Date and Time) 11th January, 1954

RATE AND ADDRESS ORD JJ COHN METROFILMS CULVERCITYCALIFORNIA

EXTRACT

466.........YOUR 347 ELIZABETH TAYLOR NOW WELL HER DOCTOR HAVING DISCHARGED HER FRIDAY STOP SHE IS AT PRESENT IN PARIS WITH WILDING AWAITING OUR CALL STOP WE ARE WORKING WITHOUT HER THIS WEEK AS THIS WAS ONLY TIME WE COULD GET ROBERT MORELY AND SHE IS NOT IN HIS SCENES STOP WE ARE STILL SCHEDULED TO FINISH WITH USTINOV FIRST WEEK IN FEBRUARY STOP CONFIDENTIALLY HIS AGENT ADVISES PETER NOW READING TWENTIETH'S SCRIPT AND IS NOT SURE HE WILL PLAY PART STOP HOWEVER IF HE DOES DECIDE TO PLAY PART HE WILL LEAVE HERE WITHOUT DELAY AFTER WE FINISH WITH HIM STOP

....

BENGOETZ+

c.c. Mr. Raymond
Mr. Zimbalist

COPY   5/12/59

File

AMERICAN SIZES ON CHARLETON HESTON

Hat	7⅝
Shirt	16½ x 36½
Coat	44 Underarm sleeve 19½
Pants	Waist 34 Inside Seam 33 Outside Seam 44
Shoes	12-C
Gloves	9½

Height: 6'2" Stocking Feet
Weight: 199 lbs.

CLEAN SHAVEN

Appendix A-6: Samples of Correspondence

Form No 126
M.G.M. BRITISH STUDIOS LTD.   ON WORKS ORDER PLEASE QUOTE   W/ N⁰ 10296

REQUISITION FOR WORKS ORDER

To Studio Manager,

Please have the following work executed :

"CLEOPATRA" T.C.F.707   A/c. 941/1

Mahogany Slips:		WALTER WANGER ROUBEN MAMOULIAN	
Door Cards:	4	PRIVATE WALTER WANGER ROUBEN MAMOULIAN	
	2	SAUL WURTZEL JACK SWINBURNE UNIT OFFICE MAKE-UP HAIRDRESSING PUBLICITY	) headed) "Cleopatra")) also Indicator) Slips
Chairbacks:		WALTER WANGER ROUBEN MAMOULIAN	
Car Park Signs:		JACK SWINBURNE JACK HILDYARD SAUL WURTZEL	
	2	T.C.F. PRODS. "CLEOPATRA"	

Job. No. :

Department	
ACCOUNTS	xx
ART	
BUILDING MAINT.	
CAMERA	
CARPS.	
CASTING	
CONSTRUCTION	x
DRAPES	x
EDITORIAL	
ELECTRICIAN FLOOR	
ELECTRICIAN MAINT.	
ENGINEERS	
ESTATE	
FIRE	
INVENTORY	
MAILING	
MAINTENANCE ENGR.	
MAKE-UP	
MEDICAL	
MODEL PATTERN	
PERSONNEL	
PLASTER	
PLUMBER	
POWER HOUSE	
PRODUCTION OFFICE	
PROPS.	x
PUBLICITY	
RESTAURANT	
RIGGERS	
SCENIC	x
SCULPTOR-MOD.	
SECURITY	x
SOUND	
SPECIAL EFFECTS	
STILLS	
STORES	x
TIMBER STORE	x
TRANSPORT	
WARDROBE	

LABOUR ....   LABOUR ....
MATERIALS ....   MATERIALS ....
TOTAL ....   TOTAL ....

Signed ....   Dept   STUDIO OPERATING

Approved ....   Date   28.10.60.

MGM British Studios

From Sound Dept.

THEATRE RESERVATIONS

Wk commencing 18th November, 1968.

Messrs: Beckett, Bruton, Carrick, Cleary, Dawson, Griffen, Honess, Jones, King, Miall, Pollock, Smith, Somner (4) Ward, Miss Coxhead.
All prods and edits concerned.

Stamp: STUDIO OPERATING 18 NOV 1968

THEATRE ONE

19th November HF 314 p/s Journey into Unknown.
20th - 22nd November r/r   "   "
27th - 29th November r/r   "   "
4th - 6th December r/r   "   "
9th - 20th December (Paramount) r/r 'Two Gentlemen sharing'.
1st Jan - 14th February Mirisch productions r/r.
24th Feb - 4th April Alfred the Great MGM 105 r/r.
7th April - 25th April Mirisch r/r.
19th May - 25th July MGM 107 r/r 'Chips'.

THEATRE TWO

18th, 19th, 20th, 24th, 25th, 26th, 27th November
  'Laughter in the Dark', Fx (Woodfall) 9484.
21st and 22nd November, 2nd and 9th December Journey into
  Unknown HF 314, fx.
28th & 29th November p/s or fx 'Strange Report' (Pinewood) 9482.
3 - 6th December and 10 - 13th December MF 313 Mirisch, fx.
16th - 20th December MGM 105 Alfred the Great, Fx.
30th December - 24th January MGM 105 Alfred the Great, Fx.
27th January - 28th March MGM 107, Chips, p/s and fx.

A.W.Watkins.

Appendix A-7
'Foremost In Europe'

Published in October 1962 as a supplement to Kinematograph Weekly, this is a detailed technical description of life in MGM British.

Metro-Goldwyn-Mayer British Studios Ltd.

Board of Directors

JOSEPH R. VOGEL (Chairman)

LAWRENCE P. BACHMANN **MAURICE FOSTER**

G. R. WEBB LL.B. **M. I. DAVIS** **R. B. HUGHES**

Studio Manager

GEORGE CATT

Heads of Department

Axtell, J.	Carpenters
Beadle, F.	Transport
Brown, G.	Security
Bryant, V.	Cleaning
Bull, W.	Plasterers
Churchill, Miss M.	Wardrobe
Clarke, C.	Accounts
Clarke, F.	Editorial
Coxhead, Miss J.	Studio Operating
Crack, K.	Plant Engineer
Dawson, T.	Estate
Fensham, B.	Scenic
Graysmark, C.	Construction
Honess, K.	Personnel
Howard, T.	Special Effects
Isaacs, W.	Buyer
Johnstone, Miss J.	Hairdressing
Mead, P.	Pattern
Merrit, G.	Engineers
Miall, F.	Drapes
Mills, P.	Publicity
Nolan, S.	Catering
Pearce, J.	Stills
Pettit, L.	Fire
Ramsay, J.	Property
Scott, E.	Art
Smart, L.	Camera
Smith, Mrs. E.	Telephones
Somner, B.	Production Supervisor
Turner, S.	Stores
Walker, N.	Asst. to Maurice Foster
Walters, F.	Electrical
Watkins, A.	Sound
Wilkinson, W.	Financial Controller

Appendix A-7: 'Foremost In Europe'

Supplement to KINEMATOGRAPH WEEKLY: OCTOBER 25, 1962

THE STUDIO THAT IS YOUR PRODUCTION ORGANISATION

by MAURICE FOSTER, director and general manager

MGM British Studios has a dual personality. It is both the owner of the finest studio in Europe and also a production company making its own films. Consequently we can offer the most comprehensive service to independent producers, covering every aspect of production.

It is fundamental to our thinking that this service only has significance in relation to the "end product," i.e., what appears on the screen. The letting of space is only one of the minor ingredients of this service.

This attitude is, I believe, one of the main reasons why the studio is in such demand and explains why so many leading producers will not, from choice, make their films elsewhere.

Before elaborating on our unique services, I would like to draw attention to the main developments that have been carried out during this very exciting year. They are set out below:—

In addition to these facilities we have engaged leading English technicians on a long term basis.

These developments are only a start and we are planning a number of exciting new projects.

Furthermore, these developments illustrate MGM's belief both in the future of the industry and the conviction that we shall continue to play an important part in it.

MGM is, of course, fortunate in that it is the most recently built of all the major British studios and, consequently, was planned as a complete unit. The layout is of such a compact design that every building and department is inter-related to overall production requirements. Our lot is the largest in Britain and covers 114 acres.

Yet, even with all these additional facili-
continued on page 7

———Twenty-two steps to progress..———

1. Two new stages (75 ft. x 50 ft.).
2. New large stage (100 ft. x 120 ft.) now being erected.
3. An outdoor tank (100 ft. x 150 ft.).
4. New office blocks.
5. Additional dressing rooms.
6. Additional cutting rooms.
7. An extension to our laboratory, providing us with full colour facilities in addition to the black and white facilities that already exist.
8. Alterations to our recording theatre which will enable us to dub in two theatres simultaneously.
9. A new sound transfer suite.
10. A fifth viewing theatre.
11. The establishment of a production and budgeting department.
12. The installation of a revolutionary accounting system, using the latest electronic calculators and tabulators, which will produce up-to-date figures in a shorter time than has ever been considered possible.
13. A film library service.
14. Large standing sets on the lot.
15. Development of several new special effects processes (including an amazing new matte technique) and the building of new equipment.
16. Installation of a new sound facility, developed by MGM in Hollywood, which enables far greater use of location sound than has been possible up till now.
17. The acquisition of a fleet of various cars which can be used both as action cars and for other general purposes at considerably lower rates than available from outside.
18. Extension of car parks.
19. Re-laying of all studio roads.
20. Redecoration of the restaurant and canteen and the inclusion of a bar.
21. The modernisation of production and producers' offices.
22. The building of many new stock sets including a complete Boeing 707 and cockpit.

Two of MGM's new stages

Your production organisation—*contd.*

ties our charges are on a strictly competitive basis with other studios. Because of this and the various special services that we are able to offer there is no doubt that films can be made more cheaply, more efficiently *and more successfully* at MGM.

Producers can be misled by assessing their costs initially on the basis of a studio contract, if they ultimately find the actual costs of their production considerably exceeding the estimates. To make the obvious point, there is no advantage in having free facilities if facilities are not there!

At MGM any producer can assess beforehand the actual costs of a production and there is no reason for these to be exceeded unless the producer requires additional facilities or exceeds his schedule.

Facilities and services are not charged to the production except where required. At MGM, construction and manual labour are not allocated to a production but taken from a pool on a day-to-day basis according to the requirements of the production.

Set pieces

Because so many big productions have been made at MGM, we have acquired a vast quantity of sets and set pieces, and these can reduce very considerably the amount of new buildings required. This is one of the many factors which enable us to build sets at lower costs than anywhere else.

Our newly-formed production department, under Basil Somner, was set up primarily to help in the organisation of our own productions, but it also provides a service that we can offer to independent producers. The department covers every facet of production from the engagement of writers through to the compiling of release scripts, or any specific operation between these two extremes. Preliminary investigations, research, permits, location recces, budgeting, and general advice on production matters are part of its function. The production staff has experience of many foreign locations and could be particularly helpful to an independent producer with overseas work.

World contacts

We also have contacts in every country in Europe and most countries elsewhere and authoritative information can often be obtained for a producer without his having to incur the expense of sending representatives abroad.

We keep in touch with most of the leading technicians as well as retaining a number of them on our permanent staff. We are thus able to help an independent in getting his crew together. However, at no time do we ever expect or ask a producer to utilise our own staff. In practice it usually works the other way round!

Our sound department, under A. W. Watkins (Watty to all), has now been completely modernised. With the additional facilities installed, we can even cope with the extremes of production demands!

Our special effects department is world renowned. Tommy Howard has won so many awards for his work (including two Oscars) that we should need almost a separate supplement to describe them all!

Our engineering shops must be amongst the finest in the world. They have equipment to handle any engineering problem and staff with a vast experience of design and development work within the industry. To give an indication of their scope; we have developed and manufactured optical and step printers, stop-motion gearboxes, special-purpose lens mounts, film-lacquering machines, motorised lamp-elevators, crab and location dollies to name just a few. New equipment is constantly being developed and the heads of our technical departments have contributed many ideas that have speeded up production.

Another of our specialist personnel is Ken Crack, plant and development engineer. Crack is a qualified engineer whose inventiveness has saved many thousands of pounds over the last few years. He is only happy when he is solving some seemingly insoluble problem.

Our publicity department, headed by Paul Mills, can help on all publicity and public relation matters. We are also establishing a promotion section and independent producers will be able to avail themselves of this service as well.

Everything

In the same way, our casting department, under Irene Howard, can offer anything from advice to complete servicing.

Yet another instance of our being predominant in Europe is provided by our estate department. Our stocks of trees, shrubs, plants and flowers cover practically every production requirement.

The complete modernisation of our accounts department will mean that independent producers will have accurate up-to-date information faster than has ever been known in the industry hitherto. This is an aspect of production on which it is

continued on page 9

Your production organisation—contd.

Left: Tom Howard directing special effects scenes on (right) MGM's new outdoor tank, which covers 15,000 square feet, with water of variable depth. The tank is fitted with wave and wind machines. The model ships were built in the studio and are electronically controlled

almost impossible to place too much importance—for unless such information is available quickly it is of no practical use.

The new laboratory, which is immediately adjacent to our stage blocks, will undertake all colour work (including "dailies") as well as release printing of both black and white and colour films. In urgent cases black and white dailies can also be handled.

From the production viewpoint it is almost impossible to over-value these facilities. For example, a completed magazine can be taken direct from the floor to the laboratory and the results seen two or three hours later. How useful this is if an urgent decision is required on set striking, or it becomes important to release an artist quickly.

Furthermore, it will be possible to see a morning's work before going home that day!

The MGM studios in Culver City, Hollywood, are, of course, the largest in the world and we have the benefit of this association.

As a result, having knowledge of the latest technical progress from America, we

continued on page 11

Lighting at the MGM studio consists almost exclusively of Mole-Richardson equipment. Large numbers of lamps are held in stock, and it has not so far proved necessary to make any additional purchases for the new stages. An enormous number of lamps was used in a big scene for an MGM romantic comedy with an airline background. The set consisted of a full-sized replica of the fuselage of a Boeing 707. No fewer than 84 Mole-Richardson two kW lamps were used for front lighting. For the background, five "Brutes" and 75 10k's were needed

DD

Supplement to KINEMATOGRAPH WEEKLY : OCTOBER 25, 1962

Your production organisation—*continued*

pride ourselves that our studio can provide all the facilities that would normally be available in Hollywood, although of course, on a smaller scale.

As an illustration of the benefits of this association, Culver City recently sent us certain tests on new lighting equipment together with special accessories built at that studio. We have carried out further experiments with this equipment and are using it for filming actual interiors and small night exteriors. The results have been exceptional and very considerable savings in cost will accrue to producers.

Flexibility

Although the expansion of our own production programme, under Lawrence P. Bachmann, means that there may be less opportunity for bringing in rental productions, we try to maintain a flexibilty in planning our own pictures so as to allow for independent producers.

This has particular significance in that present day conditions require continuity of employment. We at MGM are very concerned that there should be a spread of production throughout the year so as to maintain those levels of employment without which there can be no successful operation.

I have only mentioned here some of the more valuable aspects of our operation which, because they are unique in Europe, play such an important part in making MGM's service to independent producers so exceptional.

Labour relations

There is, however, one other matter which perhaps has more influence on production than any other and this is labour relations. In this respect, we claim that MGM has the least number of labour stoppages or disputes in the industry. This, we believe, is because there is not a single person in this studio who is not vitally interested in production and in the MGM tradition. The resulting spirit is one that plays a very large part in the success of our studio.

Finally, I would point out that:

1. The Metro-Goldwyn-Mayer organisation has a record in the motion picture industry that is second to none. Remember the whole resources of this great company have gone into the development of MGM British Studios.
2. MGM British Studios were built and planned for the express purpose of making quality films for the international market.
3. No other studios in Europe can produce a more impressive record of merit and financial success in the last 15 years.

I hope that these brief notes illustrate why we are known as The Studio That Is Your *Production* Organisation.

One of MGM's 30 dressing rooms for artists, which are connected by covered way to all stages

The very pleasant restaurant at the studios is one of the amenities available to staff and visitors

Appendix A-7: 'Foremost In Europe'

Supplement to KINEMATOGRAPH WEEKLY : OCTOBER 25, 1962

DAILIES ARE DAILY
at the most modern laboratory

by R. H. CRICKS, Hon. FBKS, FRPS

TOM HOWARD

A LARGE proportion of Metro-Goldwyn-Mayer's colour printing for European release will in future be printed in the new studio laboratory. It will have an annual output of 30 to 40 million feet of Eastman Color print film, and additional capacity for processing Eastman Color negatives shot in the studio.

The laboratory, under the control of special effects expert Tommy Howard, FBKS, FRPS, occupies two floors of a new building. It is air-conditioned throughout to maintain a temperature of 68 deg. F and a relative humidity of 60 per cent. at all times of the year—temperature and humidity being continually recorded by means of a Coley recorder.

However, it may at times be desired to work at a lower temperature in various parts of the lab. for particular purposes, and in order to obtain this an Ashwell and Nesbitt chiller unit has been installed.

Four Arri developing machines have been supplied by Rank Precision Industries, each with an output of about 5,000 ft. per hour. Each machine comprises 17 tanks, two metres in height, made of a new plastic, together with loading and take-off compensators which permits continuous operation. The machines are arranged in pairs back to back. One machine is capable of processing 35mm. and 16mm. without any change of rollers, while another will handle 35mm. and 65mm. or 70mm.

Technically an important feature of these machines is that the film remains totally immersed during the developing operation. In most machines film emerges into air at the top of the loops, possibly causing directional effects of shadows at the top or bottom of contrasty boundaries in the image. Such effects are eliminated at MGM.

Nylon brushes have been installed to

continued on page 15

Two views of the interior of the new laboratory at the MGM Studios

Supplement to KINEMATOGRAPH WEEKLY : OCTOBER 25, 1962

Dailies daily
—continued

remove the anti-halation backing from the colour stock. For the positive sound track, a viscous re-development system is provided, with micrometer adjustment of the positioning of the track. After each stage of processing, moisture is removed by squeegees controlled by a vacuum-dial gauge.

Chemicals are mixed in large stainless-steel vats, and before use are normalised in tanks lined with rigid pvc. Developer is fed to the developing tanks through an automatic dosing unit, adjustable to feed one litre of replenisher at intervals of from $\frac{1}{4}$ minute to 15 minutes.

Plumbing

The control and replenishment of the solutions necessitates a complicated plumbing system which has been carried out by A.C. Plastics. From the mixing vats no less than 1,600 ft. of high-impact pvc pipes convey the solutions to the tanks under the control of 110 valves.

Purity of water is a vital factor in the processing of colour films. At MGM, water is softened in a fully automatic plant, supplied by the American firm of Lulligan, to within $\pm \frac{1}{4}$ deg., F, by means of immersion heaters and chilled-water heat exchangers.

The four MGM printers are of a type not hitherto seen in Europe. Made by the American firm of Peterson, they provide continuous printing of picture and sound at either 90 or 120 ft. per minute. To cope with these high speeds, constant-torque motors drive the take-up at adjustable tension. Light changes are pre-set by hand and actuated by notches on the negative.

Film scratching is completely avoided by the nylon gate pads. The gates provide five different apertures for head and tail printing, in addition to CinemaScope. A feature of these machines is that they permit of A and B roll printing of release prints—a feature that may avoid duping. An automatic device permits of changing over from the A negative to the B negative at a pre-selected point.

Special attention has been given to sensitometric control. MGM have installed a Joyce Loebl sensitometer and recording densitometer together with the new Kodak sensitometer of the intensity scale type. Full analytical control will be exercised using spectrophotometers, PH meters and an impressive array of distillation glassware.

Colour scene testing will be by comparitor strips made on a Herrnfeld scene tester. A range of selected filter colour will enable the colour grader to choose the appropriate colour pack for printing.

One of MGM's mechanical horses: there are no others in Europe

A scene illustrating some of the trick work done for " tom thumb "

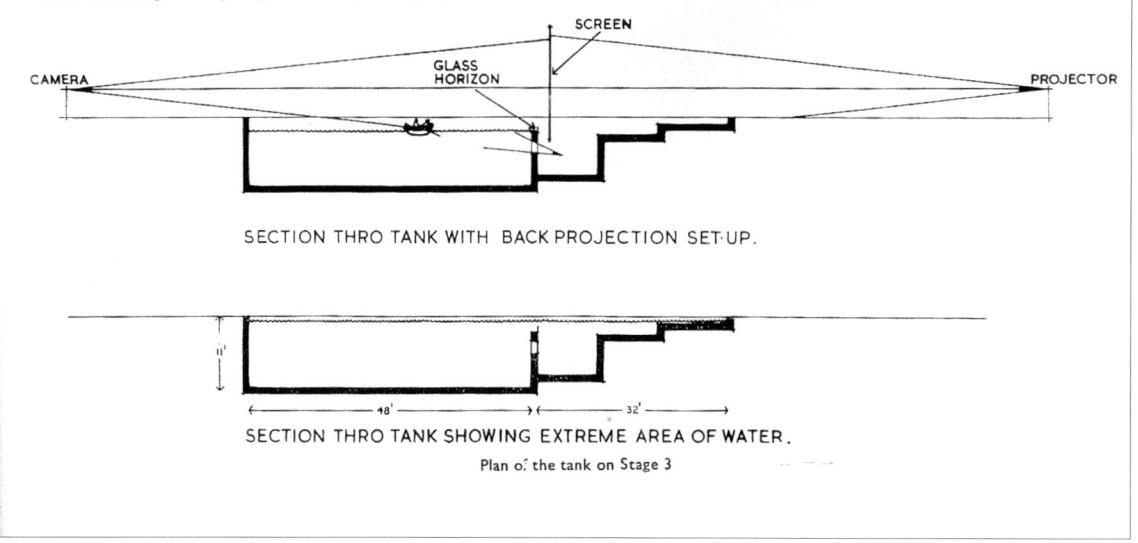

SECTION THRO TANK WITH BACK PROJECTION SET-UP.

SECTION THRO TANK SHOWING EXTREME AREA OF WATER.

Plan of the tank on Stage 3

— 234 —

Appendix A-7: 'Foremost In Europe'

Supplement to KINEMATOGRAPH WEEKLY : OCTOBER 25, 1962

The extensive new accounts block at the MGM British Studios

MORE COSTS—COSTS LESS

AT MGM, accounting is looked upon as an integral part of film making. It is as important to know how much a film is *under* budget as it is to know how much it is *over* budget.

If this knowledge is available rapidly it can considerably aid the producer in his decisions and consequently his film must benefit. Traditional methods of accounting, however, seldom match up to the speed at which this information is required.

Requirements

Knowing this, we had the problem of designing a method of accounting which would be fast, accurate and at no extra cost to production. At the same time we wanted the figures produced to be more comprehensive than normal film accounting and also easily understandable by the producer and his staff. We also had to bear in mind that the system would have to cope with "constant peaks" of production activity!

To achieve these objectives we installed, with the help and co-operation of International Computers and Tabulators, an integrated data-processing routine using the most modern high-speed, punch-card equipment. The result is a system which can only be described as spectacular. It has achieved all the required objectives and has also taken the drudgery out of accountancy.

Producers at MGM can be given information in as much detail as they wish. Daily set construction costs including labour and materials are prepared rapidly at the rate of six thousand lines of print per hour. Information required for Form C (the document which has to be submitted to the Board of Trade for British registration of a film) is no longer an onerous task, but takes merely one hour at the end of production. The system is so designed that the speed of reporting is maintained however many productions are involved at the same time.

Payroll system

From a practical point of view one of the most remarkable developments is the payroll system. An electronic calculator covers the complete compilation of wages, taking into account income tax, national health insurance, pensions, overtime at all its different rates and produces a pay slip at the end of the operation on which all this detail is printed.

The same machine is used to calculate

continued on page 19

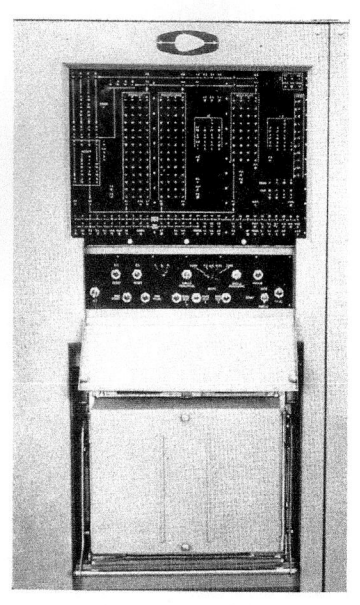

The electronic calculator

—235—

Supplement to KINEMATOGRAPH WEEKLY : OCTOBER 25, 1962

More costs—costs less—continued

the costs of materials used in set construction. The storekeeper need do no more than enter the material code number on the stores requisition to enable the calculator to work out the cost. This process, like all the others, is carried out at high speed with automatic checking of the calculation. At the same time stock control is automatically maintained and the machine informs the storekeeper of any lines that are approaching re-order level.

It would be possible to give illustration after illustration of the tremendous scope of MGM's new equipment and the way in which it not only produces information at a speed which would be absolutely impossible under manual systems but also prepares it more comprehensively and at a lower cost.

This is another example of an operation at MGM achieving greater efficiency and consequently providing both directly and indirectly, benefits for every production made at the studios.

Two of the remarkable machines that have speeded-up the costing system

General view of an accounts department office

Appendix A-7: 'Foremost In Europe'

Supplement to KINEMATOGRAPH WEEKLY: OCTOBER 25, 1962

SOUND ADVANCES AT THE STUDIOS

A. W. WATKINS

THE increased production capacity provided by the new stages has, of course, necessitated a corresponding increase in sound facilities. Nevertheless continuous research carried out by MGM's highly specialised staff has always kept the studio abreast with and often in advance of the latest sound techniques.

In recent months three newly developed pieces of equipment have been added to the existing facilities. The first, built into the Westrex re-recording console, is known as a "graphic equaliser." Designed in Hollywood, plans for this were brought to Britain by MGM and developed here. MGM was the first in Europe to use this facility and now has six, with two more on order from Leevers-Rich.

The purpose of the graphic equaliser is to enable tracks from different sources to be accurately matched in quality.

To be more precise, it serves to insert gain or loss in six separately adjustable and overlapping bands in the audio spectrum. It consists basically of six single-stage amplifiers, each with negative feedback, their centre frequencies being logarithmically spaced at 68c/s, 160c/s, 400c/s, 1kc/s, 2.5kc/s and 6.3kc/s.

Smooth curve

The gain at the centre frequencies is adjustable over a range of ±8db by means of selective feedback control. The characteristics of each circuit extend well over those of the adjacent channels, so that the resultant curve is smooth at any setting of the controls.

These amplifiers feed into a gain-equalising amplifier with pre-set gain control. The equipment is built into a ventilated housing, the controls taking the form of vertical sliders, so that the position of the knobs provides a visual indication of the final curve. This particular equipment was built to close dimensional requirements in order to fit in place of the simple high-low attenuator previously used, but a slightly larger model is being made for more general use.

The second piece of equipment is an extension of noise reduction systems, the development of which, many years ago, did much to reduce background noise due to the film itself. But the old systems could do nothing to eliminate background noise on location or from studios, cameras or lamps. The elimination of such sounds and the consequent production of a truly silent track is the object of the background suppressor developed by MGM's sound department here from information received from MGM Hollywood.

To the magnetic play-off used in re-recording is added a second magnet head, seven perforations ahead of the master head. The Westrex RA1217 recording amplifier has been modified so that its gain is normally reduced by 8 to 17db, though it may be biased back to normal by means of a DC potential. This is provided by rectifying the speech signals picked up by the second magnet head in the play-off.

The result of this arrangement is that background noise is suppressed until a fraction of a second before the commencement of speech signals, when it is allowed to provide a natural background to the speech. The degree of suppression is controllable and frequency discrimination is provided.

A third piece of equipment in use at MGM British Studios is also unique in Europe. Designed to save time in dubbing, it emanates from Mackenzie Electronics, of Los Angeles. It permits of ten different effects being mixed in with the re-recorded sound simply by pressing buttons on the console.

Basically the equipment consists of ten miniature tape re-recorders built in compact units one above the other with their respective amplifiers to the right of them.

Each carries a cassette containing $5\frac{1}{4}$ minutes of tape (at $7\frac{1}{2}$ ips) in the form of an endless loop.

The drive consists of a vertical shaft. By pressing one of the ten buttons, any one of the tapes is set in motion. A duplicate set of buttons enables them to be controlled from the re-recording console. At the end of the recording, a silver paper patch on the tape stops it.

Re-recording

The equipment has proved of immense value in adding a number of effects during re-recording sessions. The output is fed into the recording channel through an amplifier built to MGM's specification by Leevers-Rich, which raises the output to a level of ÷ 20dbm.

Yet another development of the MGM sound department is the use, particularly on location, of lanyard microphones for feature films. Excellent quality is obtained without the need to use a boom.

Joint planning by MGM's sound department and Westrex ensures that the studio will have ample facilities for handling the maximum output of all its stages. Recording may be on single or three-track magne-

Projectors in the new No. 5 preview theatre

Sound at the Studios—continued

tic and transfer facilities will be available for any type of print, single optical or three or four track stereophonic.

In the existing recording room two additional magnetic play-offs are being installed, together with an additional re-recorder and amplifiers. The existing photographic recorders are being converted to four track magnetic.

Photographic recording will thus be concentrated in the transfer suite built on to the present sound department. Here will be a multi-track magnetic reproducer which, by interchange of heads, will be able to reproduce single, three or four track recordings. There will also be single track photo-magnetic reproducers. Recording will be on a single track and a multi-track magnetic recorders.

For transfer to optical there will be a complete 35-mm. photographic recording channel producing the now standard dubilateral or four hump V.A. track.

In dubbing theatre No. 1, the console is to be modified to multi-track re-recording.

Preview theatre

The additional theatre No. 5 (Architect Kenneth Muston, ARIBA) is being constructed adjacent to the existing preview theatre No. 4.

The new theatre has been dimensioned to provide the ideal proportions for sound reproduction—a ratio of 5:3:2. The throw is 37 feet from projection lens to screen. The theatre is 21 feet in width and 17 feet 6 inches high. Maximum width of screen is 19 feet and the angle of rake is only 5 degrees.

The projection suite will be spacious with a depth of 11 feet and will be well ventilated. Below it will be the plant room.

The projectors will be Westar with, of course, Westrex sound. Besides the customary footage-counter, two other features are being provided which will make for great economies in recording time.

Reverse running

First is the system developed in conjunction with MGM engineers of reverse running of the projectors, equipped for double-film running and for the reproduction of married optical prints or unmarried 200 mil optical or magnetic single track films.

When a sequence is required to be repeated, as is continually happening during a dubbing session, the projectors are not unthreaded. The motors are simply reversed and automatically the gate pressure is lifted, enabling the film to run backwards without trouble—and, furthermore, to run at double the projection speed.

It is a remarkable fact that under these conditions the picture is found to be nearly as steady as when running normally.

This innovation must save time and money for producers, directors and especially editors, particularly during the final cutting stage.

Also provided will be remote control of focus. A viewer is able to adjust the focus himself instead of having to instruct the projectionist.

MGM has always been ready for new advances in the interests of efficiency and economy.

This new development will give 60 per cent. cheaper costs with the same high quality of reproduction.

Synchropulse

In 1952 MGM was one of the first major studios to adopt the Leevers-Rich synchropulse tape recorder for location filming and although it was first used primarily for guide track recording, confidence in both the sound quality and the reliability of this equipment soon reached the point where the tape recordings were transcribed into the final product as a standard practice.

In recent years the increasing emphasis on reducing running costs and increasing speed of production has, in many cases, led to the use of this portable equipment on the studio floor for shooting interiors.

Both dialogue and background music were recorded on synchropulse for recent productions. Following experiments by D. P. Field, the standard synchropulse recorder was modified by Leevers-Rich to the requirements of MGM's sound department, to include a four-channel mixer without any increase in the size of the equipment.

A Leevers-Rich transcription channel

The Westrex photographic recording channel

forms part of the present MGM recording department, but the steady increase of work will call for a second transcription channel as part of the planned extension of facilities.

As a result of the excellent results obtained with synchropulse recording, two additional recording channels have been developed jointly by MGM and Leevers-Rich for installation in the new stages. These will also be adaptable for location work, in that they will be capable of operating either from the mains or from batteries.

The channels will include remote control of recording, remote mixing and intercommunication and signal systems.

The power house at the studios

Appendix A-7: 'Foremost In Europe'

THE STUDIO AND ITS FACILITIES

by GRAHAM CLARKE

ELLIOTT SCOTT

MGM's two new stages 8 and 9, each measuring 75 feet by 50 feet, incorporate all the latest technical developments accrued by the company in its long history of picture making.

The new stages at MGM are in addition to the seven that have served the industry so well for so many years. It is interesting to note, for example, that over 130 major productions have been registered at the studios since 1948.

Altogether MGM's nine stages have a total clear shooting area of over 81,000 square feet. When the new large stage is completed, this will rise to 93,000 square feet.

Stages 1 and 2 have sliding, sound-proof, intercommunicating doors opening to 32 feet by 22 feet high. Stage 3 has 18,820 square feet of clear shooting area with a tank under floor level 80 feet by 32 feet by 11 feet deep, which has armoured-glass windows for underwater filming.

Stages 4 and 5, 6 and 7 also have intercommunicating doors. Stages 8 and 9 are adjacent. Stage 6 is fitted with two tanks under the floor, one 37 feet by 20 feet by 11 feet deep, the other 17 feet by 9 feet by 8 feet deep. Stage 7 is dual purpose—a shooting stage and music recording stage. It is fitted with projection, footage indicator and echo and vocal chambers.

Rare feature

Stages 1, 2, 3, 4 and 5 are 45 feet high to the rails that carry the lighting cradles. Above these are cat-walks and switchboards with 15 feet headroom. Stages 6 and 7 are 34 feet high to the rails, the new stages proportionately less. All stages have controlled temperature, ventilation and humidity—a rare feature in European studios.

For set lighting, DC current at 115/230 volts is supplied. Up to 50,000A can be supplied continuously into any or all of the stages; and, should the mains fail, a fixed diesel generator plant can be brought into use within a few minutes. This facility is unique in Europe.

A variable voltage supply is also available for remote controlled mass dimming for sunrise, sunset and theatre auditorium effects.

Compressed air, water and gas are permanently available on all stages.

There are 12 executive office suites for producers and directors, each with ample adjacent office space to accommodate staff for six productions concurrently.

Director of MGM's art department is Elliott Scott, whose work has been universally recognised. Seven suites of offices are available, each equipped for art directors, draughtsmen, set dressers and ancillary staff. The department has facilities for die-line printing and for photographic and document copying. Scott's staff has an intimate knowledge of the studio stock of wood and plaster set pieces, which is probably the most extensive in Europe. Full use of this can save thousands of pounds on an average production.

It is claimed that the make-up and hair-dressing departments are the most modern in Europe. Each has seven private cubicles for the use of stars, as well as crowd artists' dressing-rooms.

The hairdressing department, supervised by Joan Johnstone, includes a shampoo room and wig room. There are extensive stocks of make-up, wigs and hair pieces.

MGM is justly proud of its special effects department, headed by double Academy award winner Tom Howard, who is one of the small select band of British technicians who can truly be called world famous.

In addition to the new laboratory services described elsewhere in this issue the department has three main sections—back projection, photographic effects and matte painting and general effects.

Back projection is operated with blimp-

This set is typical of the fine work done in the studios

less projectors fitted with Mole-Richardson super high intensity arc lamps. The department maintains two complete equipments that can be used in interlock for dual screen projection, filling screens from a few feet for colour up to 30 feet for black and white.

The photographic effects and matte painting departments combine multiple exposure photography in conjunction with miniatures. Two fully-motorised, high-speed camera equipments running up to eight times normal speed are maintained for use with miniatures involving fire, water and smoke. Travelling matte, using beam-splitting cameras, is, of course, a speciality and some effects achieved are unique to MGM.

Howard's invention "Automotion" is a special effect that Hollywood was very pleased to learn about.

Lettering artists are permanently employed for any form of title style that may be called for.

The general effects department maintains a complete range of equipment to cover physical effects of wind, rain, fog, snow, smoke, controlled fire, explosions and all kinds of water effects. Gas-operated machine guns and other automatic weapons fitted for assimulated firing are also maintained as well as throwing devices, treadmills, wind machines and two life-like mechanical horses that are exclusive in Europe to MGM studios.

The sound department, described elsewhere, is also world-famous. A. W. Watkins has twice been nominated for Academy awards.

Experience

Many years of experience is represented by the staff of the electrical department. Frank Walter, who is in charge, has had over 30 years in the film industry.

Equipment in the camera department, run by Les Smart, includes standard and NC Mitchells, a split-beam camera, Newman Sinclair and Eymos, tracking dollies, crab dollies, Vinten Velocilator cranes, Moy heads, Nodal heads and rolling legs.

Camera maintenance department, under George Merritt, claims that no camera breakdown has ever occurred during a production, either in the studios or on location for any MGM production.

Twenty-two cutting rooms are available in the studios and more are under construction. Staff editors are Frank Clarke, who is in charge, Ernest Walters and sound editor Bob Carrick. All three have international reputations that are second to none. There is a projector Moviola for editing and matching on stage.

The library, which is, of course, being added to constantly, includes over 5,000 stock shots, 1,800 BP plates and 8,500 sound effects.

Joe Pearce is in charge of the stills department. The stills laboratory can process daily 60 (10 by 8 in.) or 100 (5 by 4 in.) Ektachrome transparencies, almost unlimited quantities of black and white negatives and upwards of 600 black and white 10 by 8 in. prints. In emergencies, six glossy prints can be produced within half an hour of receiving the exposed film. The stills studio and portrait gallery is one of the finest of its kind in the world.

The studio has an extensive wardrobe department under Maude Churchill. There are 30 artists' dressing rooms, many with private baths or showers and large rooms for male and female crowd artists. The dressing rooms are connected to the stages by covered way.

The MGM lot is the largest of its kind in Europe. It covers 114 acres and has, at one time or another, accommodated the "Ivanhoe" castle and the "Inn of the Sixth Happiness" Chinese village. An Eastern village and a Mediterranean village complete with square are part of the existing standing sets and are available to producers. Both are easily adaptable to varying designs.

The studio has an estate and garden staff under Tom Dawson for landscape and set dressing. Maintained under 5,000 square feet of glass, a large and varied collection of tropical and sub-tropical plants is always available for productions.

The construction department, chief of which is Cyril Graysmark, one of the most experienced and respected technicians in the industry, has seven branches—carpenters, scenic, model and pattern shop, plasters and clay-modellers' shop, drapery, rigging and scene dock. Sets are always prefabricated in the various shops wherever possible in order to save valuable stage space.

The transport department, in the charge of Fred Beadle, includes half-ton trucks, Landrover, open trucks, tipping trucks, pantechnicons of two- and five-ton capacity, a Rolls-Royce tracking car and a fleet of cars that can be used both for personnel transport and in production.

An extremely large stock is carried by the property department, of which Jack Ramsay is the head. He and buyer Bill Isaacs have never yet failed to find the most difficult properties, not only on time, but at the most reasonable cost.

An extremely large stock is carried by the property department

The studio always has tropical plants available

Appendix A-7: 'Foremost In Europe'

Supplement to KINEMATOGRAPH WEEKLY : OCTOBER 25, 1962

ASK ANYONE!

says GEORGE CATT

WE who have been associated with MGM since the company started to produce feature films in England are naturally proud of the traditions of quality and presentation which we have helped to establish.

All of us who, since World War II, have played a part in designing and organising our studios at Elstree are supremely confident that we have the best studio in the world to produce that quality at the lowest cost, for we have taken care that it is organised to ensure the smoothest flow of information and the most efficient progression of all work processes.

We realise, however, that it might not be possible for producers who have not worked here to share our absolute confidence.

If you need any assurance as to the quality of service provided, we say:—

Ask those producers who have worked here

To those who are concerned in our smooth organisation, the efficiency of the heads of departments, the helpfulness of the operating office which is devoted exclusively to helping all productions alike, the friendly assistance of the telephone operators, the knowledge of the transport department, and the willingness of all the service and maintenance personnel we say:—

Ask any production manager who has worked here

To those who need to be assured of our exceptionally economical building costs and unvarying high finish of the sets on all productions using the stages or of the efficiency and adaptability of the construction department (which is so well organised and controlled that the minimum of supervisory labour is employed and there is not the slightest necessity for any producer to add to his costs by employing his own construction manager) *or* that the highly developed metal shop and the extensive

continued on page 29

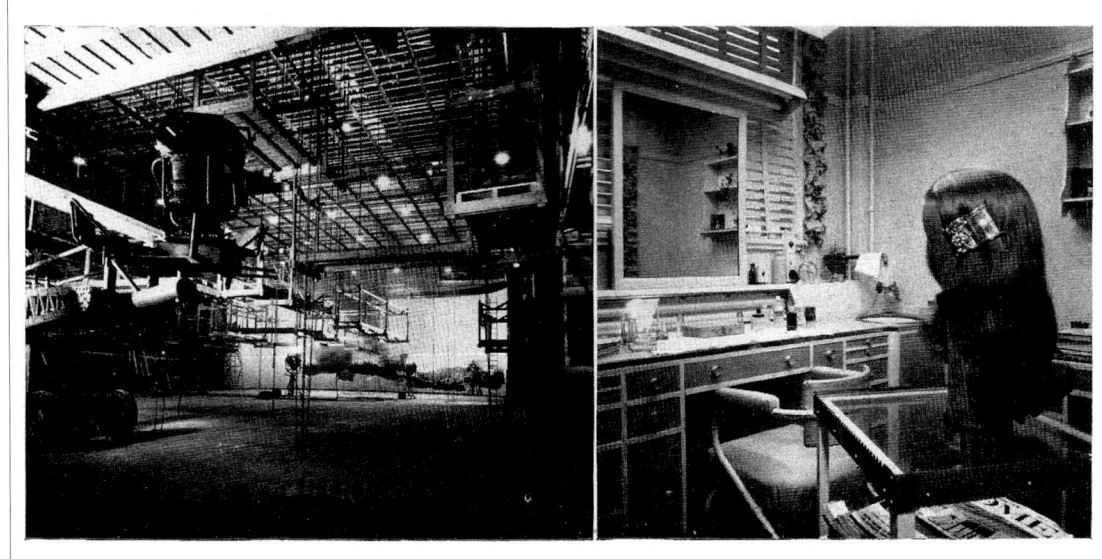

A view of Stage 3

In the hairdressing department

Supplement to KINEMATOGRAPH WEEKLY : OCTOBER 25, 1962

Ask anyone
—continued

plant nursery—both with film-trained personnel — are unique features which help to give that low cost and exceptional finish we say:—

Ask any art director who has worked here

For those who have any qualms (and it is indeed difficult for us to imagine such a person on the British film production scene) regarding the quality of our camera equipment, the skill of the camera maintenance department or of the organisation and efficiency of the floor electricians we can only say:—

Ask any cameraman who has worked here

You will have gathered that we believe that to obtain a true assessment of a studio as a film-making machine it is wise to consult the leading technicians. We hope you will take our advice for we know that:—

The best technicians prefer to work at MGM

I can say simply and sincerely that our studios are organised to make films. We provide the complete service necessary to ensure that all producers can make their films economically, efficiently and with ease.

We should be pleased and proud at any time to show the studio to anyone who is interested, so do not hesitate to call us.

We should like to show you what you are missing.

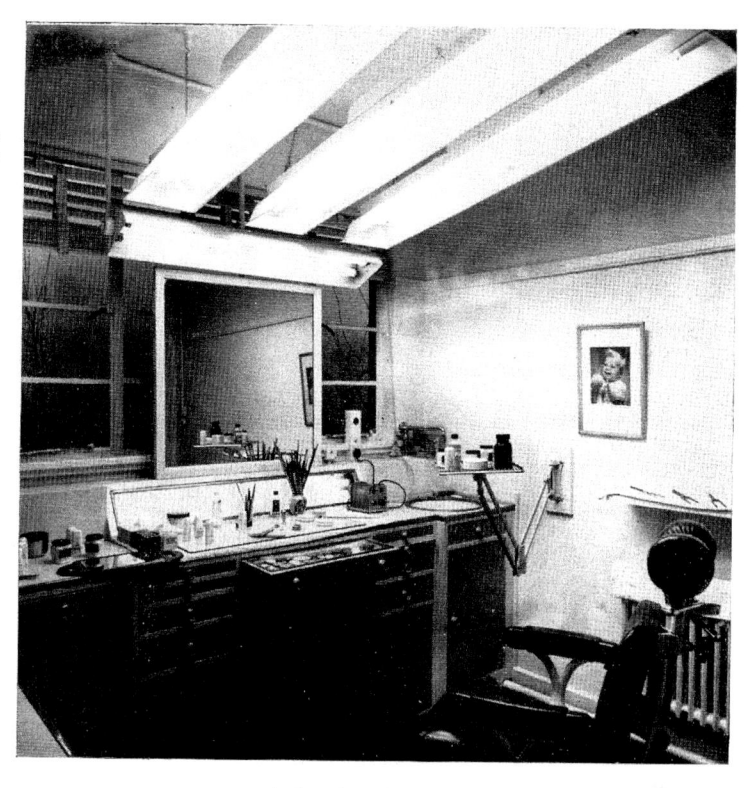

In the make-up department

In the carpenters' shop

Part of the engineering shop

Appendix A-7: 'Foremost In Europe'

30

Supplement to KINEMATOGRAPH WEEKLY : OCTOBER 25, 1962

ON THE LOT AT MGM

Standing sets include an Eastern Village (above) and (below) a Mediterranean Village and a complete jet air liner

— 243 —

Supplement to KINEMATOGRAPH WEEKLY
October 25, 1962

THE FIRST STUDIO IN EUROPE WITH FEATURE FILMS IN

CINEMASCOPE
STEREOPHONIC SOUND
TECHNIRAMA
TODD-AO
EASTMAN COLOR

THE FIRST STUDIO IN EUROPE TO USE

A & B ROLLPRINTING IN EASTMAN COLOR
SYNCHRO PULSE RECORDING
TWENTY TRACK DUBBING
AUTOMOTION
ELECTRONIC ACCOUNTING MACHINES
A BACKGROUND SUPPRESSOR UNIT
GRAPHIC EQUALISERS

THE FIRST IN EUROPE

MGM BRITISH STUDIOS

TELEPHONE: ELSTREE 2000   BOREHAM WOOD, HERTS., ENGLAND

CABLES: METROBRIT, BOREHAM WOOD, HERTS.

Appendix A-7: 'Foremost In Europe'

M.G.M. STARS FLY

PAN AMERICAN

WORLD'S MOST EXPERIENCED AIRLINE

FIRST ON THE ATLANTIC • FIRST ON THE PACIFIC • FIRST IN LATIN AMERICA • FIRST ROUND THE WORLD

Appendix A-8
The Backlot

This appendix shows the backlot when it was just farm fields in the 1940's.

The Thrift Farm sheep grazing on the front fields at MGM

The mound

MGM British Studios

A view from the Ivanhoe Castle to Thrift Farm

A view from the backlot to the studios

Towards Borehamwood

Appendix A-8: The Backlot

Thrift Farm and its famous sheep

APPENDIX A-9
The Clock Tower

The iconic clock tower stood for years after MGM British had disappeared.

Construction begins. The clock tower is erected in 1936.

The view in the 1940s.

18th July, 1946

1946

— 251 —

MGM British Studios

6th April, 1946

6th July, 1946

Appendix A-9: The Clock Tower

Awaiting demolition

Demolition underway

The end is near (Photo courtesy of Newsquest and the Borehamwood Times)

Appendix A-10
The Ivanhoe Castle

From the architect's models in 1950 to the finished construction in the summer of 1951, this appendix documents the creation of the famous 'Ivanhoe Castle'.

Detail of turret and steps

The architect's model of Torquilstone Castle 22nd May, 1950

MGM British Studios

Appendix A-10: The Ivanhoe Castle

MGM British Studios

Appendix A-11
Final Visits

These photos record visits to MGM after it closed in 1970. The first six photos are courtesy of Wilf Watters; the rest were taken by the Author.

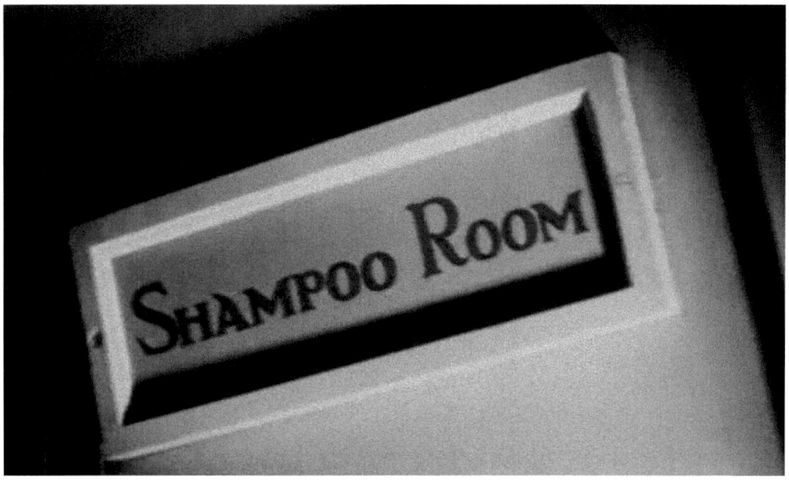
SHAMPOO ROOM

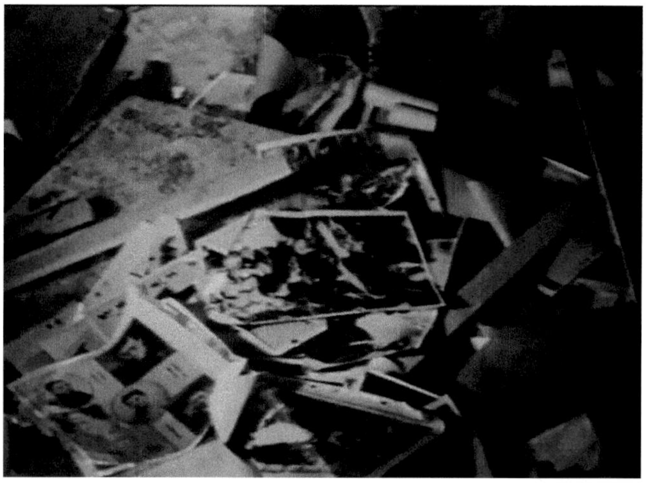

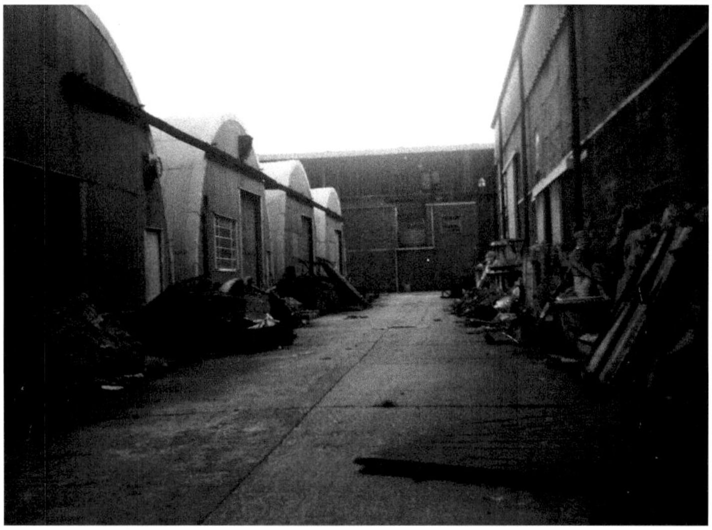

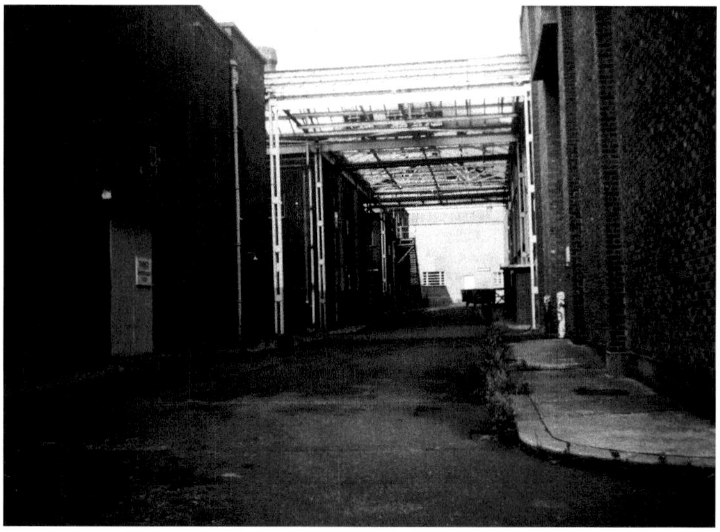

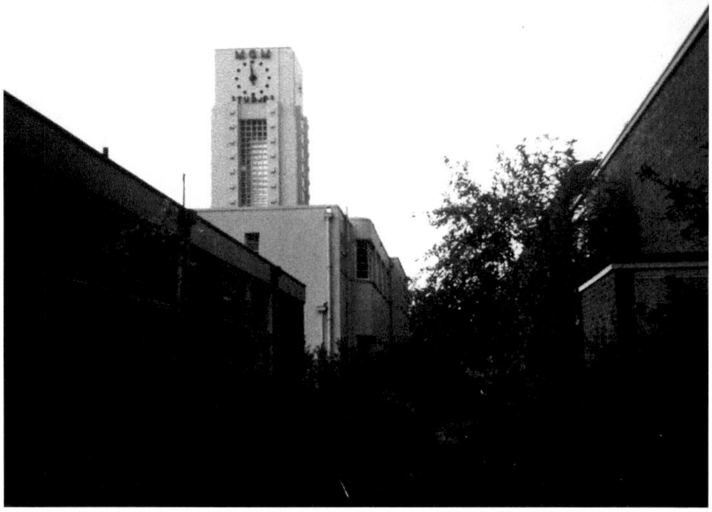

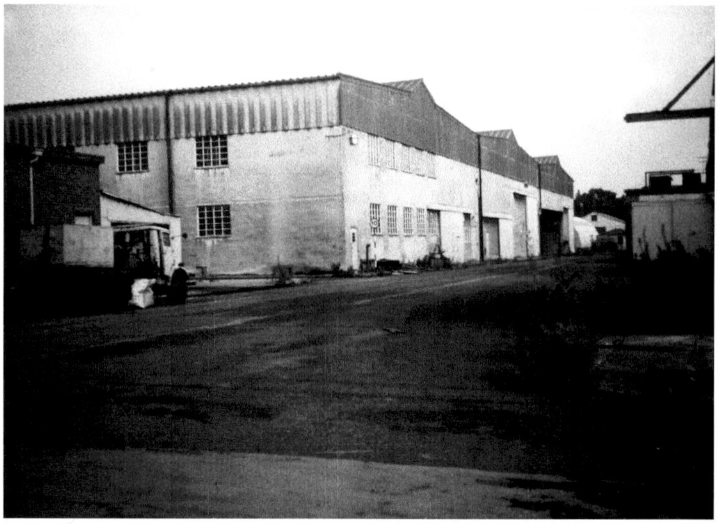

Appendix A-11: Final Visits

MGM British Studios

APPENDIX A-12
Demolition

In 1973 the studio was being used by an 'On The Buses' movie to film the demolition of a building. This provided an opportunity for the Author to record the final days of the studios.

*Notice the new Christian Salvesen Depot
being erected in the background*

APPENDIX A-13
The Backlot Fades Away

The sets on the backlot lingered on for three years after the studio buildings were demolished. These photos are courtesy of Roger Garrod and Wilf Watters.

MGM British Studios

Appendix A-13: The Backlot Fades Away

MGM British Studios

Appendix A-13: The Backlot Fades Away

Appendix A-14
The Site Today

Over the past few years members of the Friends of MGM group have visited the site. The first four photos below were from the 2012 expedition and the rest from the most recent visit in 2016.

More recently, in the Autumn of 2019 the Author was permitted to visit the site once again, as it starts its latest transformation.

Mike Grant provided the photos on this page; Bob Redman provided the rest of the photos.

September 2012 and some of the Friends gather to get their bearings on an overgrown roadway

David Lally points out an item of interest to the Author and Kieran McAleer

Aerial photos help to compare the site when it was home to MGM British Studios with the present site

Journey's end! David Lally, Mick Brady, the Author and Smudge fight off the effects of dehydration

— 271 —

2016, and houses now stand on the backlot

By the gate to the perimeter road

Rick Davy with the
Author and David Lally

Appendix A-14: The Site Today

By the Autumn of 2019, long-term site residents Sainsbury had moved from their Distribution Depot.

Once more the Author was back to witness the latest chapter in the history of the site while the last of the warehouses are being demolished and the site cleared.

The Gate House from York Way

Loading bays and the administration building

Demolition workers enter one of the buildings

Scrap to be recycled, with the Power House in the background

Loading up

Already cleared

Inside the last warehouse is still standing...

But not for much longer, as the 'burner' gets to work with his acetylene torch

The Author says farewell where Sound Stage A once stood

Demolition worker Dave shows the Author one of the cutting heads used to tear apart the buildings

Appendix A-14: The Site Today

From the other side of Elstree Way, we can see buildings on the MGM site, some of which will stay and some which are proposed to be replaced.

The view up Studio Way towards the backlot, with new housing to the left and the EUTC to the right

The EUTC (Elstree University Technical College) which trains tomorrow's film and TV stars, in front and behind the camera

Next door to the EUTC are warehouses which may be replaced by…..

…. Borehamwood's second Lidl, subject to planning approval

New branch of supermarket proposed to be built in town

Lidl wants to build a second store off Elstree Way

The Power House for the Sainsbury Depot can be glimpsed through trees. Between them and Elstree Way stands the remains of the base of the fence which once ran across the front of MGM British Studios

An artist's impression of Panattoni Park which has been planned to occupy the site of buildings currently being demolished

And so the transformation of the MGM British site continues. The Lidl retail outlet plans to occupy 1.46 hectares, while Panattoni Park will occupy 369,000 square feet. Together they will take just over 9 acres, equivalent to about 8 % of the total 115 acres of the original MGM British site.

Just how large is 115 acres? About 64 times the size of the Wembley Stadium pitch!

Appendix B

Remembering MGM British Studios

1: Local Road Names 279
2: The Film & TV Heritage Trail 283
3: The Studio Way Woodland Trail 285
4: The Elstree Project.. 289

Appendix B-1
Local Road Names

Since the 1970s the Author has been invited to suggest to the local planning authority names for roads, streets, closes and courts being built on or near film studio sites in Boreham Wood. Happily they have all been accepted.

The latest at the time of writing are for a new development next to the railway station where we have honoured Lee Marvin, Lord Lew Grade, Sid James and Bill Owen.

At the site of the old Gate Studios we named two Courts after stars who had worked at MGM and Elstree Studios, Michael Wilding (1912-1979) and Stewart Granger (1913-1993). Odette Court is named after the film made at the Gate Studios, while Whitehall Close recalls the original name of the studio.

On what had been the MGM backlot, we again chose film-themed names. Some were named after other film studios: Pinewood, Shepperton, Bray, Ealing, Denham, Cygnet, Gate and Danzigers. Lion Court is a nod to 'Leo the Lion', who remains the logo of MGM.

The majority, however, were named after film stars who had worked at one or more of the studios in Boreham Wood. The three exceptions were film producers who had links with MGM and they were Herbert Wilcox (1890-1977) who shot 'Spring In Park Lane' and 'Maytime In Mayfair' at the studio, Sir Michael Balcon (1896-1977) who moved Ealing productions to the studio in the mid 1950s and Sir Alexander Korda (1893-1956) who bought the studio for MGM. We have also acknowledged Sir Alfred Hitchcock (1899-1980) who directed 'Under Capricorn' at the studio.

The roll call of stars we have honoured who worked at MGM is lengthy:

Robert Taylor (1911-1969)	Richard Todd (1919-2009)
Sir John Mills (1908-2005)	Greer Garson (1904-1996)
William Holden (1918-1981)	Ava Gardner (1922-1990)
Spencer Tracy (1900-1967)	Ingrid Bergman (1915-1982)
Gary Cooper (1901-1961)	Gene Kelly (1912-1996)
John Gregson (1919-1975)	Grace Kelly (1928-1982)
Dame Margaret Rutherford (1892-1972)	Peter Sellers (1925-1980)
James Mason (1909-1984)	

and Dame Anna Neagle (1904-1986) who is unique in the list as she was also a local resident.

Those honoured who did not work at MGM but did work elsewhere in the town were:

Ivor Novello (1893-1951) the famous music composer and actor after whom the famous music award is named.
Vivien Leigh (1913-1967) star of 'Gone With The Wind'
veteran star Charles Laughton (1899-1962)
character actor Leslie Banks (1890-1952)
comedian Tony Hancock (1924-1968)
comedy actress Joyce Grenfell (1910-1979)
stage and screen pre-war idol Jack Buchanan (1891-1957)
actress Dame Celia Johnson (1908-1982)
American singer and actor Paul Robeson (1898-1976)
actress Merle Oberon (1911-1979)
actress Margaret Lockwood (1916-1990)

What a roll call of Hollywood and British screen greats and fitting legacy to the memory of Metro Goldwyn Mayer's British Studio.

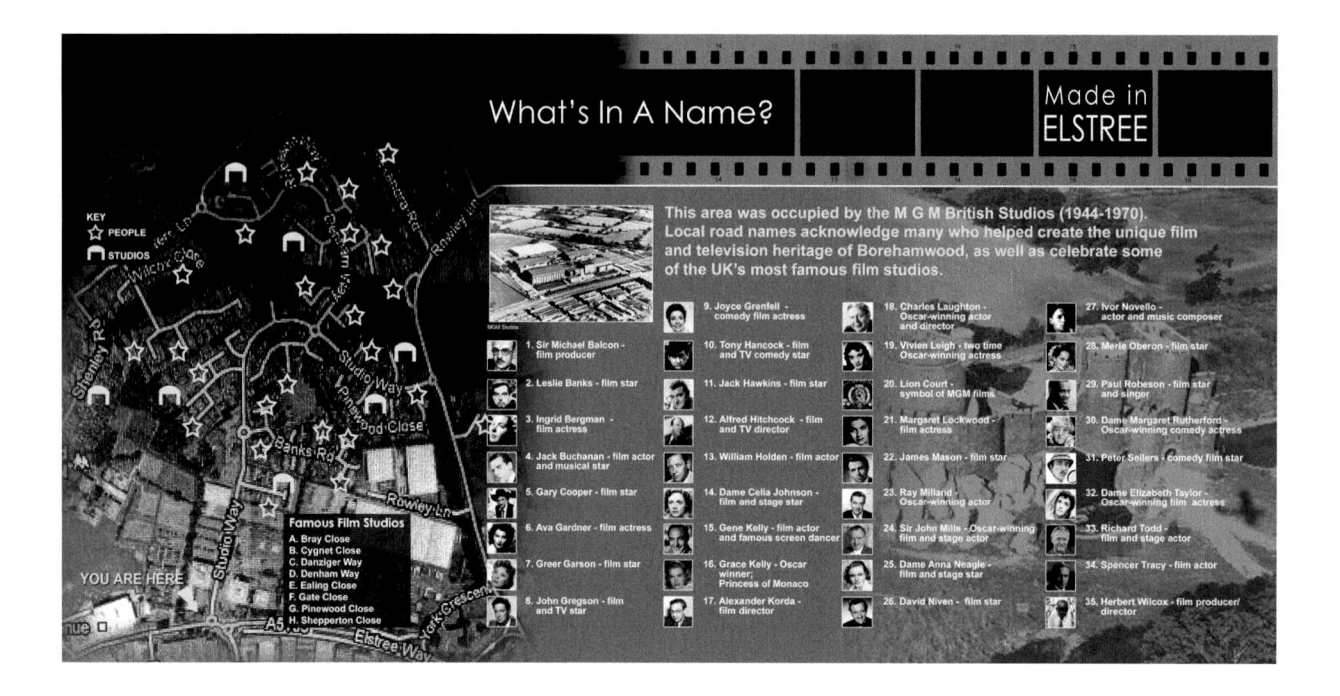

Appendix B-1: Local Road Names

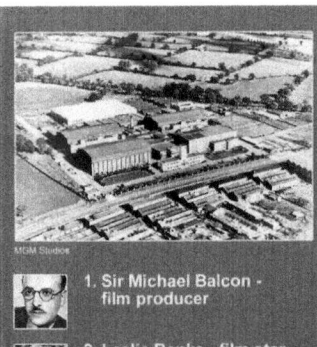

This area was occupied by the M G M British Studios (1944-1970).

Local road names acknowledge many who helped create the unique film and television heritage of Borehamwood, as well as celebrate some of the UK's most famous film studios.

1. Sir Michael Balcon - film producer
2. Leslie Banks - film star
3. Ingrid Bergman - Oscar-winning film star
4. Jack Buchanan - film and musical star
5. Gary Cooper - Oscar-winning film star
6. Ava Gardner - film star
7. Greer Garson - Oscar-winning film star
8. John Gregson - film and TV star
9. Joyce Grenfell - comedy film star
10. Tony Hancock - film and TV comedy star
11. Jack Hawkins - film star
12. Alfred Hitchcock - film and TV director
13. William Holden - Oscar-winning film star
14. Dame Celia Johnson - film and stage star
15. Gene Kelly - film star and famous screen dancer
16. Grace Kelly - Oscar-winning film star and Princess of Monaco
17. Alexander Korda - film director
18. Charles Laughton - Oscar-winning film star and director
19. Vivien Leigh - Oscar-winning film star
20. Lion Court - symbol of MGM films
21. Margaret Lockwood - film star
22. James Mason - film star
23. Ray Milland - Oscar-winning film star
24. Sir John Mills - Oscar-winning film and stage star
25. Dame Anna Neagle - film and stage star
26. David Niven - Oscar-winning film star
27. Ivor Novello - actor and music composer
28. Merle Oberon - film star
29. Paul Robeson - film star and singer
30. Dame Margaret Rutherford - Oscar-winning comedy film star
31. Peter Sellers - comedy film star
32. Robert Taylor - film star
33. Richard Todd - film and stage star
34. Spencer Tracy - Oscar-winning film star
35. Herbert Wilcox - film producer/director

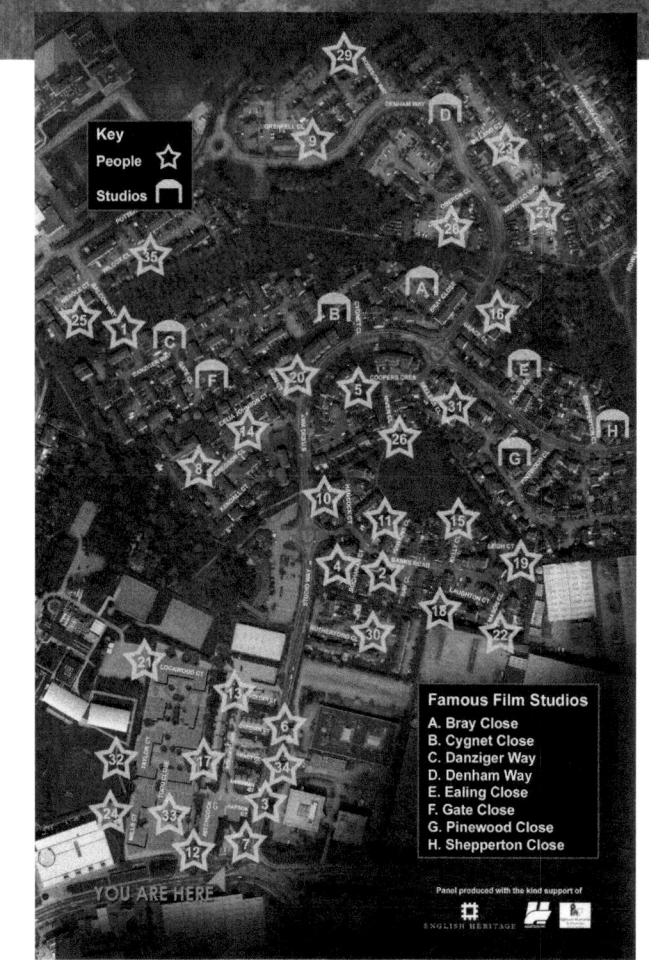

Key
People ☆
Studios ⌂

Famous Film Studios
A. Bray Close
B. Cygnet Close
C. Danziger Way
D. Denham Way
E. Ealing Close
F. Gate Close
G. Pinewood Close
H. Shepperton Close

– 281 –

Appendix B-2
The Film & TV Heritage Trail

Since 2008 the 'First Impressions' initiative has used film and TV images in public spaces in Elstree and Boreham Wood to increase awareness of and pride in our unique heritage and to create a more welcoming environment.

A key element of that programme has been the creation of a Film & TV Heritage Trail celebrating the contributions of men and women who have worked at our studios during the past 100 years.

We have put in place heritage panels along the high street, Shenley Road, from the railway station up to Elstree Studios and the BBC Elstree Centre, and beyond, as far as the site of MGM British Studios on Elstree Way.

Some of these panels incorporate the eighteen plaques awarded in 1996 to the town of Elstree and Boreham Wood by the British Film Institute to mark the centenary of film in the UK. One of these plaques honoured MGM British and was unveiled by famed film-makers Freddy Francis, a two-time Oscar winner, and Freddy Young, a three-time Oscar winner.

Photo by kind permission of 'Captured Moments'

After years of exposure to the elements, the original 18 plaques were not aging well, and so by May 2011 each plaque had been removed, cleaned and mounted on an explanatory panel with additional text and images. The explanatory panels have been designed by a professional designer and manufactured to a high standard.

There are now over 25 panels on display and each year we add more. Following a recent public poll, the latest heritage panel was installed to honour the many contributions of Harrison Ford to our local heritage. For further details of the heritage trail please visit our website at: www.ElstreeScreenHeritage.org

The MGM British Studios is commemorated with its own heritage panel, standing on Elstree Way. Beside it is the panel described in the previous section, showing the local road names chosen to celebrate our film heritage.

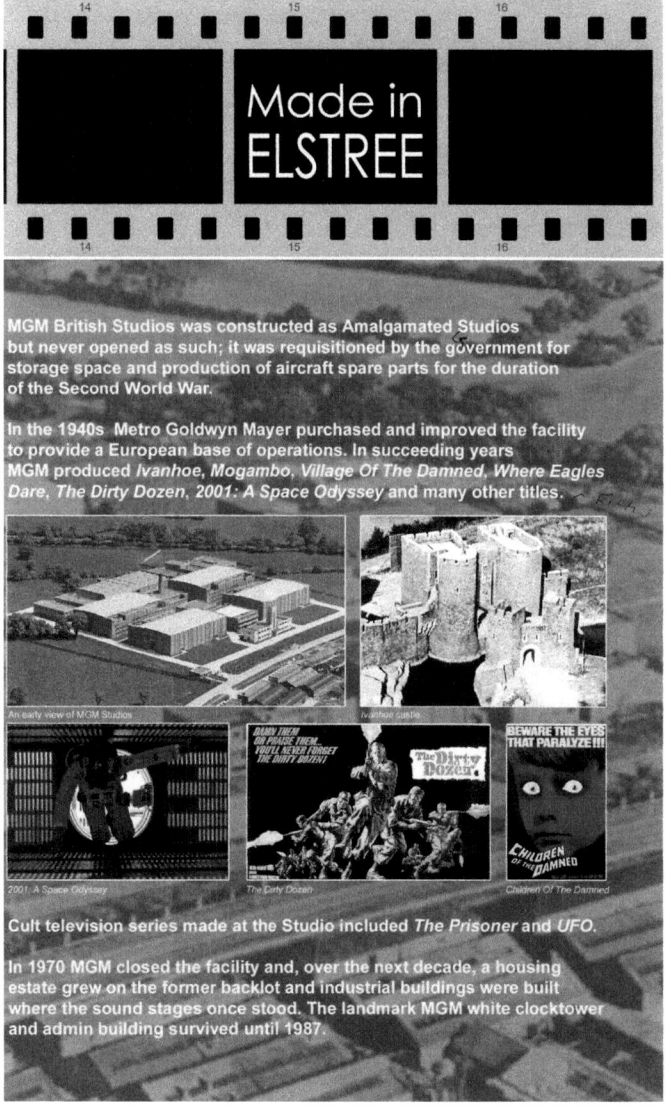

Appendix B-3

The Studio Way Woodland Trail

Until MGM British Studios closed in 1970, much of its 115 acre site was a backlot, where films could be shot without film crews needing to go 'on location'. Over more than 25 years this space was home to a castle (for 'Ivanhoe' and many other films), a Chinese village (for 'Inn of the Sixth Happiness'), a French chateau (for 'The Dirty Dozen') and on and on. TV Classics 'Danger Man' and 'The Prisoner' also regularly used the backlot.

After MGM closed, much of the backlot was redeveloped for housing but a 14 acre space was retained for the benefit of local residents. Called 'Studio Way Woodland and Potterswood Park', this open area has been popular for years.

In 2017 the Countryside Management Service of Hertfordshire County Council, in association with Hertsmere Borough Council, decided to reinvigorate the park. It also wanted to start to tell the story of the backlot, and so CMS approached Elstree Screen Heritage for help in designing interpretation panels to tell this story.

Elstree Screen Heritage soon came up with information and photos which were then displayed on five heritage panels at intervals along the trail which runs through the park.

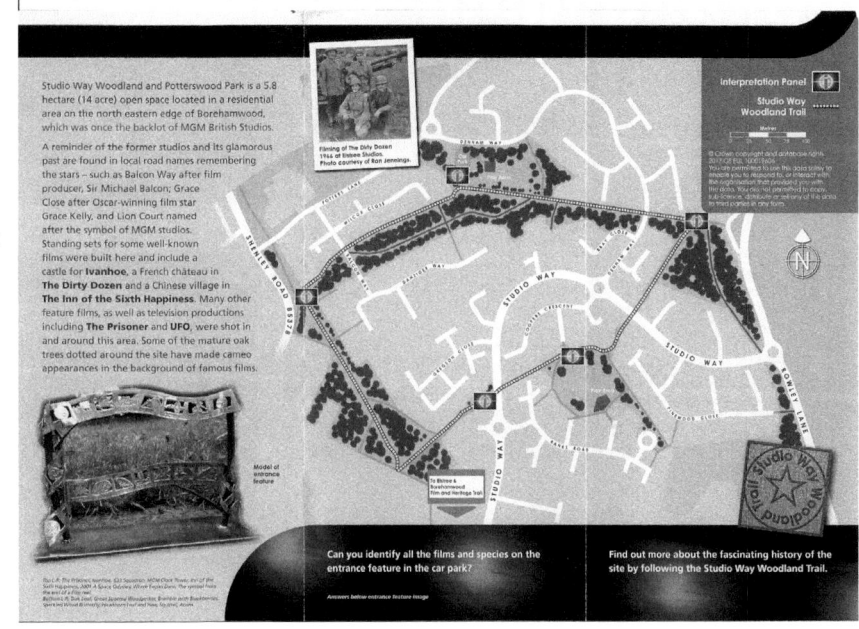

The park is open to all, so why not visit and discover for yourself the amazing history of the backlot of MGM British Studios. Parking is free, and children and dogs are very welcome!

For details please visit:

www.hertsmere.gov.uk/Parks-and-Leisure/Parks--Open-Spaces/Find-a-park-in-Hertsmere/Parks-in-Borehamwood.aspx

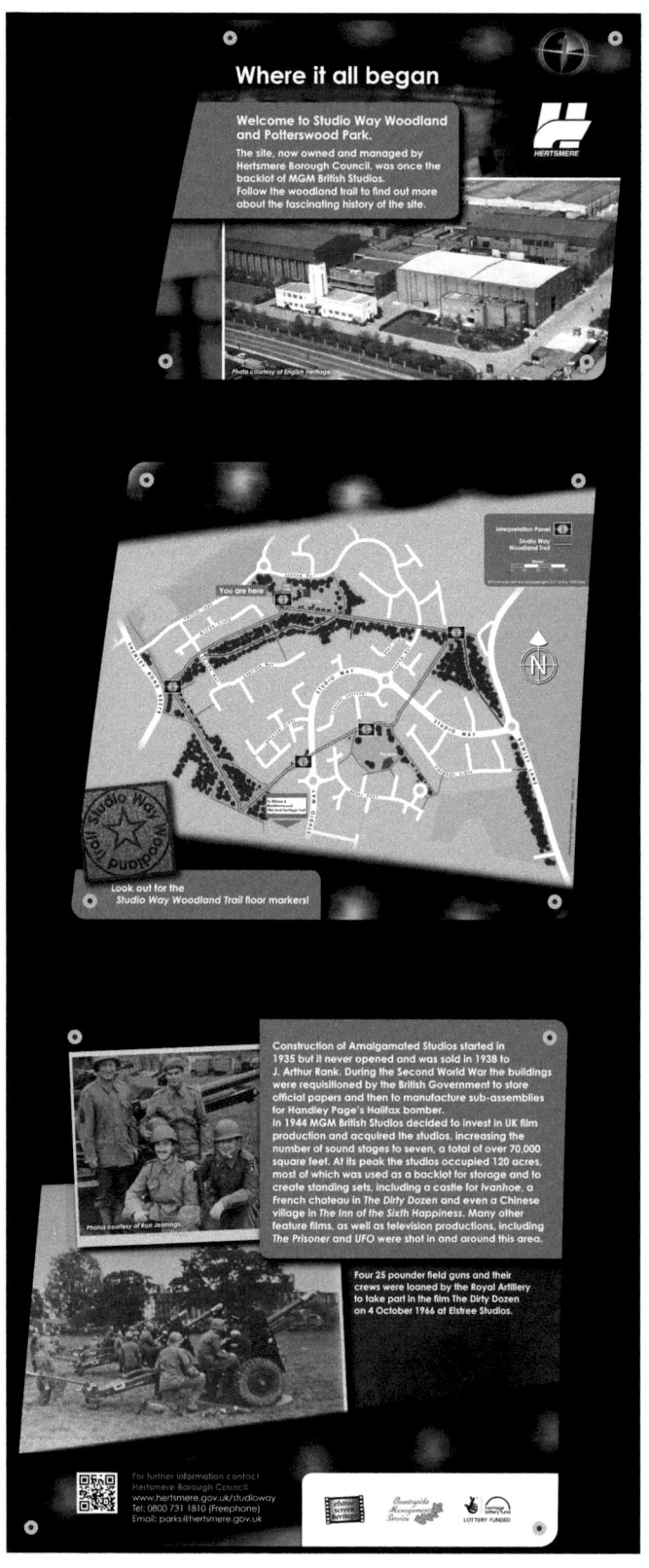

MGM British Studios

Appendix B-3: The Studio Way Woodland Trail

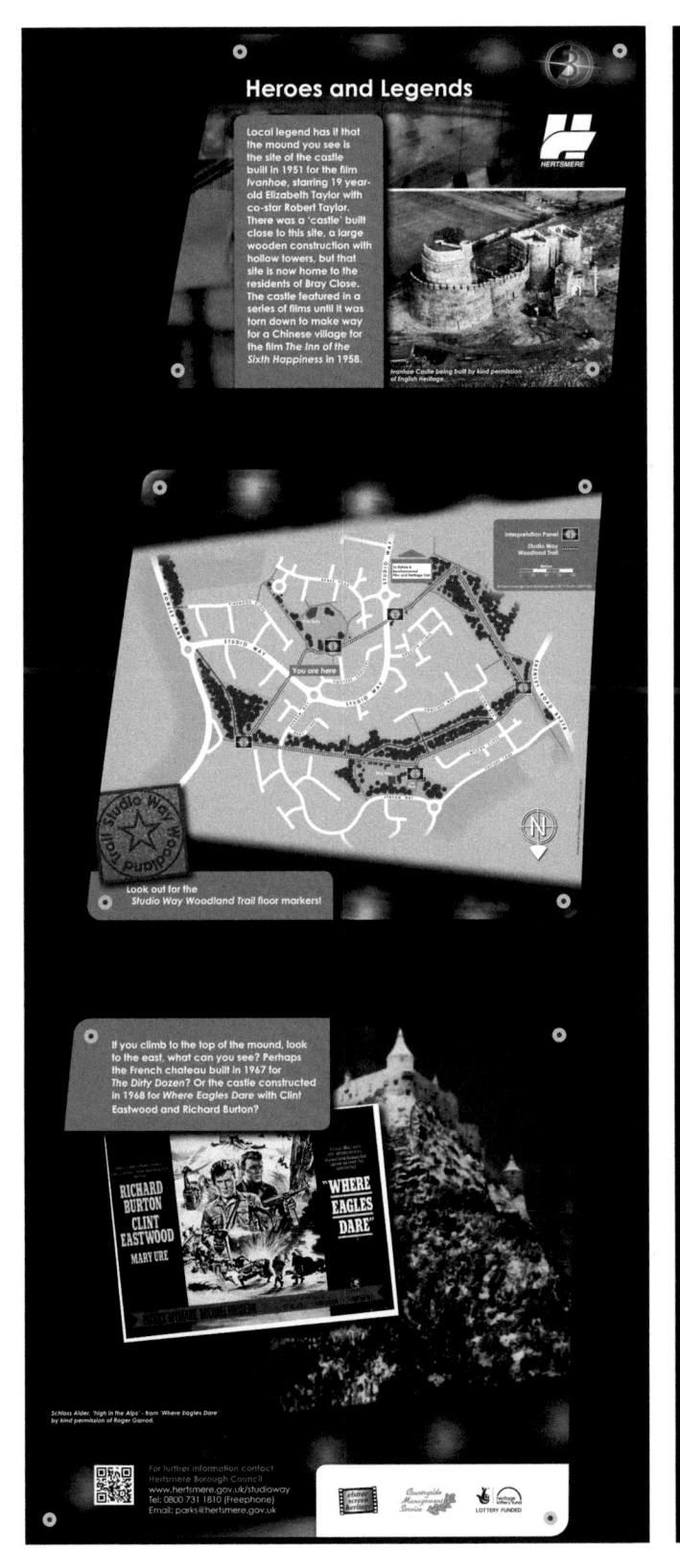

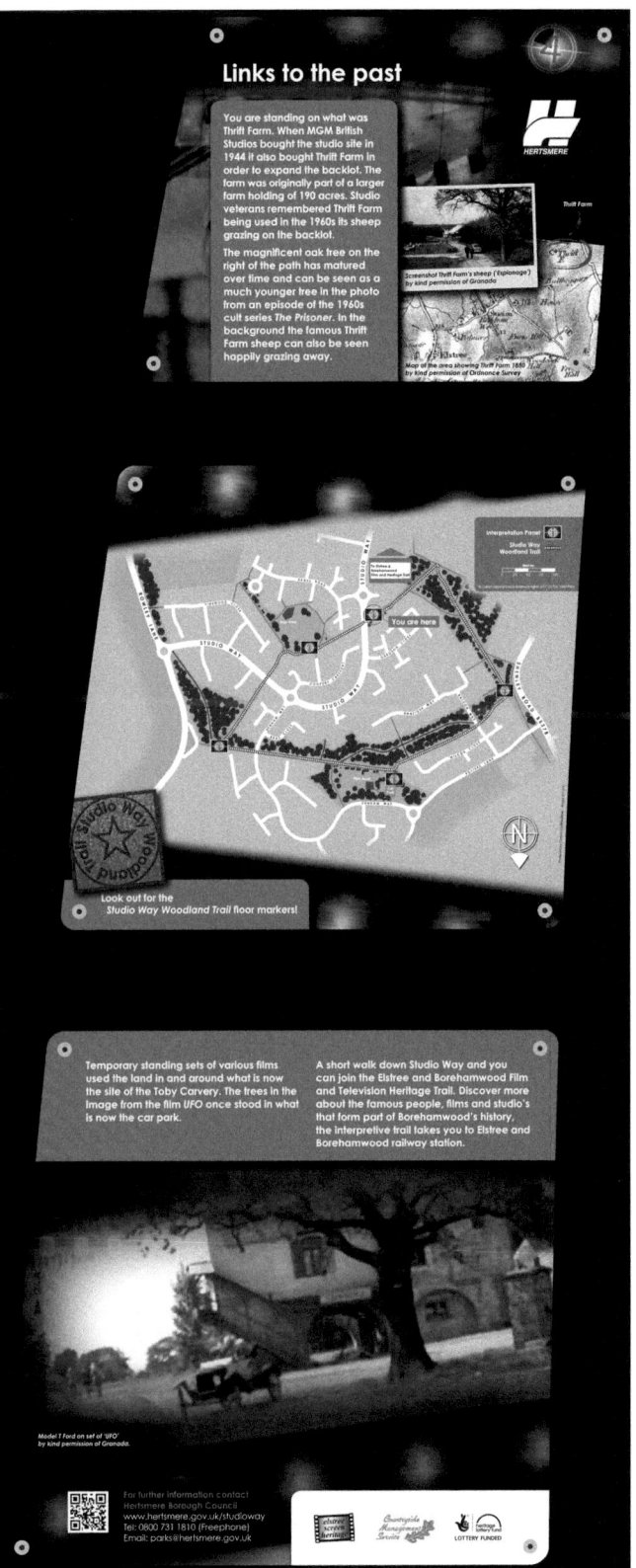

— 287 —

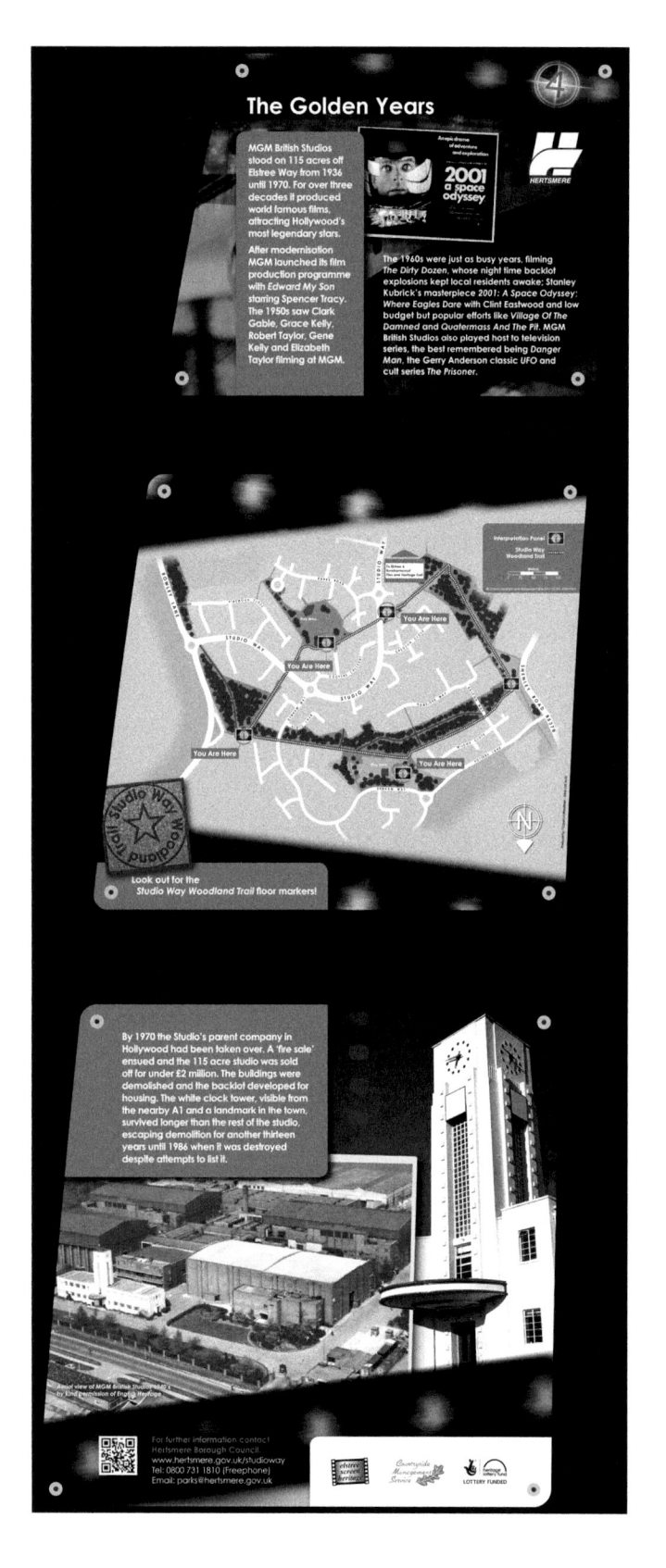

MGM British Studios

The Golden Years

MGM British Studios stood on 115 acres off Elstree Way from 1936 until 1970. For over three decades it produced world famous films, attracting Hollywood's most legendary stars.

After modernisation MGM launched its film production programme with *Edward My Son* starring Spencer Tracy. The 1950s saw Clark Gable, Grace Kelly, Robert Taylor, Gene Kelly and Elizabeth Taylor filming at MGM.

The 1960s were just as busy years, filming *The Dirty Dozen*, whose night time backlot explosions kept local residents awake; Stanley Kubrick's masterpiece *2001: A Space Odyssey*; *Where Eagles Dare* with Clint Eastwood and low budget but popular efforts like *Village Of The Damned* and *Quatermass And The Pit*. MGM British Studios also played host to television series, the best remembered being *Danger Man*, the Gerry Anderson classic *UFO* and cult series *The Prisoner*.

Look out for the *Studio Way Woodland Trail* floor markers!

By 1970 the Studio's parent company in Hollywood had been taken over. A 'fire sale' ensued and the 115 acre studio was sold off for under £2 million. The buildings were demolished and the backlot developed for housing. The white clock tower, visible from the nearby A1 and a landmark in the town, survived longer than the rest of the studio, escaping demolition for another thirteen years until 1986 when it was destroyed despite attempts to list it.

For further information contact Hertsmere Borough Council.
www.hertsmere.gov.uk/studioway
Tel: 0800 731 1810 (Freephone)
Email: parks@hertsmere.gov.uk

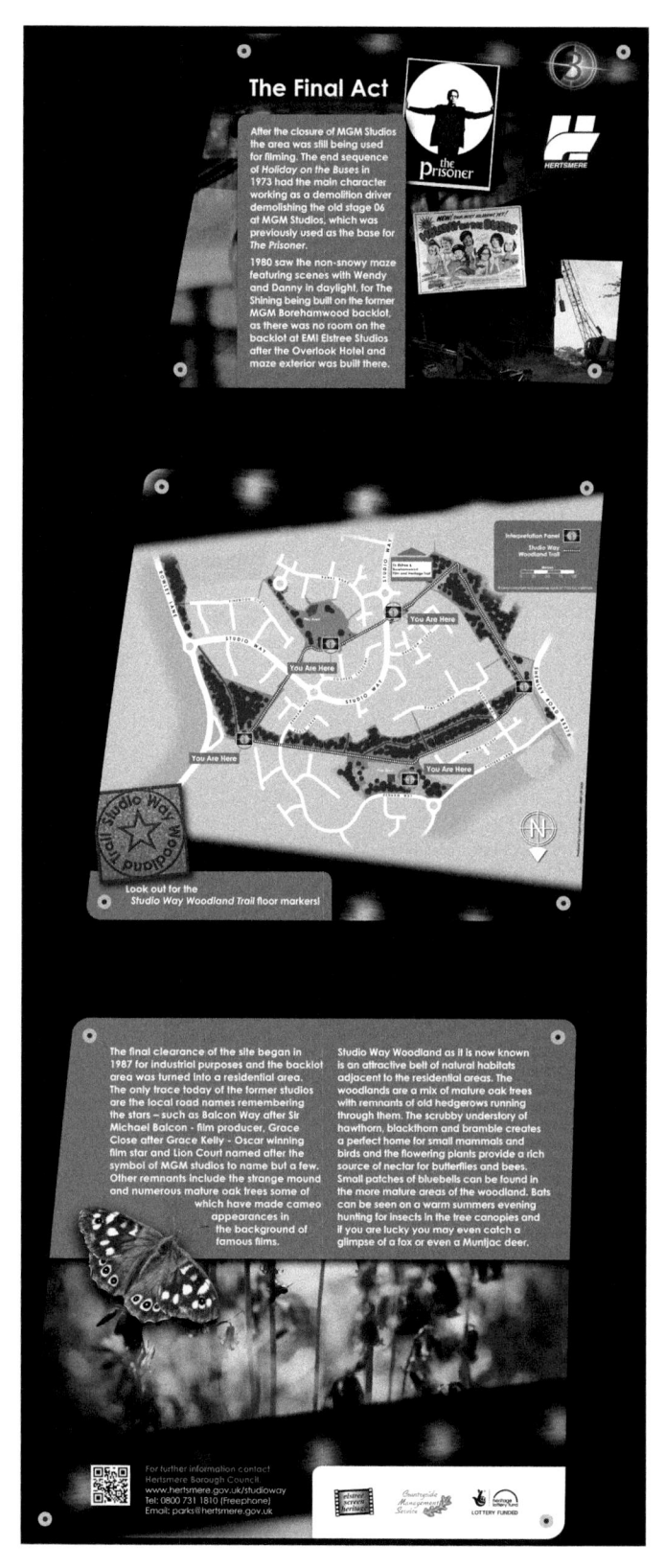

The Final Act

After the closure of MGM Studios the area was still being used for filming. The end sequence of *Holiday on the Buses* in 1973 had the main character working as a demolition driver demolishing the old stage 06 at MGM Studios, which was previously used as the base for *The Prisoner*.

1980 saw the non-snowy maze featuring scenes with Wendy and Danny in daylight, for *The Shining* being built on the former MGM Borehamwood backlot, as there was no room on the backlot at EMI Elstree Studios after the Overlook Hotel and maze exterior was built there.

Look out for the *Studio Way Woodland Trail* floor markers!

The final clearance of the site began in 1987 for industrial purposes and the backlot area was turned into a residential area. The only trace today of the former studios are the local road names remembering the stars – such as Balcon Way after Sir Michael Balcon - film producer, Grace Close after Grace Kelly - Oscar winning film star and Lion Court named after the symbol of MGM studios to name but a few. Other remnants include the strange mound and numerous mature oak trees some of which have made cameo appearances in the background of famous films.

Studio Way Woodland as it is now known is an attractive belt of natural habitats adjacent to the residential areas. The woodlands are a mix of mature oak trees with remnants of old hedgerows running through them. The scrubby understory of hawthorn, blackthorn and bramble creates a perfect home for small mammals and birds and the flowering plants provide a rich source of nectar for butterflies and bees. Small patches of bluebells can be found in the more mature areas of the woodland. Bats can be seen on a warm summers evening hunting for insects in the tree canopies and if you are lucky you may even catch a glimpse of a fox or even a Muntjac deer.

For further information contact Hertsmere Borough Council.
www.hertsmere.gov.uk/studioway
Tel: 0800 731 1810 (Freephone)
Email: parks@hertsmere.gov.uk

– 288 –

Appendix B-4
The Elstree Project

The men and women who worked in MGM British Studios are the genuine voice of the Studio. We were able to record on video first-hand accounts of life at MGM from a dwindling band of film veterans.

Of the over 65 people we interviewed, 13 of them had worked at MGM British, and we have drawn on some of their memories in this book. In this section we include a lengthy extract from our interview with Julian Senior, a unit publicist at MGM.

From May 2010 until mid-2016, volunteers from Elstree Screen Heritage worked with staff and students from the University of Hertfordshire to create a remarkable archive of interviews with veterans of film and television at all of the studios of Elstree and Boreham Wood. We called this "The Elstree Project". The University of Hertfordshire has gratefully acknowledged the unique contribution and knowledge of Paul Welsh, Chair of Elstree Screen Heritage, who prepared for and interviewed most of the film and TV veterans who took part.

Any interviews since then will have been carried out independently by the University of Hertfordshire or by Elstree Screen Heritage, reflecting the priorities of the University and Elstree Screen Heritage.

However, all past interviews will be freely accessible to the general public and academic researchers. The University of Hertfordshire remains committed to making the interviews available, with the first set becoming 'live' by 2020 on the project website: www.TheElstreeProject.org

We are grateful beyond words to everyone who agreed to share their memories of life in the studios of Elstree and Boreham Wood, with particular thanks to the veterans of MGM British Studios:

Mick Brady	Props
Ruby Burke	Tea Lady
Brian Clemens	Writer
Damian Cluskey	Carpenter
Dennis Fraser	Grip
Johnny Goodman	Production Supervisor
Jan Harlan	Producer
Brian Harris	Cameraman
Geoff Glover	Cameraman
Alf Newvell	Rigger
Kelvin Pike	Cameraman
June Randall	Continuity
Julian Senior	Unit Publicist

THE ELSTREE PROJECT – Julian Senior, Unit Publicist (JS)

Interviewed by Paul Welsh (PW)

INTERVIEWER: Can I take you back in time to when you first came into the film industry? How and when did you enter the business.

JULIAN SENIOR: I came into the business in the publicity department of MGM Studios in Boreham Wood in 1962. I'd been in South Africa and came to London. Happily my father-in-law to be had been with MGM for many years, had many contacts. He'd been a foreign manager for MGM all over the Far East and then South Africa. I was introduced to the Head of Publicity at MGM Studios, wonderful man called Paul Mills who ran the studio publicity department.

INTERVIEWER: Did you have difficulty obtaining a union ticket to get into the industry?

JULIAN SENIOR: I had to be proposed and seconded. There were three unions that covered the film industry then, but since Paul was Head of Publicity it wasn't terribly difficult. There were a lot of unit publicists around who belonged to the union who wanted to remain good friends with Paul Mills and I was proposed and seconded and in to a department of three unit publicists, on salary. It was ten pounds a week so it didn't cripple MGM.

INTERVIEWER: What were your memories of the first film you worked on, on your first few days arriving at a big film studio?

JULIAN SENIOR: It was the second most exciting thing that's ever happened to me. I can't begin to tell you what a joy, what a thrill it was to walk into an existing film studio, set up all ready and waiting. I'd arrived at this place, was being given an apprenticeship where they made movies, they made films, and it was truly exciting.

I spent six months or more living in Swiss Cottage in a bedsit, had to get two buses to get to MGM.

Clocked in and into the publicity department where I was given the most extraordinary apprenticeship. I was taught so much by the people who were there. There were two unit publicists already on staff, plus secretaries and other people, and Paul Mills was head of the department.

I spent six months captioning black and white contact sheets. Every unit filming had a unit photographer, and I spent six months captioning, you know, reel sixteen, numbers one through four, 'Sophia Loren talks to the Director on set', which meant that I had the opportunity to go on the set and talk to the publicists who were there, so that I could identify Sophia Loren.

I'd sit around with my mouth hanging open, slack-jawed, watching it all, and that's what I spent the first six months doing until I got assigned first the union ticket, and then my first film, 'Password Is Courage', with Dirk Bogarde. Black and white, shot at the studios. Barracks built at the studios and shot there. Very excited. It was as if it was yesterday.

It was a vast studio, churning out films, MGM, because the parent company at Culver City with the finance to make British films, and British films were made. This was a vast hundred and fourteen acre studio with Oscar winners left, right and centre and various divisions and departments. A front office, a contact with MGM Culver City as I say, and an opportunity to learn and to watch. And I watched, for years watched people on the set.

INTERVIEWER: What was the story you told us earlier about going on to the backlot with that first film and eating your bacon sandwich?

JULIAN SENIOR: Oh, that was, yes, the other joy was that living in a bedsit and earning ten pounds a week, there wasn't room for hefty lunches so make sure you got on a lot of sets for the bacon rolls and tea and coffee. And that first day I remember going on set and looking sideways shyly at the stills photographer to find out what was happening, to find everybody standing around the breakfast truck, of course, having bacon rolls and drinking the tea. And I took the bacon roll, free, coffee, free, tea, free, and sat down.

It was an electrician who sort of sidled up to me and he said "Get up, get up". "What d'you mean ... what have I done wrong? I know I've done something wrong". "No, just get up." And I stood up and eventually I said "Why?", and he said "Look", he said, "you've gotta realise it's all in the pay pack. If you have to take breakfast standing up, you're paid time and a half, too busy to have breakfast, if you sit down it's straight time", so everybody takes breakfast standing up." Nobody was actually working. They were standing around the breakfast ... it was wonderful.

But I learned, I learned a great deal. I also learned where not to stand, you know. Film sets are wonderful because you can quietly slip in the back and just look at all this excitement going on in front of you. And we were shooting a film, I remember Ted was the cameraman, great British cameraman, one of the best, this film it was called, it was originally called 'Dark Of The Sun', then it became 'The Mercenaries', a Willoughby Smith novel about diamond smuggling from some African country ...

The interior was shot at the studios and they'd got there together every Afro-Caribbean extra available. This was supposed to be a bar in downtown Kampala or somewhere in Uganda, and a fight breaks out, and there's a tremendous fight in this huge room. The Director said "Cut" and he said, "Everybody happy? Everybody happy? Everybody happy?" and Ted's voice cut across the stage and he said "Julian Senior" ... "No, not me", he said, "Either get blacked up or get off my set, you're in picture". And I was reflecting in one of the mirrors behind the bar and I hadn't thought about that. So, two valuable lessons I learned: be careful, stand right at the back, don't say anything, and make sure you stand up for breakfast. Two very valuable lessons.

INTERVIEWER: So you were very lucky in the sense you had the opportunity to learn on the job rather than academically learning. You were actually learning as you went.

JULIAN SENIOR: As I said, it was one of those wonderful things where you were, in fact, apprenticed. You walked on to an apprenticeship in, against a campus, almost university-like background. You know, there were the gates all around. The films were being made. You had freedom to go pretty much everywhere.

Elizabeth Taylor was the first time I ever came

across a closed set on 'The VIPs'. But you had freedom to learn as you went along. Most people did. Youngsters were taken on in every department, in every division. There were kids who learned photography in the stills department. I learned, I hope, something about publicity and marketing from Paul Mills and the guys around me. Tom Howard was an Academy Award Winner for 'Tom Thumb', and special effects, there was a huge special effects department. Watty, A W Watkins, was the Head of Sound, another Academy Award Winner. They took on apprentices.

They took on people who learned and got to understand something about film-making, just something, because there was a market for the films and MGM were one of the studios, together with Shepperton and Pinewood, and EMI of course. There was a market for those small British films, the 'Password Is Courage' style film. Today that would be a sixty, seventy million dollar film with a forty million dollar marketing budget, and unless you have a worldwide acceptance of it, you just couldn't market it.

That's what killed the industry. It got so expensive that, essentially, all these tremendous people trained and worked but the films dried up because it was just as easy and cheaper to film in Yugoslavia or Spain or somewhere else. You didn't need a studio. Look, when I first joined in the '60s it was the tail end of those wonderful days when people learned, when there were apprenticeships.

INTERVIEWER: Can you tell us about the actual role of the unit publicist? People may not understand today, what in the 1960's that meant. What would, when you were assigned to a film, what actually would you then be tasked to do?

JULIAN SENIOR: Well, one of the ... I can't talk for all unit publicists, of course, but one of the advantages of MGM was that being part of a worldwide production and distribution organisation, MGM very quickly cottoned on to the fact that every film needed to have as much information readily available to their distribution officers worldwide. They produced it, there was a product. Now, the office in Taiwan or the office in Madrid or the office in San Paulo or Manila had no idea what this film was, what this thing was until they got it, so any advance early notice ... anything you had ... would be enormously helpful. So the minute you were assigned, you first of all met the talent: the Directors and the Producers and whatever stars were there. Some interesting meetings at that stage because they were all friendly, sometimes through gritted teeth but friendly to one another.

And we put together basic information about the film: the synopsis of the story, detailed production notes which could run, you know, you're a journalist. We used to get them ten/fifteen pages worth of biographies, feature stories, word, news about the film. And then as the film drifted on, to create publicity for the film so that the offices around the world could begin to disseminate this information. But as I say, having MGM distribution office in St James's Street, and MGM film studios in Boreham Wood was the best possible way of combining a production and distribution facility.

That's what a unit publicist did. And the

unit publicist travelled everywhere with the film, stayed with them, kept the talent out of trouble when the talent needed keeping out of trouble. Suppressed the stories that you didn't want released, and tried to promote some sense of what was going on. The Producers and actors, actors are human beings, frail human beings, flawed human beings. And, think about it, they get up every morning, go to a big building, put on somebody else's clothes, wear make-up, read somebody else's lines, and then go home. David Niven became a close chum over many years, we did three MGM pictures together where I was unit publicist and he was the star.

INTERVIEWER: When you were making films then, were unit publicists encouraged to bring journalists down to the set or were they closed sets on the whole?

JULIAN SENIOR: Some films were closed sets but, yes, we were encouraged to bring journalists down on the set, for reasons that common sense just didn't work for me. I mean the film was, at best, a year away from release. Most people can't remember what they read in the newspaper this morning, rather than what they saw ... There was no way of creating an awareness.

It was more, I believe, that actors are frightened people and it was more to make the Director and the Producer and the actors and stars feel as though they were doing something worthwhile. "Look, it's in the paper." I know, I know they all ... "Oh, God, I'm in the papers again. Ohhh", you know, as all actors do and they love it. Nothing better than seeing your name and face in the paper. "Oh, I can't stand all this. Oh my God, my name's in the paper again." But they all employ publicists to do nothing but keep their names in the papers.

So we're encouraged to bring people down to the set. There <u>were</u> closed sets. Richard Burton, Liz Taylor, 'The VIPs' was at a very bad time of their lives and, as a human being, you can understand why they would want some privacy. It was a closed set and it remained a closed set until the famous closed set silent press conference that they agreed to give me. Where they said, "Oh, we'll do, we'll do a press conference but we're not gonna say a word". I said, "Well then that's not a press conference, that's just people standing around being photographed, looking pretty". She said, "That's exactly right".

And she said something to me I'll never forget. She said, "I think I'm looking gorgeous in this wonderful gown", with this wonderful, gorgeous man drinking champagne and Guinness from first thing in the morning, Burton's Black Velvet, he started on champagne and Guinness, and the two of them were just…. well I'm star struck, of course I am. Why am I ... pretending to be blasé. She said, "You know, if I look this good, that's what people want to come and see. My views on the political situation in, in China don't really carry too much weight and I understand that perfectly. What I look like is what matters". And over the years that's been a byword and it hasn't changed.

Parts of 'The Dirty Dozen' were a closed set occasionally because it was kind of dangerous. But for the most part unit publicists were encouraged to write the material that told everybody everything that was happening, or hopefully everything that was happening. We used to have a mailing list that would go to MGM offices worldwide at least once, twice, three times during the film. So that when the film eventually arrived in South America or in Hong Kong, they, they'd pre-sold some of it. The unit publicist's job, as MGM saw it in the time that I started, was just to keep the offices informed.

Keep the press informed as well. We had lists of columnists who regularly ran, you know American columnists in particular. There were two trade papers in the UK that always had to get good material, and there were the national newspapers. Six or seven daily papers and all the Sunday papers. And you're invited to bring press down and photographers down.

INTERVIEWER: Were you at, at the end of that era of Hedda Hopper and Sheila Graham, people who would want to fill every week of their radio programme with snippets from the set, gossip?

JULIAN SENIOR: Absolutely. I got to know Sheila Graham quite well. A remarkable lady. She dragged me off to Harrods one day to buy her book. She said, "Come, you must have my book, must have my book". I expected a signed copy and she dragged me into Harrods and hung back and said, "Ask how the book's selling". And I said, "Could you tell me how the book….?" and the guy said, "Oh, extremely well". She came leaping out and said, "Oh, I wrote it, it's mine. And you'll buy it, Julian, won't you buy it?" I said, "Of course I'll buy it" and I ended up paying for it.

But, yes, we kept in touch. The press in the UK were a lot more difficult, and I mean difficult only in the sense of having a tabloid newspaper to fill without a regular show business although there were some regular show business characters around. We've kept in touch and are still good friends to this day. They ran the show business columns. There weren't many of them, so we encouraged people down, get a picture, get them off, run into the Producer. The Producer was happy, MGM was happy but they didn't care too much. The title changed a dozen times before it was released. So that was part of the job, yes.

INTERVIEWER: Did you get many stars who really didn't want to co-operate with that level of publicity?

JULIAN SENIOR: Most of them had to be led kicking and screaming, and smiling eventually. The biggest stars didn't really need it or want it or believe it was necessary. It was a job. The trouble always came from people who weren't that well-known and "I've seen nothing of myself in the papers". "Well, that's because nobody knows who you are." And sometimes you can get things hideously wrong.

I worked as a unit publicist on all the 'Miss Marple' films. The 'Murder Ahoy' and 'Murder Most Foul' and 'Murder She Said'… a remarkable, wonderful lady, and on 'Murder Ahoy' she was on board a training ship. The Producer was George Brown who produced all those films, lovely man, and he signed a lad called Terence Edmond who'd come from 'Z Cars', where he was PC Sweet. He came to the set and I met him. He said, "Well, it's a good story, I've left 'Z Cars', no longer a policeman, that's it, I'm over." I said, "Mr Edmond, sir, in this film you're playing a policeman so it's really not a major step". He said, "No, no, you're right but it's worth a publicity picture, isn't it?" I said, "Yeah, of course it is", and I called up friends, a wonderful photographer called Terry O'Neil who was to become a world renowned photographer. He was the show business photographer, Terry. He knew everybody. And he came down on the set to photograph ... PC Sweet, Terence Edmond, in his uniform.

Terry shuffled over to me wide-eyed and he said, "Julian, have you seen what's going on on that set? There's a ... there's a sailing ship rigged up". I said, "I know, that's part of the film. It's a training ship." He said, "But there's, there's a lady sword-fighting and the lady is Margaret Rutherford". There was this jolly, wonderful Margaret Rutherford leaping across the stage with a sword which I hadn't seen. I was becoming blasé. Isn't that scary? I hadn't noticed it.

My job was to produce the materials that were needed and the studio had an investment. We all felt that, you see.

At that time Antonioni, who was at the studios, looked at the rushes with us one day and saw David Hemmings and said, "That's the boy". He'd already signed Terence Stamp for the film but said, "Hemmings is the boy for 'Blow Up'. That was another launch, you know, of a British career, of an English career. So all these people learned what they learned. All these people learned their jobs, and they learned their tasks and they learned by making mistakes.

Today you can't make mistakes. Today Alan Parker says, you know, "The British film industry's really just a lot of people who couldn't get Green Cards to work in America." And he may be right, which is the tragedy. Except for, down the road, there's a reborn MGM in the shape of Warner Brothers Leavesden Studios, hopefully. It's not gonna get sold off for housing. MGM British got sold off for cold storage, thank you Christian Salvesen for taking over MGM.

And MGM did that. MGM had seven hundred, or seven hundred fifty people working there and they learned their business, they learned their trade, I learned most of mine as well and the sadness is that the economic situation changed, the technology of this stuff changed so that you didn't have to have sound cameras in the studio, inside a soundproof studio. You could shoot with a rifle mike across fifty yards or a hundred yards. The technology got better. You didn't need a studio, you could shoot in a warehouse anywhere. And it became cheaper. We tried to negotiate, Paul Mills my former boss ... I'd left the year before. I left in, well that same year, 1970/69 I left and Paul Mills was acting head of the studio but it was all dribbling away.

Land prices became, property prices became what they are now, and, you know, while the unions were still fighting a perfectly legitimate battle, the studios didn't close down because of union demands. They were difficult. You know, twelve people: four production, four sound, four lighting. A minimum of twelve people every time you took a crew out.

Today people laugh at you. They put a camera over their shoulders and off they go and shoot. They've learned, they know what they're supposed to be doing. Video came in and gave them the opportunity to do that. Couldn't do that on film.

Anybody making mistakes doing things gets that much better and MGM as a studio allowed that to happen. I made an enormous, an horrendous number of mistakes, none of which were earth-shattering. MGM didn't collapse because of my mistakes, the publicity department didn't. There was a benevolent dictatorship which is the only way studios can work, you know, other than just being a renting operation. A benevolent dictator in the form of Paul Mills who was gentle, became a father to me and my children over the years, who taught me what I needed to know.

I took that away to Warner Brothers and tried to do the same thing but the world had changed. I tried to set up interns. Essentially, there was an internship happening at MGM all those years ago and it died. It died because there wasn't enough support. There should have been more support. There should have been more governmental support.

That wonderful era of the studio there, the American head of the studio Larry (Bachman) in Barnet Lane, Kubrick living in Barnet Lane. Sophia Loren, when she came over to do 'Operation Crossbow' stayed at the Edgwarebury Country Hotel just round the corner. So it was a film village. It was a village that made film.

INTERVIEWER: Can we go, Julian, go through some of the films that you would have worked on at MGM?

JULIAN SENIOR: Yes. I did work on 'Children Of The Damned'. Lovely, brilliant idea. Extraordinary idea for a film if you think about it. Something happens one night, it sounds like Cup Final night, doesn't it -- in England? Or World Cup night in England and nine months later all the women produce children, not all alike. Yes, I worked on that and did some work on 'Village Of The Damned'. A sequel is the sponge of an empty mind that says, "Well, this worked quite well last time, if we do much the same thing, it may work again". No, films are original ideas, and other than big blockbuster things they don't work.

INTERVIEWER: Do you remember 'The Dirty Dozen'?

JULIAN SENIOR: I worked on 'The Dirty Dozen' for a long, long time and that's interesting, because the Producer was, of course, Ken Hyman who, although an American, son of Elliott Hyman, Ken is English. He lives in Chelsea - Ken and Caroline - and they were great supporters of the British industry at that time. A great supporter of movies. Ray Anzarut was the line Producer and the Director was Robert Aldrich. "A thing of beauty, a thing of beauty, let's shoot it again" was his basic phrase. And, of course, 'The Dirty Dozen' had the collection of extraordinary actors, quite extraordinary actors. But just think of what was done. Just think of what MGM did to assign that sort of movie to a crew that was, other than the editor who worked with Aldrich, the crew was essentially all British, everything.

Gerry Crampton was the stuntman who was paid per fall off the roof. I went rushing up to him and he gave me a big wink and he said "Is everything okay?" "Yes, okay", and "No, there's nothing wrong with any of the cameras, nothing wrong with any of the cameras". And the Director said, "They're fine" and Gerry went "Oh". And I said, "What's the matter? Why are you sighing?" and he said, "It's a hundred and fifty pound a fall, every time I fall ... nothing better for me that the camera gets stuck or there's a hair in the gate or something goes wrong with the sound".

So 'The Dirty Dozen' was a collection of terrific people from Savalas and Bronson and Clint Walker. Clint Walker familiarised himself with the English countryside. He was a, a country boy, Clint Walker. Six foot six and beautiful, gorgeous boy. Big, powerful former football player. Talked real slow. Moved real slow. And we were driving to a location through Hertfordshire, Markyate , and we passed a piggery. And we were, I don't know, maybe a hundred yards, two hundred yards past, down a small country lane and Clint said to me, "Hey, Julian" .... "Yes", and he said, "D'you see the size of some of those hogs?". I thought, "Oh, yes, I, I did, Clint, yes", and he said, "I could almost throw a saddle over some of them". My God. It doesn't get much better than that.

And then I spent a lot of time actually working with Clint Eastwood. Maybe it's a thing with cowboys. He was wonderful. Telly Savalas was wonderful. Brilliant, brilliant actor, also without a theatrical training, no theatrical training. And Bob Aldrich, the Director. The local people in Boreham Wood as you know got a little uptight about it because there were lots of explosions and gun batteries and all sorts of excitement going on, all of which we loved. And it went on well into the night and there were a lot of very irritated people after a while.

And then at two o'clock one morning, when we weren't shooting, there was a sudden and very mysterious explosion and the whole thing shattered to the ground. Local people decided "That's it, we're gonna get some sleep" and the shed had burnt to the ground ... the structure they put up was just bits and pieces of broken timber. I remember walking to Bob Aldrich across the set, kicking bits of timber going, "Well, we can use that piece". "No, we can't use that piece again". They actually literally rebuilt it.

Trini Lopez played a young Mexican criminal. Trini's boss was Frank Sinatra and Trini was expected in Vegas and, of course, films drifted over and on and on and on. Trini's manager was a man called Bullets Durgan. Can you actually imagine picking up the telephone and saying, "Hi, this is Bullets". Bullets called me up and he said, "Hey, kid, we've gotta get Trini back. I said, "Why, anything, Bullets. Anything you want". And I went to see Aldrich; he said "You've gotta finish the movie, you've gotta finish the movie" and Bullets came on set and was absolutely out of 'Guys And Dolls' with a Panama hat with a little headband and a very smart suit and a big cigar, yeah. He said "Frank wants him back in Vegas, kid". And there's a point at which you realise that arguing with Frank may not be the healthiest option in the world, so Trini left, sadly.

What happened to his character? His parachute got caught up in the tree and he died. That was the end of Trini and he was heartbroken. I remember going with him when he was packing, leaving the Dorchester, and he was almost in tears. He said, "This could have been my big break, Julian". "Yes, it could have been", and that's what the studios was. The studios was a big break for a lot of people, in truth.

'The VIPs' took over everybody's lives, and 'The Yellow Rolls Royce' was quite extraordinary. Imagine going on to a set and you're a young unit publicist, and you're going to talk to Orson Welles. You're going to talk to the man who made ... it was almost, get on stage and realise that you're going to say something that's gonna be total gibberish. And you go ... and then there's a pause and "I'm terribly sorry, I'll try that again". And we had that standing joke because every time I came on the set again, he said "D'you want a second take. I was so embarrassed I could not speak.

INTERVIEWER: Did you ever collect autographs? Were you ever tempted or anything like that?

JULIAN SENIOR: No, no, no, no. Only because every time I came on set, and certainly every time I brought a journalist on, the crew would stand around and the comments were wonderful. "Working today, Julian? That's nice" from somewhere up in the, in the gangways up there. No, I, I never collected autographs.

INTERVIEWER: Which stars did you meet?

JULIAN SENIOR: Peter Ustinov, I worked with him on 'Hot Millions' with Karl Malden and Maggie Smith and Bob Newhart, and he was a quite extraordinary man, Ustinov. Quite extraordinary. Eric Till was the Director, Canadian born. The crew were wonderful because Ustinov would mimic the crew. He'd mimic their voices to such an extent that there was a photographer who worked with me on the film called Bert and I was actually having a conversation with him behind a flat, you know one of those removable flats. I thought it was George. It was Ustinov.

It was an interesting film, talking about predicting the future of computers and the man who pays himself. You ever, do you know the background to that, that film was just wonderful where the idea was that here was a man who was so adept. He was our first hacker and he hacked into the computer and created a lot of phoney businesses across Europe and kept paying himself through this huge company. Collected all the money. Maggie Smith was wonderful.

Yeah, 'Hot Millions' was that and Ustinov signed a book of short stories to me which typically Ustinov, I'm not sure it was actually a compliment or a slap in the mouth cos he actually said "Dear Julian, thanks for making everything that could have been and probably should have been more difficult". I spent a lot of time wondering over that, you know "What was he talking about?"

Margaret Rutherford invited me round for tea, you know, in one of the 'Miss Marple' things, and went over to Gerrards Cross where she lived and went for tea with her and she spent a good deal of time talking to a plush toy. I realised at that point that it was just perhaps time now to move on and, of course, her husband (Stringer Davies) was in all the films with her, as you know, always her side-kick. A cab driver or somebody helping out. Lovely couple. I was bowled over by her because this was a great, amazing woman. "I am not a comedienne, I am an actress". "Okay, but you make me laugh, it's funny".

INTERVIEWER: Would you, if you were starting out today, if you were twenty years old and starting out today, would you choose this as a career, as it is today? Not going back to how you would have looked back on it forty/ fifty years ago, but would you now say "I still would like to go into the film business as a career"?

JULIAN SENIOR: It's difficult. I mean, the first response is to say, "In a heartbeat, because I'd miss so much of it so much", but the truth is that what I would really like to do is to be able to develop people. There are one or two others who feel this way, they're friends of mine - Gerry Lewis who for years was EMI Paramount. I had lunch with him the other day and my former boss, there were three of us, a combined age of about seven hundred, all thinking to ourselves "You know what we should do is set up some sort of lecture course, something, some way of, of getting attached to a film school or to a major, one of the major film companies and actually just teaching people a little bit about something of the business that they're going into." You know, I can't think of what happens today to a young designer. What does a young production designer do? They have to get themselves affiliated to a film production designer. Well, go to one of the art colleges and get the degrees but get yourself affiliated so that you get close to understanding what the designer is actually doing.

INTERVIEWER: In terms of the actual studio, the buildings, the facility itself, what are your classic memories of the actual studios?

JULIAN SENIOR: Well, you can very easily become wrapped up in what's happening at a studio and you do. The building of sets was quite remarkable from, you know, production designers, initial drawings, right through to the completion, the day they move the cameras in. That was always fun. But the building sets was quite, quite extraordinary.

The thing that struck me, I used to wander round the backlot, it was called the backlot, isn't that a lovely phrase? I think it's now a collection of little houses all made out of ticky-tacky where the lot used to be, what a shame. What happened was that the place is littered with staircases. Staircases are unique. I mean, if you're converting your little flat or you're converting a mansion, you have to build a staircase for that house.

And, of course, they have to build staircases for each film, for every film and it has to fit within the set. And when I used to walk on the backlot at MGM, I'd find dozens of staircases in various stages of disrepair, with wallpaper trailing beside and, and banisters a little wonky. But staircases just pointing at the sky. Staircases going nowhere. Something I won't forget.

INTERVIEWER: We spoke earlier about the atmosphere at the studio and, and the friendliness of it all. Was it, in part, driven by family links? A lot of people had brothers, sisters, aunts, uncles, dads, mums, all working together.

JULIAN SENIOR: Absolutely. It's back to the discussion we had earlier about apprenticeships. You know, you had to have somewhere where newcomers could learn the business. Where better to learn the business than working for your uncle or your dad or your mum? We mentioned the Ibbotson family, Arthur Ibbotson the cameraman and his sister who was a remarkable hairdresser, make-up and hairdressing. It was a way of getting in.

It was not quite Bourneville, building an entire village for its employees or Rowntree or any of those people. It was a benevolent, benevolent dictatorship. That's it, that's how you run a studio. Benevolent dictatorship. Somebody who has all the decisions, has all rights to make the decisions but is actually quite a nice person.

But the apprenticeships at the studio that I talk about, the people who came in were all the time we met them. Bert the still photographer, his daughter was in the business as well, brought in through him into one of those family films. In fact, if I'm not mistaken, she was in, she was an extra in one of those 'Damned' films. I mean 'Village Of' or 'Children Of'. The guy who worked in stills, Arthur, his daughter was there as well. There were people that you met and ran into all the time. Sadly, my children weren't old enough to work there, or else I would have put them to work.

INTERVIEWER 2: You told us you met Lee Marvin when he was staying in London.

JULIAN SENIOR: I worked with him on 'Dirty Dozen', yeah. Because the day before we'd been on the Eamonn Andrews Show, which I will never forget either. If you're still rolling …

'The Dirty Dozen' threw up a number of characters. The funniest of whom, because I think he was the most talented, was Lee Marvin. Lee was, in many ways, when I met him on 'The Dirty Dozen', a slightly bitter man. He'd won an Academy Award for 'Cat Ballou'. If you remember he was the cowboy on the horse, the drunken horse. He and the horse always drunk. Great opening shot of Lee leaning against the wall and the horse leaning against the wall with him. He'd been taken on that picture as an instructor to try and teach whoever the star would be how to handle the six-guns cos he was very good.

The start date of the film got closer and closer and the studio could never settle on anybody. And finally, with ten days to go, they said, "Why don't we give it to Marvin?" And Lee Marvin took on the role and obviously trained all these other clowns, actors, and he won an Academy Award, but he was very bitter about that in many ways because his whole career had taken off simply because there'd been nobody else. Won an Academy Award. Brilliant man.

Actually knew a good deal more about the inside of the pubs in London than I think anybody did. Lee liked a drink or two, or twelve. One of the jobs as a unit publicist I had was to get a little publicity for him and take him on the Eamonn Andrews Show, which was a late night Saturday night talk-show. Now anything late night was dangerous with Lee. In fact, anything after ten o'clock in the morning was dangerous with Lee because he was pretty well oiled at that stage.

We went to the studios at Twickenham. Lee had had more than enough and I arrived and said to one of the floor managers, "Who else is on tonight?" Stupid, I should have found out before, and they said, "Richard Harris". Well, that's like running into an explosives store with a lighted match. How can you put Richard Harris and Lee Marvin together?

They met one another, took an instant dislike to one another, and within five minutes were rolling on the floor of the green room thumping each other. And I was the unit publicist and mesmerised, against the wall. I couldn't move cos I could hear Eamonn Andrews saying "And in London tonight, filming on 'The Dirty Dozen', we hav ..." and I thought "No, he's never gonna get off the floor". Lee got up off the floor, straightened his tie. One eye was closing. And he went on and did the show. Lee Marvin and Richard Harris rolling around the floor fighting.

But the funniest, well, sad but funny story? I went over to see him one evening after work. It was about eight-thirty at night, and he had a small rented mews house in Old Barrack Yard, just about where St George's Hospital is. I came in, we had a drink, I took a drink with Lee and sat down and e chatted. His face was already, I think, magenta coloured and I knew there was gonna be trouble this evening, and suddenly he said to me, "Hey, kid, what time do you have?" and I said, "It's about five to nine". He said, "Ah" and he got up and walked out.

And I sat for a while and I realised after ten minutes he wasn't coming back. There was no more Lee Marvin. I thought, "Well ... I'm going home" so I got up and walked out. The door was wide open and standing outside Old Barrack Yard, leaning against a wall like a cigar-store Indian, was Lee Marvin. Puce in the face. I said, "Lee, what are you doing out here?" He said, "Studio always sends a car at nine o'clock, kid". I said "Nine o'clock in the morning, Lee". "Ahhh". He actually hadn't made the change. He hadn't actually noticed that it was nine o'clock at night.

He was a wonderful man. The film ran over and over and over and I said "Lee, aren't you getting bored?". He said, "Bored?" He said, "Every day on this film beyond my contract is a week's fishing in Mexico for me". I said, "I love it. Good for you."

APPENDIX C

Filmography

This list does not include films served on location by MGM staff or films which used the studios only for postproduction, special effects or for renting the backlot facilities.

The author welcomes any additional titles.

1946
Brighton Rock	(91 mins, cert A, b/w)

1947
While I Live	(85 mins, cert U, b/w) (The Dream Of Olwen)
Idol Of Paris	(92 mins, cert U, b/w)
Spring In Park Lane	(92 mins, cert U, b/w)

1948
The Guinea Pig	(97 mins, cert U, b/w)
Edward My Son	(112 mins, cert A, b/w)
Under Capricorn	(116 mins, cert A, colour)

1948
Conspirator	(87 mins, cert U, b/w)
Maytime In Mayfair	(96 mins, cert U, colour)
The Miniver Story	(104 mins, cert U, b/w)

1950 & 1951
Calling Bulldog Drummond	(80 min cert U b/w),
The Hour Of Thirteen	(78 mins, cert A, b/w)
Ivanhoe	(107 mins, cert U, colour)

1952
- Never Let Me Go — (94mins, cert U, b/w)
- Time Bomb — (72 mins, cert U, b/w)
- Invitation To The Dance — (93 mins, cert U, colour)

1953
- Seagulls Over Sorrento — (92 mins, cert U, b/w)
- Mogambo — (116 mins, cert U, colour)
- Knights Of The Round Table — (115 mins, cert U, colour)
- Saadia — (87 mins, cert U, colour)
- Betrayed — (108 mins, cert U, colour)

1954
- The Dark Avenger — (85 mins, cert U, colour)
- Beau Brummell — (111 mins, cert U colour)
- Prize Of Gold — (100 mins, cert A, colour)
- That Lady — (100 mins, cert A, colour)
- Gentlemen Marry Brunettes — (95 mins, cert A, colour)
- Flame And The Flesh — (104 mins, colour)
- Stranger From Venus — (75 mins, cert U, b/w)

1955
- Another Time, Another Place — (95mins, cert A,, colour)
- The Gamma People — (78 mins, cert A, b/w)
- Safari — (91 mins, cert A, colour)
- Around The World In 80 Days — (175 mins, cert U, colour)
- The Adventures Of Quentin Durward — (100 mins, cert U, colour)

1956
- The Barretts Of Wimpole Street — (105 mins, cert U, colour)
- Stars In Your Eyes — (96 mins, cert U, b/w)
- Port Afrique — (91 mins, cert A, colour)
- The Little Hut — (90 mins, cert A, colour)
- Odongo — (85 mins, cert U, colour)
- Beyond Mombassa — (90 mins, cert U, colour)
- Zarak — (95 mins, cert A, colour)

Fire Down Below (115 mins, cert A, colour)
Anastasia (105 mins, cert U, colour)
Sea Wife (81 mins, cert A, colour)
The Man In The Sky (87 mins, cert U, b/w)
Bhowani Junction (109 mins, cert A, colour)
The Man Who Never Was (103 mins, cert U, colour)
Fire Maidens From Outer Space (80 mins, cert U, b/w)

1957

I Accuse (99 mins, cert U, b/w)
Action Of The Tiger (93 mins, cert U, colour)
The Safecracker (95 mins, cert U, b/w)
Barnacle Bill (87 mins, cert U, b/w)
It's Time For Me To Go Now TV pilot
Island In The Sun (119 mins, cert A, colour)
The Shiralee (99 mins, cert A, b/w)
How To Murder A Rich Uncle (75 mins, cert A, b/w)
Davy (85 mins, cert U, colour)
High Flight (102 mins, cert U, colour)
Gideon's Day (91 mins, cert A, colour)
OSS TV series
Lucky Jim (95 mins, cert U, b/w)
No Time To Die (102 mins, cert U, b/w)

1958

Doctors Dilemna (90 mins, cert U, colour)
Inn Of The Sixth Happiness (158 mins, cert U, colour)
Corridors Of Blood (86 mins, cert X, b/w)
The Angry Hills (105 mins, cert A, b/w)
Count Your Blessings (102 mins, cert U, colour)
Dick And The Duchess TV series
Dunkirk (134 mins, cert U, b/w)
First Man Into Space (77 mins, cert X, b/w)
Nowhere To Go (87 mins, cert U, b/w)
Tom Thumb (92 mins, cert U, colour)

1959

Serious Charge	(99 mins, cert X, b/w)
Libel	(100 mins, cert A, b/w)
The Rough And The Smooth	(99 mins, cert X, b/w)
A Touch Of Larceny	(91 mins, cert U, b/w)
House Of Seven Hawks	(91 mins, cert U, b/w)
Gorgo	(77 mins, cert X, colour)
Jazz Boat	(96 mins, cert A, colour)
Beat Girl	(85 mins, cert X, b/w)
Too Hot To Handle	(100 mins, cert X, colour)
The Day They Robbed The Bank Of England	(85 mins, cert U, b/w)
In The Nick	(105 mins, cert U, b/w)
The Wreck Of The Mary Deare	(104 mins, cert U, colour)
Rendezvous	TV series
The Scapegoat	(91 mins, cert A, b/w)
Village Of The Damned	(91 mins, cert A, b/w)

1960

The World Of Suzie Wong	(126 mins, cert A, colour)
Let's Get Married	(91 mins, cert U, b/w)
The Millionairess	(90 mins, cert U, colour)
Invasion Quartet	(87 mins, cert U, b/w)
The Green Helmet	(88 mins, cert U, b/w)
Secret Partner	(91 mins, cert A, b/w)
Five Golden Hours	(89 mins, cert U, b/w)
Mr Topaze	(97 mins, cert U, colour)
Danger Man	TV series

1961

Murder She Said	(86 mins, cert U, b/w)
She'll Have To Go	(90 mins, cert U, b/w)
Postman's Knock	(87 mins, cert U, b/w)
Light In The Piazza	(101 mins, cert A, colour)
Satan Never Sleeps	(125 mins, cert A, colour) (The Devil Never Sleeps)
The Inspector	(111 mins, cert A, colour)
Village of Daughters	(86 mins, cert U, b/w)

Appendix C: Filmography

I Thank A Fool	(100 mins, cert A, colour)
Nine Hours To Rama	(125 mins, cert A, colour)
Zero One	TV series
The Password Is Courage	(116 mins, cert U, b/w)
Kill Or Cure	(88 mins, cert U, b/w)
In The Cool Of The Day	(91 mins, cert A, colour)
Come Fly With Me	(109 mins, cert U, colour)
The Haunting	(112 mins, cert X, b/w
Cairo	(91 mins, cert A, b/w
Dead Man's Evidence	(67 mins, cert U, b/w)
Saturday Night Out	(96 mins, cert X, b/w)
The Dock Brief	(88 mins, cert U, b/w)
Private Potter	(89mins, cert U, b/w)
Live Now Pay Later	(104 mins, cert X, b/w)
The Marked One	(65 mins, cert A, b/w)
Maniac	(96 mins, cert X, b/w)
Follow The Boys	(95 mins, cert c,olour)
Tomorrow At Ten	(80 mins, cert A, b/w)
Master Spy	(74 mins, cert U, b/w) (Checkmate)
List Of Adrian Messenger	(98 mins, cert A, b/w)
King Of The Seven Seas	(103 mins, cert U, colour)
Four Hits And A Mister	TV series
Murder At The Gallop	(81 mins, cert U, b/w)
One Step Beyond	TV series
The Day Of The Triffids	(94 mins, cert X, colour)

1963

Impact	(61 mins, cert U, b/w)
The VIPs	(119 mins, cert A, colour)
Murder At The Gallop	(81 mins, cert U, b/w)
The Girl Hunters	(103 mins, cert A, b/w)
Clash By Night	(75 mins, cert A, b/w)
Espionage	TV series
Swinging UK	(28 mins, cert U, colour)
Echoes Of Diana	(61 mins, cert U, b/w)
The Chalk Garden	(106 mins, cert U, colour)

Children Of The Damned	(88 mins, cert X, b/w)
It's All Over Town	(55 mins, cert A, b/w)
Night Must Fall	(105 mins, cert X, b/w)
633 Squadron	(94 mins, cert A, colour)

1964

Murder Most Foul	(90mins, cert A, b/w)
The Americanisation of Emily	(115 mins, cert X, b/w)
A Shot In The Dark	(103 mins, cert A, colour)
Hysteria	(85 mins, cert X, b/w)
The Hill	(123 mins, cert X, b/w).
Danger Man	TV series
Murder Ahoy	(93 mins, cert U, b/w)
The Yellow Rolls Royce	(122 mins, cert A, colour)
Young Cassidy	(110 mins, cert A, colour)
The Alphabet Murders	(90 mins, cert U, b/w)
Operation Crossbow	(116 mins, cert A, colour)
The Secret Of My Success	(96 mins, cert A, colour)

1965

Lady L	(124 mins, cert c,olour)
The Comedians	(160 mins, cert c,olour)
The Cuckoo Patrol	(76 mins, cert U, b/w)
The Liquidator	(104 mins, cert A, colour)
Where The Spies Are	(113 mins, cert A, colour)
Return From The Ashes	(105 mins, cert X, b/w)
Up Jumped A Swagman	(88 mins, cert U, colour)
The Eye Of The Devil	(90 mins, cert X, colour)

1966

One Eyed Jacks Are Wild	TV pilot
Stranger In The House	(104 mins, cert X, colour)
Casino Royale	(131 mins, cert U, colour).
The Prisoner'	TV series
The Vampire Killers	(107 mins, cert A, colour)
The Dirty Dozen	(140 mins, cert X, colour)

Appendix C: Filmography

2001: A Space Odyssey   (135 mins, cert U, colour)
Blow Up   (111 mins, cert X, colour)

1967

Dark Of The Sun   (100 mins, cert X, colour)
Quatermass And The Pit   (97 mins, cert X, colour)
Battle Beneath The Earth   (91 mins, cert U, colour)
Decline And Fall   (113 mins, cert A, colour)
Attack On The Iron Coast   (90 mins, cert U, colour)
Submarine X-1   (90 mins, cert U, colour)

1968

Hammerhead   (99 mins, cert A, colour)
Where Eagles Dare   (155 mins, cert A, colour)
Hot Millions   (106 mins, cert U, colour)
Goodbye Mr. Chips   (147 mins, cert U, colour)
Journey Into The Unknown   TV series
Inspector Clouseau   (105 mins, cert U, colour)
Assassination Bureau   (110 mins, cert A, colour)
Mosquito Squadron   (90 mins, cert U, colour?)
Alfred The Great   (122 mins, cert A, colour)

1969

The Private Life Of Sherlock Holmes   (125 mins, cert A, colour)
Bushbabies   (100 mins, cert U, colour)
Captain Nemo And The Underwater City   (106 mins, cert U, colour)
The Walking Stick   (101 mins, cert A, colour)
One More Time   (93 mins, cert A, colour)
My Lover My Son   (96 mins, cert X, colour)
Julius Caesar   (117 mins, cert U, colour)
UFO   TV series
No Blade Of Grass   (97 mins, cert A, colour)